MW00531739

This book belongs to:

Helen Dinsmore

RECLAIMING ISRAEL'S HISTORY

RECLAIMING
ISRAEL'S
HISTORY

ROOTS, RIGHTS, AND THE
STRUGGLE FOR PEACE

DAVID BROG

REGNERY
PUBLISHING
A Division of Salem Media Group

Regnery® is a registered trademark of Salem Communications Holding Corporation

Cataloging-in-Publication data on file with the Library of Congress

ISBN 978-1-62157-590-0

Published in the United States by
Regnery Publishing
A Division of Salem Media Group
300 New Jersey Ave NW
Washington, DC 20001
www.Regnery.com

Manufactured in the United States of America

10 9 8 7 6 5 4 3 2 1

Books are available in quantity for promotional or premium use. For information on discounts and terms, please visit our website: www.Regnery.com.

Distributed to the trade by
Perseus Distribution
www.perseusdistribution.com

For Hila

CONTENTS

PREFACE

Criticizing Israel is not anti-Semitic, and saying so is vile. But singling out Israel for opprobrium and international sanction— out of all proportion to any other party in the Middle East—is anti-Semitic, and not saying so is dishonest.

—Thomas L. Friedman, 2002[1]

There was a time when Israel could do no wrong. Before 1967, Americans and most other Westerners typically saw Israel as an embattled outpost of democracy heroically defending itself from Arab multitudes determined to destroy it. Israel's civilians were gutsy. Israel's soldiers were gallant. Israel's wars were good.

This myth of the perfect Israel could not last. No nation is so noble and no cause so pure. Israel has committed sins both small and large. Israeli soldiers have killed innocent Arab civilians—and not always by mistake. Israeli commanders have expelled Arabs from their villages and destroyed their homes—and not always in cases of clear military necessity.

We now know about these Israeli transgressions in detail. We know about them because Israeli scholars have documented them. And we know about them because the Israeli media has publicized them. Such is life in a free society.

The problem is that the very facts that helped destroy one false narrative are now being used to construct a new one. The myth of the perfect Israel is being replaced by the myth of the evil Israel. Israel's exceptionally multiracial and multicultural society is condemned as "apartheid." Israel's unparalleled efforts to defend its citizens while minimizing harm to Palestinian civilians are dismissed as "massacres." A complex reality in which the Palestinians have rejected repeated Israeli offers of statehood is dismissed as "occupation."

Slanders such as these are fragile creatures. They can survive only in a rarefied environment empty of all context and history. Those seeking to spread such lies must disconnect Israel's actions from their underlying motives. And once the rationale is removed, the noblest defense is transformed into the ugliest aggression. The Allies had a very good reason to invade France on D-Day. This reason is why the men who fought and killed that day are heroes, not villains. Context is key.

Those seeking to tell the truth about Israel today need not revive the old fantasy. But we must confront the new lies. Most important, we must provide the context within which Israel has made difficult decisions and taken controversial actions.

WHY ISRAEL?

In revisiting these controversies, we will be placing Israel under a microscope. Such an invasive examination will inevitably highlight flaws that were invisible from afar. The very act of inspection is, practically speaking, an act of criticism. Only the perfect would emerge from such scrutiny undiminished.

So perhaps before proceeding to examine Israel, we should first pause to examine ourselves. Most of us who dissect Israel's founding and subsequent struggles have never made a similar study of any other nation, including our own. So why Israel? Does our focus on Israel speak to the special nature of Israel's sins? Or does this singular scrutiny reflect instead a flaw animating Israel's accusers?

Israel's critics are quick to claim the former. They don't deny their special focus on Israel. They rationalize it by reference to Israel's alleged crimes. The modern anti-Israel narrative focuses on a trio of Palestinian grievances in particular: occupation, statelessness, and refugeedom.

OCCUPATION AND STATELESSNESS

The crux of the modern complaint against Israel is that it is occupying the land on which the Palestinians want to build their state, thereby rendering them stateless. Those leading the attack typically speak of "occupation" and "statelessness" as crimes so outrageous that they invalidate any defense. As Palestinian President Mahmoud Abbas phrased it in 2014, "We are the only people on earth still living under occupation. Not acceptable."[2]

The underlying claim is true. The Palestinians are indeed stateless. But the issue of causation is more complex. Just because the Palestinians are stateless does not mean that Israel is to blame. National suffering, much like personal pain, can be self-inflicted.

The fact is that the Palestinians have been offered a state of their own in practically all of the West Bank and Gaza—and in even larger territories—on five separate occasions. The first offer was made in 1937. The most recent offer was made in 2008. The Palestinians turned down each of these deals. This history of independence offered and rejected should at least give critics pause before they point their fingers at Israel.

It's also important to note that statelessness is not the singular, insufferable condition that so many suppose it to be. President Abbas's protestations notwithstanding, the Palestinians are not the only "occupied" people on the planet. Far from it. *The Encyclopedia of the Stateless Nations* chronicles the claims of 350 stateless nations. And the encyclopedia's author is quick to stress that these 350 examples represent only "a fraction" of the world's stateless nations. He profiled only those stateless nations that are actively seeking their independence.[3]

There are multiple stateless nations that have never organized or sustained independence movements. In fact, according to the United

Nations, "only 3% of the world's 6,000 national groups have achieved statehood."[4] Some of these stateless nations are relatively new ones—such as the Palestinians—who developed their national identities after World War I, World War II, or even later. Other stateless nations are ancient ones—such as the Kurds—who have had their own separate identities for centuries.

Some of these stateless nations are small and obscure, such as the 790,000 Jejuvians of Korea and the 1.3 million Majeerteens of Somalia. Other stateless nations are large yet still obscure, such as the 23 million Ibos of Nigeria or the 11-million-strong Baluch community in Iran, Afghanistan, Pakistan, and India. Other stateless nations have higher profiles, such as the 6.5 million Tibetans in China and the 70 million Tamils of south India and northern Sri Lanka.

Nor is statelessness merely a Third World problem. The *Atlas of Stateless Nations in Europe* profiles thirty such nations. Here too the author chose to include only those stateless nations with active independence movements. These include the Basques and Catalans in Spain, the Bretons and Corsicans in France, and the Manx and Welsh in Great Britain. Hungary alone has thirteen stateless national minorities on its soil.[5]

Two wrongs don't make a right. Nor do 350. But this multiplicity of stateless nations raises an obvious question: Why is only one of these alleged wrongs the subject of so much of the world's focus, passion, and outrage? Why are so many people so deeply troubled by Palestinian statelessness but have no such concern about—or even knowledge of—the statelessness of so many older and larger national groups? What is it about the Palestinians that causes so many to care so much?

When passions are aroused, religion is often involved. The large majority of Palestinians are Muslim. Maybe we focus on the Palestinians because in our post-colonial, multicultural era we have developed a particular sensitivity to the occupation of Muslims. But if this is the case, then how do we explain the fact that so many other stateless Muslim nations receive so much less attention? In the Caucasus region alone, the Abkhaz, Balkars, Chechens, Ingush, and Dagestanis are all Muslim peoples seeking their independence from Russia. How many of us have even heard of these nations? Over ten million Muslim Uighurs seek their independence from China. How many of us can even pronounce their name?

Or perhaps our focus on the Palestinians flows from the fact that a minority of Palestinians are Christian. It would make sense for observers in the predominantly Christian West to take an outsized interest when their coreligionists are the ones suffering statelessness. Yet this theory fails to explain the existence of so many stateless Christian nations that receive no such attention. In the Muslim world alone, the Assyrians, Chaldeans, and Copts are Christian nations that have long sought independence from the majority Muslim states in which they live. These Christians are facing increasingly serious persecution at the hands of Islamic militants. Yet the West remains largely indifferent to their plight.

Maybe it's not religion at all but another category—nationality—that drives our concern. The Palestinians, Muslim and Christian alike, are an Arab people. Filmmakers have long glorified the Arab struggle for independence in movies such as *Lawrence of Arabia* and *The Battle of Algiers*. Perhaps we fixate on the Palestinians because we share a core conviction that Arabs must be free.

But like the prior examples, this theory fails to explain the existence of so many stateless Arab nations that suffer in anonymity. There are, for example, over 6.8 million stateless Hejazis spread out between Jordan and Saudi Arabia. The Arab Alawites lack a state of their own, as do the Arab Druze.

THE PLIGHT OF THE ARABISTANIS

The obscurity of the Arabistani people stands as a clear rebuttal to any claim of a special Western compassion for stateless people in general and stateless Arabs or Muslims in particular. The Arabistanis (also known as Ahwazis) are an Arab people numbering some five to eight million.[6] All of the land the Arabistanis claim is occupied by Iran, rendering them stateless. Their efforts to win their independence have been brutally suppressed.

The Arabistanis have a long history. The Arabs conquered Arabistan from the Persians in the seventh century. As Arabs gradually settled this region, most of its indigenous inhabitants assimilated or disappeared. The Persians eventually re-conquered this territory in the sixteenth century and renamed it Khuzestan. But despite Persian efforts to shift the demographic balance, Arabistan's population has remained overwhelmingly Arab.

Unlike the relatively new Palestinians, the Arabistanis have had a separate national identity for centuries and have enjoyed long periods of self-rule. In 1821, the Persians permitted the Arabistanis to establish an autonomous emirate. In 1857, the Emirate of Arabistan was allowed to enter into diplomatic relations with other states. In 1923, Arabistan revolted and declared independence from Persia. Persian troops crushed this rebellion the following year.

When Reza Shah Pahlavi rose to power in 1925, he centralized the Iranian government under his firm control. He terminated Arabistan's traditional autonomy and outlawed the public use of the Arabic language. In 1936, the last Arabistani emir, Sheikh Khazaal, was imprisoned and murdered in Tehran.[7]

After the Ayatollah Khomeini deposed the shah in 1979, the Arabs of Arabistan dared to dream that their long night of oppression had finally ended. They took to the streets to demand the return of the autonomy that the shah had denied them for so long. But Khomeini violently crushed the protests. When the Arabistanis launched a new round of demonstrations in 2005, the Iranians repressed them with even greater brutality. Over 130 Arab protestors were killed, and many more were imprisoned.[8]

Like the Palestinians, the Arabistanis have even resorted to terrorism to publicize their plight. In 1979, a group of Arabistani nationalists founded the Democratic Revolutionary Front for the Liberation of Arabistan (DRFLA). In April 1980, six armed DRFLA terrorists seized the Iranian Embassy in London and took twenty-six hostages. They threatened to blow up the building and kill the hostages if ninety-one Arab prisoners were not released from Iranian jails. The standoff ended when British forces stormed the embassy and killed most of the DRFLA gunmen.

Arabistan's Arabs face discrimination in education, employment, politics, and culture.[9] More than half of the province's population lives in poverty.[10] Even where the majority of students are Arab, schools are not permitted to teach in Arabic.[11] And Iran's government has undertaken active efforts to ethnically cleanse Arabistan of its Arabs. According to Amnesty International, "Land expropriation by the Iranian authorities is reportedly so widespread that it appears to amount to a policy aimed at dispossessing Arabs of their traditional lands. This is apparently part of a strategy aimed at the forcible relocation of Arabs to other areas while facilitating the transfer of non-Arabs into Khuzestan."[12]

The Arabistanis will not win their freedom any time soon. Ninety percent of Iran's oil revenues come from wells in Arabistan.[13] Simply put, an Iran without Arabistan is an Iran without oil.

THE PALESTINIAN REFUGEES

There is no logical explanation for the vast gap in attention paid to these two stateless Arab peoples, the Palestinians and the Arabistanis. So perhaps statelessness isn't the issue at all. Perhaps what truly troubles us is not that the Palestinians are stateless, but that so many Palestinians are homeless. Maybe it's the Palestinian refugee problem that drives the world's concern.

The Palestinians have certainly suffered displacement. Israel's 1948 War of Independence produced approximately seven hundred thousand Palestinian Arab refugees. But the reality of Palestinian pain does not necessarily mean that Israel is to blame.

The fact is that the large majority of these Palestinian refugees chose to flee a war that their leaders started and their Arab neighbors escalated.

Even the minority of refugees forcibly expelled by Israel lived largely in villages that had been rendered strategic targets by this war that Israel had so desperately sought to avoid. This direct link between Arab aggression and Arab dislocation should at least temper the outrage of those seeking to blame this suffering on Israel.

It is also important to note that homelessness, like statelessness, is not the rare historical injustice that so many claim it to be. The tragic reality is that the world is awash in the displaced and dislocated. In recent years, the war in Afghanistan has produced over 2.5 million refugees. The Iraq War has produced over 1.5 million refugees. By early 2016, the Syrian Civil War had produced well over 4 million refugees. Yet we in the West rarely pause to contemplate the massive scale of this suffering.

What is common today was epidemic last century. Two world wars and the subsequent birth of multiple new nation states permanently pushed many millions from the lands of their birth. Yet despite the vast numbers involved, most of us have never heard of these refugees.

In some cases the refugees were forced from their homes not by war, but by the peace that followed. After World War I, the victorious allies carved the defeated Ottoman Empire into a number of new states. As part of this process, they decided to try to end the ethnic tensions between Greeks and Turks that had sparked so much conflict over so many centuries. The solution they prescribed was radical: a massive population exchange. Under the supervision of the League of Nations, all ethnic Greeks living in Turkey were expelled to Greece and all ethnic Turks living in Greece were transferred to Turkey. Close to two million people were thus forced from the only homes they had even known and sent to live in a new land.[14]

These expulsions generated little outrage at the time or in the decades that followed. Quite to the contrary, most observers saw this population exchange as a great success. As Winston Churchill noted in a 1944 speech to Parliament, "The disentanglement of populations which took place between Greece and Turkey after the last war...was in many ways a success, and has produced friendly relations between Greece and Turkey ever since...."[15]

The British certainly had this example of peace through separation in mind when they granted India its independence in 1947. As the British withdrawal neared, violence between India's Muslims and Hindus escalated. The British addressed this crisis by partitioning their massive colony into two countries: Hindu-majority India and Muslim-majority Pakistan.

In the months immediately following partition, however, this interreligious violence only intensified. The bloodshed eventually triggered a massive population exchange, as religious minorities sought safety among their coreligionists. Over seven million Muslims fled India for Pakistan. And approximately seven million Hindus and Sikhs fled Pakistan for India.

Why have most Westerners forgotten these Muslim refugees from India but remain laser focused on the Muslim refugees from Palestine? The dual crises that created these two homeless populations occurred within one year of each other, in 1947 and 1948 respectively. And the Muslim exodus from India was over nine times larger than the Muslim exodus from Palestine.

Perhaps we have forgotten these Indian refugees because they were part of a population exchange. Both sides—Hindu and Muslim—suffered horribly from this upheaval. Likewise, the Greek and Turkish refugees of 1923 were part of an exchange with shared suffering on each side. The Palestinians, by contrast, are widely believed to be the only refugees to flow from Israel's wars in 1948 and 1967.

But this perception of one-sided Palestinian suffering is as wrong as it is widespread. The wars in 1948 and 1967 did produce Jewish refugees—and they did so in numbers that actually surpassed the number of Arab refugees.

The tragic fact is that Israel's victories in these wars outraged the Arab world. As a result, each conflict was followed by waves of anti-Jewish riots, confiscations, murders, and expulsions in every Arab country that had a Jewish population to persecute. These upheavals ultimately forced approximately eight hundred thousand Jews from their homes in Arab lands. Many of these Jewish communities had predated the birth of Islam and the Arab conquest that followed.

There is only one reason why relatively few people are even aware that such Jewish refugees ever existed: most of them found new homes in Israel.

THE GERMAN REFUGEES

If there were something about refugees that truly captivated our consciences, then most Westerners would certainly be outraged by a far larger refugee crisis that happened much closer to home only a few years before the Palestinian exodus: the expulsion of approximately twelve million ethnic Germans from Eastern Europe following World War II. There are many striking parallels between the Palestinian and German refugees. There's just one critical difference: most people have no idea that these millions of German refugees ever existed.

In the seventh century, the Arabs emerged from their homeland on the Arabian Peninsula and conquered most of the Middle East and North Africa. In the thirteenth century, the Germans ventured from their homeland in central Europe and settled large swaths of Eastern Europe. These two nations on the move came to dominate their respective regions.

World War I marked a disappointing turning point for both of these far-flung peoples. In the Middle East, the post-war settlement opened Palestine to Jewish immigrants who threatened to eventually transform the Arabs living there into a minority. In Eastern Europe, the post-war treaties divided the former Austro-Hungarian Empire into a handful of new, non-German successor states such as Czechoslovakia, Poland, and

Hungary. As a result, the millions of ethnic Germans living in these new countries were *immediately* transformed into minorities. Most of these Germans lived in centuries-old communities in German-majority regions that had always been considered an integral part of the German homeland.

Eventually, both the Arabs and the Germans launched wars to rectify these perceived injustices. German resentment was the first to boil over. The liberation of these German minorities and their reunification with their German brethren was a central plank in the Nazi platform. The fulfillment of this sacred pledge was a major motive behind the Nazi aggression that sparked World War II.

As German troops conquered their communities, many East European Germans welcomed them as liberators. Some of these ethnic Germans served in the Gestapo, the Wehrmacht, and the SS and participated in their atrocities. Others refused to join the Nazis and even fought against them. But when the war was over, almost all of East Europe's ethnic Germans bore the brunt of a brutal revenge.

As World War II drew to a close, the Czech and Polish governments in exile openly declared their intention to expel their ethnic German populations. The United States and Britain were quick to express sympathy. President Roosevelt wrote the following to the prime minister of the Polish government in exile: "If the Polish Government and people desire in connection with the new frontiers of the Polish state to bring about the transfer to and from the territory of Poland of national minorities, the United States Government will raise no objection, and as far as practicable, will facilitate such transfer."[16]

The Germans that Roosevelt was agreeing to expel had ancestors living in Poland long before the first Englishman had set foot in North America.

Winston Churchill was even more explicit. Referring to these German communities in a December 15, 1944, speech before Parliament, he stated, "Expulsion is the method which, so far as we have been able to see, will be the most satisfactory and lasting. There will be no mixture of populations to cause endless trouble.... A clean sweep will be made. I am not alarmed at the prospect of the disentanglement of populations, nor even by these large transferences, which are more possible in modern conditions than they ever were before."[17]

These were not mere empty words. In August of 1945, the victorious allies met in Potsdam. Winston Churchill and Joseph Stalin were joined by America's new president, Harry Truman. Here, these three leaders formally agreed to the mass expulsion of ethnic Germans from East Europe. Article XII of the Potsdam Protocol reads, in part, "The Three Governments having considered the question in all its aspects recognize that the transfer to Germany of German populations, or elements thereof, remaining in Poland, Czechoslovakia and Hungary will have to be undertaken. They agree that any transfers that take place should be effected in an orderly and humane manner."[18]

Those seeking to defend this agreement stress that the alternative might well have been worse. While the negotiations were taking place, ethnic Germans were already being brutalized across Eastern Europe. The Soviets were slaughtering ethnic Germans in Poland and deporting the rest to labor camps in Siberia. The Czechs were forcing ethnic Germans into abandoned Nazi concentration camps and then deporting them to Germany in cramped cattle cars or in forced marches that many did not survive.

The Americans and the British hoped that by agreeing to these transfers they could at least ensure that they were carried out more humanely. And this deal with the devil ultimately did pay some dividends. The worst of the post-war atrocities were ended. Conditions were improved. And the daily transports of ethnic Germans from their ancient communities to new homes in a truncated Germany continued until 1947.

Eventually, between ten and fifteen million ethnic Germans were expelled from Poland, Czechoslovakia, Hungary, and Yugoslavia. Over two million died before finding new homes in Germany.[19] Through immigration and intermarriage, every fourth German citizen has roots in these destroyed eastern communities.

When Winston Churchill wrote his history of World War II, he predicted that this post-war arrangement was a time bomb that would explode in a future war much as the treaties ending World War I had. He believed that these millions of displaced Germans would empower yet another expansionist German leader to liberate their former homes and pave the way for their triumphant return.

Churchill was wrong. Shortly after the war, these German refugees formed two large organizations to represent them: the United Eastern German Association and the Central Union of Expelled Germans. In 1949, these organizations collaborated to draft a "Magna Carta" of expellee rights. In this enlightened document, the expellees declared their intention to "renounce revenge and retaliation." Instead they committed themselves—"by means of hard, tireless effort"—to "contribute to the reconstruction of Germany and Europe."[20]

That is exactly what they did. These millions of displaced Germans were a highly trained labor force. And they were hungry for opportunity. The combination of their enterprise and the Marshall Plan's capital sparked an economic miracle. During the course of the decade that followed, Germany quickly rebuilt and resumed its position as Europe's economic powerhouse.

The Czech and Polish Germans came from communities that were often more than seven hundred years old. They could have resisted relocation to a foreign corner of the German homeland. They could have formed a Sudeten Liberation Army or a Popular Front for the Liberation of Prussia to reclaim their lost homes. German terror groups could have killed innocent Czechs and Poles to publicize their plight and dramatize their demands.

The fact that these millions of German refugees chose a different path is of enormous significance. It demonstrates that not every people with a grievance must respond with rage. It shows that it's possible to look forward in hope rather than look back in anger. This is what the Turkish and Greek refugees did. This is what the Jewish refugees from both the Arab world and Europe did. This is what most of the Hindu and Muslim refugees from India and Pakistan did. In fact, this is pretty much what every refugee group in the history of refugees has done, with one notable exception: the Palestinians.

The contrast between the German and Palestinian responses to their respective military defeats is instructive. It is a contrast that has been highlighted by those at the forefront of studying the history of the German refugees. Alfred de Zayas, one of the chief chroniclers of the German expulsions, has stressed that "Unlike the Palestinian expellees who became terrorists in spite of millions of dollars of United Nations help, the German expellees transformed Marshall Plan Aid into work which not only enabled them to survive but also gradually to rebuild their lives in a liberal, democratic—and peaceful—society."[21]

Not only did these German refugees respond constructively, but so too did the Germany into which they were forced. Unlike the Arab states to which the Palestinians fled, Germany did not confine the German refugees to camps. It did not bar them from becoming citizens. And it did not seek to use them as political pawns to preserve a German claim to the formerly German lands from which they came.

Quite to the contrary, Germany welcomed these refugees as full citizens of a new, smaller Germany. And it invested significant resources in supporting and integrating them. In September 1952, for example, Germany passed the Equalization of Burdens Law. This generous legislation sought to enlist the entire German people in alleviating the suffering of the

German refugees. German tax dollars were put to work providing expellees with sufficient training, housing, and health care.[22]

This generation of Germans recognized their responsibility for the tragedy of World War II. And they taught their moral clarity to their children. Even as the details of this German refugee crisis became public knowledge during the 1960s, young Germans refused to allow their elders to claim the mantle of victim: "The Generation of 1968 claimed that their fathers should not be permitted to complain about their own misery during and after the war."[23] In sharp contrast, 1968 was the year that the Popular Front for the Liberation of Palestine carried out the first Arab airline hijacking, launching an era of Palestinian terrorism that would seek to highlight Palestinian misery after the war they started in 1948.

In 2009, Germany decided to open a museum dedicated to the history of the German expellees. Poland's prime minister cautioned Germany not to use this museum as a vehicle to criticize Poland's post-war expulsions. A German government spokesman responded by promising that "the federally funded memorial would not attempt to reinterpret the history of the war and its aftermath, and reiterated Germany's admission of blame for starting the war and all its consequences."[24] That same year Hamas, a Palestinian terrorist organization that refuses to admit any Palestinian blame for anything, fired hundreds of rockets and mortars at Israeli cities and towns.

THE UNITED NATIONS AND THE PALESTINIANS

There is one way in which the Palestinian refugees are in fact unique. The United Nations has created a special organization for Palestinian refugees that both defines them differently and cares for them separately from every other refugee population on earth. In so doing, the international community has been a full partner in helping the Palestinian refugees preserve their status and nurture their grievances.

The United Nations High Commissioner for Refugees (UNHCR) is the body that cares for all of the world's refugees except for the Palestinians. The UNHCR defines a "refugee" as someone who is driven from "the country of his nationality" by a well-founded fear of persecution. This definition imposes two important limitations on the category it creates. First, refugees do not transfer this status with their genes: any children born to them in exile are not considered refugees. Second, refugees lose their refugee status as soon as they are granted citizenship in a new country.

After the 1948 Arab-Israeli War, the United Nations established a new organization dedicated exclusively to the Palestinian refugees: the United Nations Relief and Works Agency (UNRWA). UNRWA defines a "Palestine refugee" as anyone who was displaced by the 1948 War plus the "descendants of Palestine refugee males, including legally adopted children." In other words, Palestinian refugees pass their refugee status to their children in perpetuity.

In addition, UNRWA continues to recognize a Palestinian refugee as such even if he or she has obtained citizenship in another country. For example, there are approximately two million Palestinian refugees currently living in Jordan. They are all counted as refugees even though over ninety percent of these individuals are full Jordanian citizens.

Thus instead of dramatically shrinking from generation to generation like every other refugee population, the number of Palestinian refugees is growing exponentially. According to UNRWA's website, "When the Agency began operations in 1950, it was responding to the needs of about 750,000 Palestine refugees. Today, some 5 million Palestine refugees are eligible for UNRWA services."[25] If Palestinian refugees were defined the same way as all other refugees, the number of Palestinian refugees in 2014 would be closer to 30,000.[26]

WHY THE PALESTINIANS?

Our obsession with Israel is not caused by Palestinian statelessness or homelessness. There is nothing unique about Palestinian loss or suffering. Tragically, the world has done far worse to far more people to whom we pay far less attention.

What is truly unique about the Palestinians is not what they have suffered, but how they have responded to their suffering. The Palestinians are the only refugee population from the World War II era to remain frozen in time. They alone remain in camps. They alone have nurtured a culture in which the keys to houses that no longer exist are often more cherished than the lives of their children.

Most significantly, the Palestinians have consistently sought to address their grievances by resorting to terrorism—the intentional targeting of civilians with violence. Yasser Arafat did not invent terrorism in the 1970s. When the Palestine Liberation Organization (PLO) began hijacking Israel-bound planes and slaughtering Israeli schoolchildren, they were treading a well-worn path. The earliest expressions of Palestinian nationalism in the 1920s and 1930s involved the murder of Jewish civilians in Jerusalem, Jaffa, Safed, and Hebron.

A century of Palestinian terror has produced a perverse public relations payoff. Rather than blame the Palestinians for resorting to so violent a tactic, the world's morally challenged have concluded that a people so especially outraged must have been uniquely wronged. If so many Palestinians are willing to strap bombs to their bodies and blow themselves up, we're told, then Israel must be guilty of some truly terrible crimes.

But Palestinian terror is not a reflection of Israeli misdeeds. It is a mirror held up to the Palestinians themselves. The Palestinian choice to respond to their suffering with generation after generation of violence reveals far more about the true source of Palestinian pain than any excuse they might offer.

There is another reason for the world's special focus on the Palestinians. Israel's defenders are often too quick to invoke it, and Israel's critics are typically too fast to dismiss it. Yet as hatred of Israel grows out of all proportion to Israel's actual sins, it is increasingly difficult to deny the role that anti-Semitism plays in this obsession with the Jewish state.

Let's be clear. It is not anti-Semitic to criticize Israel. Israel often deserves to be criticized, and Israelis themselves are typically the ones leading the charge. But it is anti-Semitic to criticize *only* Israel. Those who ignore the sins of all other nations and are outraged only by Jewish sins—real or imagined—are doing exactly what all anti-Semites have done throughout history. They are singling out Jews for our common human failures. And, more often than not, they are exaggerating if not outright imagining the Jewish transgression.

While anti-Semitism may be fueled by blind hate, anti-Semites rarely recognize their motive. Anti-Semites *never* criticize Jews simply for being Jewish.[27] They *always* criticize Jews for some alleged crime or offense. These sins are shared by all humanity, but the Jews are singled out for blame. Some Jews were capitalists—yes. But Europe's anti-Semites turned capitalism into a purely Jewish enterprise. Some Jews were communists—absolutely. But the Nazis turned communism into a uniquely Jewish conspiracy. Some Jews committed murder—of course. But the infamous "blood libel" turned every unsolved murder into a Jewish plot to obtain blood for their dark religious rituals.

Today, Israeli Jews are nationalists. They believe in building a nation state that preserves a special focus on one specific people and culture. The Jews did not invent nationalism. And in a world with hundreds of independent nation states—and hundreds more peoples seeking the same—they are certainly not the sole practitioners thereof. But they are somehow blamed for nationalism's sins every bit as much as they were blamed for those of capitalism and communism in decades past.

Today, Israeli Jews are counter-terrorists. Israel is on the front lines of a new type of asymmetrical warfare against terrorist organizations dedicated to murdering civilians on both sides of the conflict. Countries across the globe are now confronting this very difficult military and moral challenge. Yet Israel's Jews continue to suffer the lion's share of the blame for the casualties that such warfare inevitably produces.

Arab journalist Khaled Abu Toameh sums up the media's priorities with the phrase "no Jews, no news."[28] What he means is that the media tends to ignore the death and suffering of Arabs unless there is some way to blame Israel for it. Yes, there are articles about the hundreds of thousands of Arabs being intentionally slaughtered by their fellow Arabs in Syria. But this coverage lacks the frequency, intensity, and outrage of the articles written when Israel accidentally kills Arabs—in exponentially smaller numbers—in its ongoing battle against Hamas and other terror organizations.

The answer to the question "why Israel" is often that Israel is the Jewish state. Recognizing this fact does not require one to excuse Israeli misdeeds or ignore Palestinian suffering. All it requires is an admission of the obvious.

This book will not seek to reestablish the myth of the perfect Israel. Nor will it portray Israel as the monster it is increasingly said to be. What follows is largely the story of thoughtful Israeli leaders struggling with oversized challenges. Don't be surprised if you find yourself agreeing with their decisions. Once the historical dots are connected and the context colored in, the picture that emerges is almost always understandable—and often quite admirable.

PEACE THROUGH TRUTH

By what mystical geography are we not at home there [the Middle East] too, we who descend from the same indigenous populations since the first human settlements were made? Why should only the converts to Islam be the sole proprietors of our common soil?

—Albert Memmi, 1975[1]

The 1950s and 60s were decades of liberation struggles across the Third World. One by one, colonized peoples rose up against their European masters and demanded their independence. When this freedom was too long withheld, armed revolt often followed.

In those pre-digital days the powerful idea of national liberation was spread primarily by books. Frantz Fanon's *The Wretched of the Earth* is credited with sparking the bloody Algerian revolt against France. But across North Africa and beyond, colonial police frequently found nationalist rebels in possession of another book. This volume—*The Colonizer and the Colonized*—set forth the author's militant program in stark terms: "Revolt is the only way out of the colonial situation, and the colonized realizes it sooner or later. His condition is absolute and cries for an absolute solution; a break and not a compromise.... For the colonial condition cannot be adjusted to; like an iron collar, it can only be broken."[2]

1

The Colonizer and the Colonized was written by an Arab nationalist named Albert Memmi. Memmi was a leading intellectual of the
Destour, the party that won Tunisia's independence from France. Memmi
was born, raised, and educated in Tunisia. But he was different from
most of his nationalist comrades, and this difference would ultimately
force him to flee the very homeland he had helped to liberate. Albert
Memmi is a Jew.

Memmi saw no contradiction between his Arab and Jewish identities. Since the Arabs are a people, not a religion, he believed that one
could be a Jewish Arab every bit as much as one could be a Muslim Arab
or Christian Arab. But his Arab colleagues, friends, and neighbors disagreed. As Memmi would write years after leaving his homeland, "Jewish Arabs—that's what we would have liked to be, and if we have given
up the idea, it is because for centuries the Muslim Arabs have scornfully,
cruelly, and systematically prevented us from carrying it out. And now
it is far too late to become Jewish Arabs again."³

Far from being accepted as fellow Arabs, Tunisia's Jews were a
despised and often persecuted minority. And the situation in Tunisia was
the rule for the Arab world in general. As Memmi noted, "The supposedly
'idyllic' life led by Jews in the Arab countries is all a myth!... As far back
as memories can take me, in the stories told by my father, my grandparents,
my aunts and uncles, cohabitation with the Arab was not only uneasy but
filled with threats, which were periodically carried out.... Never, I repeat,
never—except perhaps for two or three eras with very clear boundaries in
time...have Jews lived in the Arab countries otherwise than as diminished
people in an exposed position, periodically overcome and massacred so
that they would be acutely conscious of their position."⁴

Memmi recalled his own grandfather wearing the distinguishing
marks on his clothing that Tunisian Jews were once required to display.
And he remembered his grandfather's stories of being hit on the head by
passing Muslims—a ritual called the *chtaka*—as a way to remind Jews
of their inferior status.⁵

Memmi also remembered the terror sparked by rumors of an imminent anti-Semitic attack: his father rushing home from his store, windows

and doors being hastily bolted, the fear of a child who grasps that his parents may not be able to protect him from this danger.[6]

THE WRETCHED OF THE EARTH

Reflecting on his life, Memmi realized that he and his fellow Arab Jews were double victims: they had been colonized by the colonized. If the colonized people of the Third World were, in Fanon's term, the "wretched of the earth," then the Jews of the Arab world were more wretched still. As Memmi argued, "The Arabs were colonized, it is true. But weren't we? What have we been for centuries if not dominated, humiliated, threatened, and periodically massacred? And by whom? Isn't it time our answer was heeded: by the Moslem Arabs."[7]

Memmi had been a loyal soldier in the fight for the liberation of the colonized Arabs. But he refused to accept anything less for his own people, the twice-colonized Jews. Thus Memmi supported Jewish national liberation—also known as Zionism—and argued that the Jews should build their independent state in the Middle East to which they too were indigenous. He urged Muslim Arabs to understand that Jews from Arabs lands also needed to "live free like them," and that the State of Israel offered them the opportunity to do so "on a scrap of the immense common territory which belongs to us too, though it is called Arab."[8]

When Memmi wrote these words, Arab leaders were largely in the thrall of a philosophy known as pan-Arab nationalism. This movement saw all Arabic speakers—from Morocco's Atlantic coast to Iraq's eastern frontier—as part of one large Arab people. And this movement claimed the massive expanse of land on which these Arabs lived as one extended Arab homeland. Thus Memmi and almost all of his contemporaries typically spoke of Israel in the context of this vastly larger Arab world.

After Israel crushed four Arab armies in six days in 1967, this pan-Arab dream began to fade. Pan-Arab nationalism disintegrated into a series of smaller nation-state nationalisms.[9] Among the Arab groups asserting a new and narrower identity were the Arabs living in the former British Mandate for Palestine. For the first time, a majority of Palestine's Arabs began to see themselves as part of a separate Palestinian people. And for the first time, a majority of Palestine's Arabs began to seek independence instead of integration into the larger Arab world around them.

Memmi responded to this sudden shift with instant generosity. He called for the creation of a Palestinian state in 1969, years before the United Nations or even the Arab League got around to doing so. But while this veteran Arab nationalist was quick to support the Palestinian cause, he saw nothing in this new movement that delegitimized Jewish nationalism. As he noted in 1973, "Certainly the Palestinian Arabs' situation is tragic, just as ours is; but it must be recalled…that they are scarcely any more numerous than we are, and that they too often come from elsewhere, just like us. When you come right down to it, the Palestinian Arabs' misfortune is having been moved about thirty miles within one vast nation. Is that so serious? Our own misfortune, as Jews from Arab countries, is much greater, for we have been moved thousands of miles away, after having also lost everything. And today there are 1,300,000 of us, i.e. half the population of Israel."[10]

While Memmi was able to embrace both Palestinian and Jewish nationalism, the Palestinians took a less constructive approach. From the start, Palestinian leaders linked their national liberation to the destruction of Israel. The Palestinians did not seek a state alongside the Jewish state; they demanded a state that would replace the Jewish state. In so doing, they were setting the stage for endless conflict. As Memmi presciently cautioned, "The Palestinians' right to existence, and even to a national existence, must be recognized; but they must not, in turn…proclaim that what they too want is the reconquest of *all* Palestine and 'the end of the Zionist State'…in other words, the same impossible apocalypse."[11]

Many decades have passed since Memmi issued this warning. In the intervening years, the half of Israelis who came from Arab countries have extensively intermarried with the half who came from Europe. As a result, a very large majority of Israelis now trace their roots back to the Arab world.

But while Israel's people have changed, Palestinian policy has not. The Palestinians have ignored Memmi's advice. They have largely refused to de-link their national aspirations from the destruction of Israel. This refusal is the only reason that the Palestinians remain stateless to this very day.

The first leader of the Palestinian national movement—Amin al-Husseini, the Mufti of Jerusalem—was dedicated to the destruction of the Jewish community in Palestine well before there even was a State of Israel. Husseini's years as a Berlin-based Nazi collaborator during World War II were no aberration. His support for the extermination of the Jews was the logical conclusion of his zero-sum mindset, in which the fulfillment of Palestinian rights was inextricably linked to the denial of Jewish rights.

Husseini's successor, Yasser Arafat, shared the same zero-sum approach. After Arafat took over the Palestine Liberation Organization in 1968, the organization ratified a new charter that explicitly denied the existence of a Jewish people and the legitimacy of a Jewish state. And Arafat's PLO became a pioneer of international terrorism as it sought to destroy Israel through armed struggle.

But then things seemed to change. The United States had long maintained that it would not recognize the PLO unless it first renounced terrorism. Facing increasing irrelevance, Arafat eventually decided to meet this American demand. In 1988, he held a press conference in which he seemed to speak a formula that had been arranged in advance with American diplomats.

But Arafat's words that day were unclear, and his intentions less clear still. Munib al-Masri, one of Arafat's oldest friends and colleagues, was with Arafat while he negotiated his statement. Al-Masri related that the Americans had asked Arafat to say, "We totally and absolutely renounce all forms of terrorism." Yet, according to al-Masri, Arafat could not bring himself to say the words. Instead, what he actually said at the press conference was: "We announce tourism! We announce all forms of tourism!"[12]

Whatever Arafat really said that day, his actions proved his true intentions. Arafat signed the Oslo Accords with Israel in 1993 and accepted control of increasing portions of Gaza and the West Bank pursuant thereto. But in 2000 the Palestinians launched a bloody *intifada* against Israel, characterized by suicide bombers' blowing up Israeli restaurants, buses, and cafes. It was later proven that Yasser Arafat had directly ordered and funded many of these attacks.

Arafat died in 2004. He was succeeded by his loyal lieutenant, Mahmoud Abbas.

Unlike his predecessors, Abbas renounced terrorism and seems to have stuck to it. In recent years, he has not been directly implicated in planning or funding terrorist attacks against Israelis *before the fact*. But his hands are hardly clean. The Palestinian Authority he runs makes monthly payments to the families of terrorists who died or were arrested while attacking Israelis.

Yet this tactical shift aside, Abbas has done little to free the Palestinians from their original national sin of linking their liberation to Israel's destruction. To the contrary, Abbas has actually strengthened this linkage by teaching his people that the Jews have no rights in the land and that the Palestinians have no responsibility for the conflict. Yes, Abbas talks about compromise and a two-state solution. But in the environment that he has created, such talk sounds treasonous to Palestinian ears.

Abbas spreads this anti-Israel narrative every time the Palestinian Authority names a street after a suicide bomber or broadcasts a television program praising jihad against the Jews. So ingrained is Abbas's belief in Israel's illegitimacy that it even spills over into his English-language public relations efforts.

THE LONG OVERDUE PALESTINIAN STATE

In May of 2011, Abbas published an op-ed in the *New York Times* entitled "The Long Overdue Palestinian State." This piece was a passionate plea to the United Nations to recognize a "State of Palestine" in the West Bank and Gaza Strip. On the surface, it appeared that Abbas was merely making a modest request for what Albert Memmi and so many others already supported back in 1969.

But beneath this humble headline lay some dangerous deceptions. In making his case for the future, Abbas repeatedly lied about the past.

Abbas opened with his personal story: "Sixty-three years ago, a 13-year-old Palestinian boy was forced to leave his home in the Galilean city of Safed and flee with his family to Syria.... Though he and his family wished for decades to return to their home and homeland, they were denied that most basic of human rights. That child's story, like that of so many other Palestinians, is mine."

He then tied his personal tragedy to the larger, national tragedy suffered by his people: "The last time the question of Palestinian statehood took center stage at the General Assembly, the question posed to the international community was whether our homeland should be partitioned into two states. In November 1947, the General Assembly made its recommendation and answered in the affirmative. Shortly thereafter, Zionist forces expelled Palestinian Arabs to ensure a decisive Jewish majority in the future state of Israel, and Arab armies intervened. War and further expulsion ensued."

Finally, Abbas summarized the peace process that began in the early 1990s to resolve this conflict through a two-state solution. He asserted, "We have been negotiating with the State of Israel for 20 years without coming any closer to realizing a state of our own."

Abbas thus sought from the United Nations the justice he claimed he could not obtain through these negotiations: the long overdue Palestinian state.[13]

Westerners are growing increasingly uncomfortable with the word "lie." They find it too judgmental. These days it's far more acceptable to speak of competing "narratives." So what Abbas was doing in this op-ed, many would claim, was simply sharing the "Palestinian narrative."

But in the admirable effort to transcend subjectivity, we dare not abandon reality. When it comes to the Arab-Israeli conflict, there are certainly dueling narratives. But there are also hard facts. And when people knowingly distort these facts they are, in fact, lying. More than any other aspect of this conflict, lies about Israel are responsible for stoking Palestinian rage and sparking Palestinian violence.

If Abbas's narrative is true, then Israel is guilty of unrepentant theft and ethnic cleansing. And a proud people will not sacrifice justice for peace. But if Abbas is wrong—if his black-and-white tale masks a very different reality—then compromise ceases to be capitulation. Compromise instead becomes a courageous act that can deliver both peace and justice.

In the long run, insisting upon the truth is not a petty impediment to peace. Demanding the truth is the only way that peace can ultimately be achieved.

With these considerations in mind, let us fact-check Abbas's Palestinian narrative. Starting with the personal, neither Mahmoud Abbas nor his family was "forced" to leave Safed. They chose to flee Safed. Our source for this fact is none other than Abbas himself. Speaking in Arabic during a 2009 interview on Al-Filistiniya TV, Abbas explained, "People were motivated to run away.... Those of us from Safed especially feared that the Jews harbored old desires to avenge what happened during the 1929 uprising. This was in the memory of our families and parents.... They realized the balance of forces was shifting and therefore the whole town was abandoned on the basis of this rationale—saving our lives and our belongings."[14]

But even the more honest Abbas of 2009 was concealing more than he revealed. The events of "the 1929 uprising" were hardly as noble as the word "uprising" implies. Abbas is referring to a massacre. More specifically, in August 1929 local Arabs invaded Safed's Jewish quarter and engaged in an orgy of destruction, rape, and murder—a pogrom.

David HaCohen, a prominent Jewish leader who rushed to the scene, later wrote the following first-hand account: "The pogrom began on the afternoon of Thursday, August 29, and was carried out by Arabs from Safed and from the nearby villages, armed with weapons and kerosene. Advancing...they looted and set fire to houses, urging each other on to continue with the killing. They slaughtered the schoolteacher, Aphriat, together with his wife and mother, and cut the lawyer, Toledano, to pieces with their knives. Bursting into orphanages, they smashed the children's heads and cut off their hands. I myself saw the victims."[15]

In total, eighteen of Safed's Jews were killed and approximately eighty were wounded that day.[16] Over two hundred Jewish homes were looted and burned.[17]

This was no isolated outburst. What happened in Safed was replicated in towns and villages across Palestine that summer. By the time the violence had ended, the Arabs of Palestine had murdered 133 Jews and injured an additional 339.[18] As Britain's Peel Commission would later note, "There was little retaliation by the Jews."[19]

So much for expulsions. Abbas and his family voluntarily fled Safed. And they fled because they remembered those terrible days nineteen years earlier when their community had massacred their Jewish neighbors and burnt down their homes. They feared that the Jews would finally seek their revenge.

After he misrepresented what happened to his family, Abbas proceeded to distort what happened to his people. Israel did not start the 1948 War in an effort to drive out Palestine's Arabs. Palestine's Arabs started this war in an effort to destroy the Jewish state.

On November 29, 1947, the United Nations voted to partition Palestine into two states—one Jewish and one Arab. Jews in Palestine and around the world had worked desperately to secure the votes of wavering nations. When partition passed, they rejoiced.

The Arabs—those living in Palestine as well as neighboring Arab states—had aggressively opposed the partition plan. They were determined to prevent the creation of a Jewish state on what they viewed as exclusively Muslim Arab land. Every Muslim nation in the General Assembly voted against partition.

As the sun rose over Palestine the morning after the UN vote, Palestinian Arab gunmen murdered seven Jews returning home from their long night of celebration. In the following months, militias from approximately half of Palestine's eight hundred Arab villages attacked Jewish villages and neighborhoods across the country.[20] The 1948 War began as a civil war, with Palestine's Arabs attacking Palestine's Jews in an effort to prevent the creation of a Jewish state.

When the British Mandate for Palestine officially ended on May 15, 1948, the Arab effort to destroy Israel went international. Egypt, Syria, Transjordan, and Iraq invaded the fledgling Jewish state in an effort to accomplish what Palestine's Arabs had failed to do alone. Lebanon later joined the war. Suddenly, the tiny and pathetically equipped Jewish army faced a war on multiple fronts against armies far larger, better armed, and better trained than their own.

Before Palestine's Arabs began this war, there were no Palestinian refugees. Not one. But during the course of this war—a war that the Jews had sought desperately to avoid—approximately seven hundred thousand Palestinian Arabs became refugees. The overwhelming majority of these refugees were individuals who chose to flee their homes in order to escape the fighting. Others fled because they were ordered to do so by certain Arab leaders and commanders.

But that's not the full story. In the middle of a war in which they were fighting hundreds of Palestinian Arab militias at home while facing a multi-front Arab invasion on their borders, the Israelis were confronted with bleak strategic choices. Ultimately, Israeli commanders were authorized to conquer Arab villages and expel their inhabitants when strategic considerations necessitated. Israeli commanders exercised this authority inconsistently, expelling some Arab communities while leaving many others in place.

Reasonable people can certainly debate the morality of each and every Israeli battlefield decision. Secure in the knowledge of Israel's ultimate victory, it's especially tempting to look back and conclude that some of Israel's wartime actions were not strategically justified. Such critiques are legitimate, even valuable. But they don't transform an effect into a cause. The military emergency that forced Israel to confront such tough choices was entirely of Arab making.

So it turns out that Abbas has it exactly backward. The Arab states did not invade Israel to help the Palestinian refugees. It was the Arab invasion that *produced* the Palestinian refugees. Had the Arabs accepted the UN Partition Plan and agreed to the creation of a Jewish state, there would have been a Palestinian state back in 1948. And had the Arabs accepted the partition of Palestine, there would not have been so much as one Palestinian refugee.

Toward the end of his op-ed, Abbas shifted his focus to the peace process begun in Oslo in 1993. Abbas was actually telling the truth when he wrote that these negotiations have not produced a Palestinian state. But his clear implication is that Israel is somehow to blame for this failure. Thus the United Nations must deliver the Palestinian state that Israel has refused to offer.

The reality is quite different. In 2000, Israeli Prime Minister Ehud Barak offered the Palestinians a state in the Gaza Strip, the Arab neighborhoods of East Jerusalem, and ninety-two percent of the West Bank. Later that year, Barak accepted the Clinton Parameters that increased this offer to ninety-four percent of the West Bank plus additional land from Israel proper. In 2008, Prime Minister Ehud Olmert expanded the offer further still, to ninety-four percent of the West Bank plus additional land from Israel proper equal in size to the six percent of the West Bank that Israel sought to retain. Yet Arafat, and then Abbas, turned down these increasingly generous offers. Arafat did so violently. Abbas did so quietly.

If Abbas wanted a Palestinian state, he did not need to seek one from the United Nations. He could have simply said yes when he was offered one in 2008. At the very least, he could have made a counter offer. He did neither.

SPEAKING TRUTH TO TERROR

There are extremists on both side of the Arab-Israeli conflict who lie about and delegitimize the other side. What's most disappointing about Abbas's lies is that he's no fringe figure; he's the president of the Palestinian Authority. And he's the most moderate leader that the Palestinians have ever had.

But while he may recognize the damage that terror has done to the Palestinian cause, Abbas fails to understand the damage done by his deceit. The de-legitimization of Israel is the mother's milk of terror. By convincing Palestinians that there is no justice in Israel's claims, this anti-Israel narrative transforms brave compromise into cowardly surrender. Thus while Abbas may reject the tactic of terror, he has been strengthening the motive for terror. Abbas has been sowing the wind. Both Israelis and Palestinians are reaping the whirlwind.

A HISTORY OF REJECTIONISM

The following pages will tell the tragic story of two small peoples claiming the same small territory. In what may be the only case of its kind, both peoples claim to be indigenous to this land.

One of these peoples—the Jews—is an ancient nation with deep historic, religious, and demographic ties to the land. But this long history of connection to the land is tempered by the long absence of so many Jews from it. The Jews are the indigenous people who were gradually forced out of their land and have been steadily returning to it ever since.

The second of these peoples—the Palestinians—is a new people. The Palestinian national movement was born in the 1920s only after, and partly in response to, this modern Jewish return. It would take decades, until after the 1967 War, for a majority of Palestine's Arabs to embrace this new identity. But this historical deficit is balanced by demography. The people who would become the Palestinians formed a majority of Palestine's population before the birth of the State of Israel.

When two peoples claim the same piece of land, an obvious compromise is to split that land between them. Indeed, this solution—the partition of Palestine into a Jewish state and an Arab state—has been repeatedly proposed since the earliest years of this conflict.

Each time this suggestion was made, the Jews (later the Israelis) accepted it. And each time this offer was made, the Arabs (later the Palestinians) rejected it. Sometimes, as in 1967 and 2008, Palestine's Arabs quietly rejected these offers. Other times—as in 1937, 1947, and 2000—this Arab rejection came in the form of violent attacks against Jewish civilians.

In 2005, Israel tried another tactic. Rather than wait for a peace treaty, it unilaterally removed every last settler and soldier from the Gaza Strip and handed full control to Abbas's Palestinian Authority. The Israelis saw this gesture as a "down payment for peace" that would ease tensions and demonstrate to both sides the value of compromise. Instead, the Palestinian terrorist group Hamas seized Gaza in a bloody coup and began firing missiles into Israel by the thousands.

To point out that one side has a history of compromising while the other has a history of rejectionism is not to claim that one side is perfectly good while the other is purely evil. The truth is that each side to this long conflict has blood on its hands. Each side has made mistakes. Each side has produced extremists who have committed atrocities.

But the fact that this picture isn't perfectly black and white must not blind us to the clear patterns that are present. The conflict between the Arabs and Jews in Palestine persists because one side—the Arab side—has linked their national liberation to the other side's destruction. The Palestinians, despite their moderates, have refused to share the land. The

Israelis, despite their hardliners, have repeatedly offered to do exactly that.

For peace to reign, terror must end. And for terror to end, Palestinians must accept that Jews have a right to independence in the Land of Israel every bit as much as they believe that they themselves have a right to independence in Palestine. In short, the recognition of Israel's moral legitimacy is a prerequisite for peace. It is to this mission that the following pages are dedicated.

CHAPTER ONE

THE JEWISH CLAIM

In spite of all the troubles inflicted on them by the Muslims, the Jews refuse to leave the Land.

—Christian pilgrim to Jerusalem, 1491[1]

There's a popular version of the history of the Jewish people in the Land of Israel. Most observers—both friend and foe—know it well. The tale begins millennia ago when the Jews were rooted in their land and living out the stories of the Bible. Then they made a decision that forever changed the course of Jewish history: they rebelled against Rome. In 70 AD, Roman legions crushed the Jewish revolt and destroyed the Jewish temple. Those Jews who weren't killed were expelled.

Thus began an exile of the Jewish people from their ancestral homeland that would last almost two thousand years. In the centuries that followed, Jews would long for their land. They would pray daily to return to it. Every year at Passover they would proclaim, "Next year in Jerusalem." But only with the birth of the modern State of Israel in 1948 would the Jews actually make their way back home.

There is a certain romance to this story. A land and a people, separated for two thousand years, finally reunited. There's just one problem: it isn't true.

Yes, the Romans did crush the Jewish revolt in the year 70. And yes, they did kill, enslave, and exile many hundreds of thousands of Jews. But even after the Romans had done their worst, millions of Jews remained in their land. These Jews would continue to cling to their native soil—and constitute a majority in it—for many centuries to come. There was no two-thousand-year separation.

In addition, Jews living in the Diaspora did not merely pray to return home. They *did* return home. Century after century they braved high seas and highway bandits, poverty and persecution to make their way back to the Land of Israel. When conditions permitted, they built businesses, schools, and cities. And when word of such progress spread, thousands more Jews streamed home to join them.

More often than not, however, returnees encountered far less favorable conditions. The Romans and later the Byzantines pursued policies intended to drive the Jews from their land. Then, from the Arab invasion in the seventh century until the British conquest in the twentieth, the Land of Israel was ruled by Muslims. With a few notable exceptions, these new overlords subjected their Jewish subordinates to centuries of unrelenting prejudice and persecution. Muslim authorities typically enforced the Islamic laws requiring that Jews (and Christians) be relegated to second-class status. And many Muslims went well beyond those dictates to rob, attack, and murder members of this vulnerable minority. Disease and earthquakes intervened on a regular basis to multiply the man-made misery.

When times were tough, the Jewish community dwindled. The early decades of the nineteenth century were a particularly bad time for Palestine's Jews. As persecution grew more brutal, natural disasters grew more frequent. By mid-century—before the birth of the modern Zionist movement—it's estimated that only thirty thousand Jews remained in Palestine out of a total population of approximately five hundred thousand.[2]

This snapshot of Palestine's Jewish population before the first wave of modern Zionist immigration has become a central pillar of the case against Israel. Since the Jews were a minority in the land at the time the Zionist project began, it is argued, they had no right to return and build their state there. At some point during their long exile, the Jews lost their rights to their homeland. There is a statute of limitations on being indigenous.

But this one population statistic reveals little about the true record of Jewish life in the Land of Israel. It ignores centuries of Jewish presence, Jewish return, and Jewish construction. It likewise overlooks centuries of oppression by the foreigners who conquered and governed this territory. Simply put, Palestine's Jewish community would have been exponentially larger had it not been repeatedly decimated by so many generations of Muslim rulers and Arab neighbors.

It takes a special kind of audacity to drive the Jews from their ancestral land through violence, persecution, and misrule and then point to the small size of the Jewish population as proof that their rights have somehow lapsed. The Arabs of Palestine were hardly passive observers of the reality they cite.

The history of the Jews in their land is a powerful rebuttal to the false narrative that dominates the modern debate.

THE BAR KOCHBA REVOLT

After their victory in 70 AD, the Romans destroyed the Second Temple and most of Jerusalem along with it. But the majority of Judea's Jews were not city dwellers; they lived in the towns and villages that dotted the Judean hill country. Even after the war, this countryside remained overwhelmingly Jewish.

As the second century dawned, the Jews were still a majority in their land. And they were still a disgruntled majority. In the year 132, Simon Bar Kochba led a second major revolt against Roman rule. Bar Kochba and his rebels surprised the Romans and captured hundreds of cities, towns, and villages, including Jerusalem. They established an independent Jewish government to rule the lands they liberated and minted coins proclaiming the "freedom of Jerusalem."

But the mighty Roman Empire could not be long defied. The Emperor Hadrian sent a massive, multi-legion force to Judea and unleashed them to scorch the earth. The Roman historian Dio Cassius chronicled the destruction of 50 Jewish towns and 985 Jewish villages. In the process, he noted, the Romans killed 580,000 Jewish men. "Of those who perished by famine and disease," he added, "there is no one [who] can count the number."[3] By the summer of 135, Hadrian and his legions had killed Bar Kochba and suppressed the revolt.

This time, however, the Romans did not stop at physical destruction. They tried to destroy the Jewish religion by outlawing the study of the Torah and executing an entire generation of rabbis. They sought to crush the Jewish economy by expropriating the country's most productive land and taxing the rest at exorbitant rates. And they attempted to sever the connection between the Jewish people and their land by changing the country's name from "Judea"—the source of the words "Jews" and "Judaism"—to *Palestina*, or Palestine.

Rome's ethnic cleansing of Judea would be the greatest tragedy to befall the Jewish people until the Holocaust. But as in the Holocaust, the destruction was not complete. Even after the Romans had finished their massacres, expulsions, and expropriations, Jews remained in their land. In fact, they remained a majority in it.

The Romans had razed the Jewish heartland around Jerusalem. But Galilee—distant, rural, and mountainous—survived the Roman backlash. Many of Galilee's Jewish communities actually grew, as tens of thousands of Judean refugees made their way north.

THE THIRD JEWISH REVOLT, THE MISHNA, AND THE JERUSALEM TALMUD

The Romans ruled Palestine for the next two and a half centuries, until the empire finally split in two. During these years there were some relatively benign emperors and periods of peace. But for Palestine's Jews, the overwhelming pattern was bitter oppression, heavy taxes, and steady decline.

When Constantine became emperor in 306, he brought a new passion to Roman persecution. As Rome's first Christian emperor, Constantine initiated efforts to Christianize Jesus's home country. Constantine's son Constantius accelerated his father's work, delegating much of the day-to-day oversight to his cousin, Constantius Gallus. In his zeal for Christianizing Galilee, Gallus crossed new lines. Jews complained that he built churches in the heart of Jewish towns and encouraged violent attacks on synagogues.

In response, the Jews of Palestine did something shocking. They mustered the numbers and the courage to rebel against Rome for a third time. According to the Church father Jerome, "Gallus persecuted the Jews, who slaughtered his entire garrison in the night and then afterwards declared open revolt. He [Gallus] killed thousands of people, even infants, and destroyed the towns of Caesarea, Tiberias and Lydda and set fire to many others."[4]

By some reports, Jewish fighters advanced as far as the gates of Jerusalem. Yet despite the initial success they achieved, the Jews simply lacked the manpower and the resources to hold out for long. The Romans crushed the revolt within a year. In the process, they destroyed Galilee's largest Jewish cities and killed several thousand Jews.[5]

As Palestine entered the fifth century, Jews were still the majority in Galilee and a significant minority beyond. Jerome, who lived near Bethlehem, complained that most of the people in Palestine were still Jews.[6] A contemporary Christian document notes, "The Christians were not numerous in these countries (Palestine, Phoenicia and Arabia); the Jews and Samaritans dominated...in this region."[7]

Beyond merely surviving the Romans, Palestine's Jews produced some of Judaism's most important texts while under their rule. For centuries, most of Jewish law had been transmitted orally from teacher to student. After the Romans killed off a generation of rabbis during the Bar Kochba revolt, however, the survivors decided that the time had come to preserve these traditions in writing. Working in Galilee, Rabbi Judah Hanasi and his colleagues completed a compilation of this "Oral Law" around the year 220. The book they produced—the Mishna—is second only to the Bible in its importance to the Jewish faith.

Over the next two centuries, hundreds of scholars in Tiberias, Caesarea, and other Galilee towns continued to dispute and elaborate the meaning of the Mishna. In the early fifth century, these debates were summarized in a massive multi-volume work known as the Jerusalem Talmud. In time a similar work written by Jews living in Babylonia—the Babylonian Talmud—would take a place of precedence in Jewish life. But the Jerusalem Talmud remains one of Judaism's most significant texts, and the primary authority on all laws relating to the Land of Israel.

In addition to being central works of Jewish theology, the Mishna and the Jerusalem Talmud are also detailed records of Jewish history. These books are replete with references to the Jewish communities that dotted Palestine's landscape from the second to the fifth centuries. These and other historical sources provide a record of at least 373 Jewish towns and villages in Palestine during this era. The majority of these communities—205—were in Galilee. But, despite intensive Roman persecution, there were still 101 Jewish villages in the Jerusalem region and 67 in the Transjordan and coastal plain.[8]

BYZANTINE PERSECUTIONS AND THE END OF PALESTINE'S JEWISH MAJORITY

In 395, the Roman Empire split into western and eastern halves. The eastern half, which included Palestine, came to be known as the Byzantine Empire. The next 250 years of Byzantine rule were an unmitigated disaster for Palestine's Jews. Following Constantine's example, the Byzantines were determined to Christianize the birthplace of their faith. They would ultimately achieve the success that had eluded their Roman forebears.

The Byzantine emperors steadily reduced the Jews to second-class citizens in their own land. In 429 they terminated Jewish autonomy. Then they proceeded to strip the Jews of a series of rights enjoyed by other Byzantine subjects, including holding public office and bearing witness against Christians in court. Jews were prohibited from building new synagogues and expanding existing ones. And as Jewish social status plumbed new lows, physical attacks on Jewish homes and institutions rose to historic highs.[9]

The fifth century marked an important turning point in the demographic history of Palestine. At the start of the century, Jews likely comprised a majority of the total population. By century's end, after decades of Byzantine persecution, the Jews had almost certainly become a minority in their homeland for the first time.

THE FOURTH JEWISH REBELLION AND THE PERSIAN CONQUEST OF PALESTINE

In 614, the armies of an expanding Persian Empire advanced southward from Damascus into Galilee. Palestine's Jews recognized this invasion as an historic opportunity to free themselves from their Byzantine oppressors. The Jewish leaders Nehemiah ben Hushiel and Benjamin of Tiberias raised and equipped a Jewish army to fight alongside the Persians.

Well over a century had passed since Jews were the majority in their land. But they were still a substantial minority able to field a sizable fighting force. The Christian historian Eutychius estimates that twenty thousand Jewish soldiers joined the revolt.[10] Other sources place this total closer to twenty-five thousand.[11] While most of these rebels came from Galilee, Jewish volunteers streamed in from the south of Palestine and as far away as Cyprus.

This joint Persian-Jewish force marched south and quickly conquered Jerusalem. The Persians rewarded their Jewish allies by giving them control of their ancient capital. With Jerusalem in Jewish hands for the first time in centuries, Jews streamed back to the city from throughout the region. There they built homes and synagogues and even began making arrangements to rebuild their Temple.

This renaissance was short-lived. In 617, the Persians made peace with the local Christians and betrayed the Jews. Jewish rule over Jerusalem was terminated a mere three years after it had begun.[12]

This Persian perfidy was quickly eclipsed by an even greater tragedy. The Byzantines re-conquered Jerusalem in 629 and immediately took their revenge. They massacred most of Jerusalem's Jews.[13] Those Jews who survived fled to the hills, the desert, and the safety of neighboring territories. There they waited and prayed once again for deliverance from the Byzantine yoke. They would not have to wait very long.

THE ARABS CONQUER PALESTINE

The year 633 was a turning point in Arab history. That's the year the Prophet Mohammed's successor, Abu Bakr, completed the conquest of the Arabian Peninsula. Mohammed's followers were now free to expand their empire beyond their desert homeland. In the years that followed, they surged forth from Arabia and conquered most of the Middle East and North Africa.

One of the Arabs' first objectives was to seize the neighboring territories of *Bilad al-Sham*—the area comprising present-day Israel, Syria, Lebanon, and Jordan—from the Byzantines. In 636, the Arabs won a decisive victory at the Battle of Yarmouk. In 638, they conquered Jerusalem. In 640, they took Caesarea, the last Byzantine stronghold in Palestine.

The Palestine that the Arabs invaded still had a significant Jewish population. And Palestine's Jews still had the same intimate knowledge of the land and burning hatred of the Byzantines that had made them such a valuable asset to the Persians. When the Arab armies arrived, many Jews were happy to reprise their role as allies and guides to an enemy of their Byzantine oppressors.

As the Arab invaders approached Hebron, for example, they "marveled" at the city's massive walls and concluded that "there was no opening by which they could enter it."[14] The Arabs were able to conquer

Hebron only after local Jews showed them a damaged section of the wall that could more easily be breached.[15]

A similar scene played out in the port city of Caesarea. With the sea on one side and massive walls surrounding the other three, this city was able to resist the Arab invaders longer than any other in Palestine. The Arabs succeeded in seizing Caesarea only after some of the city's Jews led them to a secret entrance through an ancient aqueduct.[16]

After the Arab conquest, the Jews had every reason to celebrate. Their new rulers were initially far more tolerant than the Byzantines they had replaced. As a reward for Jewish support, Caliph Omar permitted seventy Jewish families to return to Jerusalem and build a synagogue on the Temple Mount.[17] As word of these new freedoms spread, Jews who had fled the Byzantines began returning home and rebuilding their towns and villages.

THE MUSLIM PERSECUTION BEGINS

This Arab beneficence did not last for long. In the vast lands they so quickly conquered—from Africa's Atlantic coast all the way to the Fertile Crescent—the Arab Muslims were a tiny minority ruling over a multitude of other peoples professing different faiths. At the time, North Africa was overwhelmingly Christian. Persia was mostly Zoroastrian. Palestine was largely Christian and Jewish.

This new empire, won by force of arms, would ultimately be maintained by force of culture. The Arabs aggressively promoted their Islamic faith and Arabic language to their masses of new subjects. For pagans and members of smaller religious cults, the marketing was quite forceful: they were given a choice between conversion to Islam and death.

The members of the larger religious communities—Jews, Christians, and Zoroastrians—were offered a less drastic alternative. They were permitted to continue practicing their faiths so long as they submitted to a series of special rules and restrictions. These new laws rendered them second-class citizens in their native lands.

First and foremost, the members of these faiths—known by the derogatory term *dhimmis*—were required to pay two special taxes. Every adult male dhimmi was required to pay a heavy tax called the *jizya*. In addition, dhimmis who worked in agriculture had to pay the *kharaj*, a fee for the right to farm what was now considered Muslim land. As applied in Palestine, the kharaj had the effect of driving Jews off the land and into the towns and cities. The jizya had the effect of driving Jews to Islam or out of the country altogether.

Beyond high taxes, dhimmis were forced to submit to a series of humiliating legal restrictions. They were prohibited from holding public office and from testifying against Muslims in court. They were not allowed to wear fancy clothing or to ride upon "noble" animals such as horses or camels. They were barred from constructing new houses of worship and repairing existing ones.

Finally, the Arabs elevated Islam over these preexisting religions by appropriating their holy sites. In Palestine, the Muslims built mosques on every major Jewish site including the Temple Mount in Jerusalem, the tomb of the patriarchs in Hebron, Elijah's altar on Mount Carmel, the tomb of Jethro in Kfar Hittin, the tomb of Jonah in Kfar Kanah, and the tomb of Samuel outside of Jerusalem.[18] As Muslim claims were asserted, Jewish rights at these sites were typically curtailed or terminated altogether.

These oppressive policies gradually transformed the entire region— from North Africa to Persia—into one massive Muslim bloc. Yet this change came slowly in some corners of the Muslim empire, especially in Palestine. Arab historians writing at the beginning of the tenth century suggest that the Muslims did not yet constitute a majority in Palestine.[19] Even toward the close of that century—after more than three centuries of Muslim rule—the famous Arab geographer al-Maqdisi wrote that Christians and Jews still outnumbered Muslims in Palestine.[20]

Al-Maqdisi's testimony highlights a surprising fact. He wrote not only at the turn of the century, but at the turn of the millennium. Almost one thousand years had passed since the Romans supposedly expelled the Jews from their land. The Jews had suffered centuries of Roman, Byzantine, and Arab ethnic cleansing. Yet they still had a substantial presence in their land. Palestine's cities still had sizable Jewish populations. And Palestine's countryside was still dotted with over fifty Jewish towns and villages.[21]

THE CRUSADERS AND THE RETURN OF CHRISTIAN PERSECUTION

At the close of the eleventh century, the Crusaders invaded Palestine to wrest control of Christian holy sites from Muslim "infidels." But the Muslims were not the only "infidels" they encountered. A sizable Jewish community still lived in Palestine. And most of these Jews decided to fight alongside the Muslims to defend their homes and their very lives.

When the Crusaders reached Jerusalem in 1099, Jerusalem's Jews bravely fought to defend their city. A contemporary Crusader account praised the skill of these Jewish fighters, noting that among all of the city's defenders, "the Jew is the last to fall."[22] When the Crusaders ultimately conquered the city, they massacred Muslims and Jews alike. Survivors were sold as slaves or ransomed for large sums. Jews were once again banned from their holiest city.

In their rush to reach Jerusalem, the Crusaders had initially bypassed the port of Haifa on Palestine's northern coast. In 1100, the Crusaders returned and laid siege to the city. Most accounts indicate that a majority of the city's defenders were Jews.[23] And these Jews surprised the Crusaders by holding out for over a month. The Christian historian Albert of Aachen noted that Haifa's Jews fought "with great courage, to the shame and embarrassment of the Christians."[24] When the city fell, the Crusaders massacred most of its inhabitants and sold the survivors into slavery.

By this time, the Crusaders had also defeated and massacred the Jews of Acre, Caesarea, and Hebron.[25] Further resistance made little sense. Palestine's remaining Jewish communities—mostly in the upper Galilee—surrendered and were largely spared destruction. Among the surviving outposts were Tiberias, Safed, and at least ten Jewish villages in the nearby countryside.[26] Once again, Galilee endured as a center of Jewish life in a newly conquered Palestine.

SALADIN LIBERATES PALESTINE. THE MAMLUKS DESTROY IT

The Jews subsisted under a harsh Crusader regime for the better part of ninety years. When Saladin defeated the Crusaders and restored Muslim rule in 1187, the Jewish community rejoiced.

This unusually humane conqueror issued a proclamation urging the Jews to come back to their former homes.[27] As always, Jews seized the opportunity to return. They came from nearby hiding places and from communities as far away as Yemen, North Africa, Spain, and Germany.[28] Between 1209 and 1211, a group of three hundred rabbis from England and France immigrated to Palestine.[29] Most went to Jerusalem, determined to rebuild the Jewish community in their holiest city.[30]

But for the Jews of Palestine, the good times never lasted very long. Saladin and his successors relied upon a caste of slaves—the Mamluks—to form the bulk of their army. In 1250 these slaves seized power for themselves. The Mamluks would rule Palestine until the Ottoman conquest in 1517. While they may have been good soldiers, the Mamluks proved to be exceptionally incompetent rulers.

Palestine's coastal cities had traditionally been trading centers that energized the nation's economy. But the Crusaders had demonstrated that the very port cities that connected the country to commerce also opened it to invasion. The Mamluks decided that the best way to prevent future Christian conquests of Palestine would be to destroy these points of entry. So they systematically razed all of Palestine's major coastal cities, including Haifa, Caesarea, and Acre.[31] Palestine's seaboard was abandoned to encroaching desert and sand dunes. Most of it remained that way until the twentieth century.

Through disastrous policies such as these, the Mamluks plunged Palestine to new social and economic depths. Commerce moved north to Syria and south to Egypt. As trade left, people followed. Palestine's population plummeted by two-thirds.[32]

As Palestine's economy shrank, so too did Mamluk tax revenues. This drove the Mamluks to double down on misrule by hiking taxes. And while everyone's taxes went up, the pain was not evenly inflicted. The jizya—the tax imposed upon all non-Muslim males—reached historic highs.

The Mamluks were also exceedingly strict in their enforcement of the dhimmi rules, often adding new humiliations to those required by Islamic law. As one Christian observer noted approvingly in the early years of the sixteenth century: "Brother, I wish you to know how these dogs of Jews are trampled upon, beaten and ill-treated, as they deserve.... They live in this country in such subjection that words cannot describe it. And it is a most extraordinary thing that there in Jerusalem, where they committed the sin for which they are dispersed throughout the world, they are by God more punished and afflicted than in any other part of the world. And over a long time I have witnessed that."[33]

As the Jewish and Christian communities collapsed under the weight of Mamluk misrule, the Muslims became an increasingly larger percentage of Palestine's shrinking population. It was during the reign of the Mamluks that it first became possible to speak of Palestine as a Muslim country.[34] To the spoilers of the land went the demographic victory.

Despite these calamities, the Mamluk period was punctuated by repeated waves of Jewish immigration. These infusions of new Jews from Spain, Italy, North Africa, and Syria likely saved Palestine's shrinking Jewish community from disappearing altogether. In fact, so many Jews left Spain for Palestine during this era that Spanish authorities, fearing for their economy, prohibited the "transportation of Jews to the East."[35] The Vatican, wary of competition for control of Jerusalem's holy sites, prohibited sea captains from transporting Jews to Palestine.[36] Italy's major ports actively enforced this order for decades.[37]

THE OTTOMAN GOLDEN AGE AND THE JEWISH RENAISSANCE

In 1517, the Ottoman Turks conquered Palestine from the Mamluks. They would rule this territory for the next four hundred years, until the end of World War I. Palestine was now part of a great and powerful Muslim empire on the rise.

In sharp contrast to the Mamluks, the Ottomans had a history of benevolence toward the Jews. And this auspicious situation grew more favorable still during the reign of Sultan Suleiman "the Magnificent." This forward-thinking Muslim leader pursued policies that benefited his empire and all of the communities living in it, including the Jews. His reign—from 1520 to 1566—was the Ottoman Empire's "Golden Age."

Suleiman understood that prosperity was a product of security and stability. He therefore invested in fortifying the cities of his realm with strong defensive walls. From 1537 to 1540, Suleiman built the wall around Jerusalem which stands to this very day. In 1549, he built a wall around Safed. No longer would the inhabitants of these cities live in fear of Bedouin or Druze marauders riding in and destroying all they had built.

Suleiman also recognized that Palestine faced a unique economic challenge. This land, which had grown so desolate under the Mamluks, needed a larger population to prosper. Suleiman decided to open Palestine to immigration. And he warmly welcomed the one group of people who most desperately wanted to come: the Jews.

For the first time since the Romans destroyed Jerusalem, Palestine was being governed by a benign ruler who permitted and protected Jewish immigration. And for the first time in centuries, there was a mobile population of Jews with the resources to take advantage of this opportunity. Spain's large and prosperous Jewish community had been expelled in 1492. The Jews of Portugal had been forced from their homes five years later. Most of these exiles had settled in the Mediterranean basin—primarily in North Africa, Italy, and the Ottoman port of Salonika. While some settled there for good, many others viewed these places as mere way stations on their journey home to the Land of Israel.

When Suleiman opened Palestine's doors to them, these waiting Jews rushed in. Many of these immigrants went to Jerusalem, where they quickly doubled the Jewish population. But the majority went to the town of Safed in Galilee. By the middle of the sixteenth century, the Jewish population of Safed had risen to fifteen thousand.[38]

The Golden Age of the Ottoman Empire would also be a golden age for Jewish Safed. Many of the city's new immigrants brought capital and skills with them, and they transformed Safed into a major textile center. There in the Galilee hills they built businesses that controlled the entire production process, from importing wool to weaving cloth to shipping finished garments. They secured markets for their products in Damascus, Constantinople, and beyond. By the middle of the century there were approximately three thousand looms operating in Safed.[39]

As Safed grew, Jewish agricultural villages sprang up around it. By 1549, there were at least a dozen Jewish villages in Galilee. In addition to supplying Safed with food and wool, these villages exported fruits, grains, wool, and sheep by way of Palestine's Mediterranean ports.

An Italian Jew who visited Safed in 1535 summed up the progress in a letter home: "He who saw Safed ten years ago, and observes it now, has the impression of a miracle. For more Jews are arriving here continually, and the tailoring trade grows daily. I have been told that more than 15,000 suits have been manufactured in Safed during this year, besides fancy suits. Every man and every woman who works woolen fabric earns an abundant living."[40]

This thriving economy enabled Safed to support a revival in Jewish scholarship. Famous rabbis from the Spanish and Portuguese exiles converged on the city. Students from around the world flocked to study under them. In the intellectual ferment thus produced, some of the greatest scholars in Jewish history wrote some of Judaism's most important works.

Foremost among Safed's intellectuals was Rabbi Joseph Caro. In Safed, Caro wrote the *Shulchan Aruch*, the preeminent codification of Jewish law. For centuries, observant Jews had had to cull the rules binding on them from the Talmud's multiple volumes. By collecting these rules in one work and organizing them in a logical fashion, Caro relieved Jews of this burden and helped to standardize practices across the Jewish world.

Beyond Jewish law, Safed also emerged as the center of a more esoteric discipline: Jewish mysticism, or *Kabbalah*. Jewish tradition holds that Rabbi Shimon Bar Yochai wrote the core work of Kabbalah, the *Zohar*, while hiding from the Romans in a cave near Safed. Thus once conditions permitted, Kabbalah scholars flocked to this town. All of the rabbis most responsible for developing the doctrines of modern Kabbalah lived and taught in Safed, including Rabbi Moses Cordovero, Rabbi Isaac Luria, and Luria's chief disciple, Rabbi Chaim Vital.

While Safed flourished, the nearby city of Tiberias still lay in ruins. As one contemporary traveler noted, "Tiberias was formerly a great city...but now it is desolate and waste.... No man can go there from fear of the Arabs."[41]

In 1558, a prominent Ottoman Jewish family launched an ambitious effort to rebuild Tiberias. That year Dona Gracia Mendes, a wealthy Jewish refugee from Spain, purchased a lease for the town and its nearby villages from Suleiman. She placed her nephew, Don Joseph Nasi, in charge of the construction. In the winter of 1564–1565, Don Joseph completed building the city's walls. Then he built a synagogue and a Jewish college.

Following Safed's lead, Don Joseph developed a textile industry in Tiberias. He imported wool from Spain, Turkey, and the Balkans. He also planted mulberry tree plantations so that silkworm cultivation could provide a local supply of silk.[42] The commerce that flowed from Don Joseph's investments spurred the growth of Tiberias, as well as a number of Jewish villages surrounding it. As a French visitor observed, "We look around Lake Tiberias and see the villages of Beth Saida and Korazim. Today Jews are living in these villages and they have built up again all the places around the lake, started fishing industries and have once again made the earth fruitful where once it was desolate."[43]

As word of this revival spread, thousands of European Jews— including entire Jewish communities—packed up to return to their ancestral home.[44] But many of these immigrants never made it. This was an era when the Knights of Malta engaged in piracy and preyed on vessels traveling from Italy and Greece to Palestine. When they captured human cargo, they either sold them into slavery or held them for ransom. A letter survives from the Jews of Pesaro to Don Joseph seeking his help to pay such a ransom: "For the terrible news has reached us of the capture by the Knights of Malta of some 102 of our brethren—our coreligionists who were on board ship bound to settle permanently in Eretz-Israel."[45]

THE LONG OTTOMAN DECLINE

The Ottoman Golden Age was short-lived. When Suleiman died in 1566, he was succeeded by a series of less enlightened men. By the late sixteenth century, the imperial authorities in Istanbul were losing their grip on their far-flung provinces. With the Ottomans no longer able to defend it, Safed was once again vulnerable to attack from Bedouin, Druze, and local Arab villagers. As security deteriorated, so too did the economy and public health. Natural disasters and famine sped the downward spiral.

In 1567, Bedouin and Druze tribesmen rode into Safed and ransacked the town. In 1587, Safed was attacked again and its Hebrew printing press—the only printing press in the Middle East at the time— destroyed. In 1599, Safed suffered a devastating combination of drought, plague, and famine. Local Druze raided Safed in 1604, 1628, and again in 1636. In 1660, Lebanese Druze raided and razed both Safed and Tiberias.[46]

By the end of the seventeenth century, Safed was a ruin. Tiberias was a ghost town. Raids, pillage, hunger, and disease had taken a similar toll on almost all of the Jewish villages that had sprung up around these once thriving centers.[47]

The eighteenth century was a largely bleak expanse of continued decline for Palestine and its Jews. The same familiar hits—both man-made and natural—just kept on coming.

It was during this century that Palestine's population reached lows not plumbed since the dark days of the Mamluks. It's estimated that there were only 250,000 people in the entire country during this period. Others place the total even lower, at a mere 100,000.[48] The French writer Volney estimated that from the northern line of Caesarea-Tiberias south the population was a mere 50,000.[49] Westerners who visited Palestine during this era stressed the desolation and poverty they witnessed.

From the start of the century until its finish, Palestine's Jewish population hovered between 6,000–8,000.[50] This community would certainly have shrunk further, or disappeared altogether, had it not been replenished by repeated waves of immigration.

Many of these Jewish immigrants returned during the reign of the Zaydan clan. In the 1720s, this Bedouin family filled the power vacuum created by the Ottoman decline and consolidated its control of northern Palestine. From the 1730s through the 1770s, a Zaydan sheikh named Dahir al-Umar was the de facto ruler of Galilee.

Dahir was a forward-thinking leader. Like Suleiman before him, Dahir understood that growing the region's sparse population was a prerequisite to developing his domain. And like Suleiman, he realized that the easiest way to attract immigrants was to invite the one group of people who would jump at the chance: the Jews.

Dahir reached out to a prominent Jewish leader, Rabbi Haim Abulafia of Smyrna, and invited him to oversee the reconstruction of Tiberias. Rabbi Abulafia arrived in 1740 with a large group of followers. With Dahir's help, these new immigrants built homes, synagogues, and schools and planted vineyards and olive orchards.[51] As a new Tiberias rose from the rubble, more immigrants streamed back to live there.

The Ottomans eventually grew to resent Dahir's growing power and decided to reassert their control over Galilee. In 1775, Ottoman forces defeated Dahir and replaced him with a loyal officer named Jezzar Pasha.

Jezzar is best remembered for his bad temper and excessive cruelty. His unfortunate predilection for mutilating his enemies—and even some of his friends—earned him the nickname "the butcher." But sadism aside, Jezzar recognized the importance of the Jews to the region's development. He therefore followed Dahir's lead and welcomed Jewish immigrants to Galilee. He decided to rebuild Safed, which had been leveled in the earthquake of 1759, and lured Jews there with an offer of reduced taxes and customs duties. He even delegated much of the local administration to his top advisor, a Syrian Jew named Haim Farhi.[52]

As always, Jews were quick to seize an opportunity to return to their land. In 1777, over three hundred Hasidic Jews from Russia and Lithuania moved to Safed and rebuilt the Jewish quarter. Their positive reports to their brethren back home inspired further waves of Hasidic immigrants to Safed and Tiberias.[53]

In 1799, the pattern of Jewish return followed by Jewish decline was interrupted by a new force. Napoleon Bonaparte invaded Palestine as part of his campaign to conquer the Ottoman Empire. Marching north from Egypt, his forces took Jaffa and continued up the Mediterranean coast. Like the Persians and the Arabs before him, Napoleon believed that the Jews could be valuable allies in seizing this land they loved so deeply and knew so well. In an effort to win their support, Napoleon issued a proclamation calling on the Jews of Asia and Africa to rally to his banner and help him fight for the "restoration of Jerusalem."

Napoleon's appeal reads like a Zionist manifesto. Addressing himself to "the rightful Heirs of Palestine," Napoleon wrote,

> Israelites, unique nation, whom, in thousands of years, lust of conquest and tyranny have been able to deprive only of their ancestral lands, but not of name and existence!
>
> Arise, then, with gladness, ye exiled! A war unexampled in the annals of history, waged in self-defense by a nation whose hereditary lands were regarded by its enemy as plunder to be divided…it offers you at this very time, and contrary to all expressions, Israel's patrimony![54]

After Jaffa, the coastal city of Acre loomed as the next great obstacle between Napoleon and his ultimate goal of Constantinople. Napoleon lay siege to Acre and tried to persuade its Jews to rebel. But Acre's Jews remained loyal to their Ottoman overlords. In fact, Acre's leading Jewish family—the Farhis—financed Jezzar Pasha's defense of the city. Napoleon ultimately abandoned his attempt to take Acre and retreated back down the Mediterranean coast.

The Jews benefited little from their fidelity. As Napoleon withdrew his forces, local Arabs attacked the Jews of Safed and Jerusalem. Safed's Jewish quarter was completely destroyed. Jezzar "the butcher" eventually grew angry with his Jewish funder and advisor Haim Farhi and had his nose cut off. Jezzar's son and successor later had Farhi executed.

THE NINETEENTH CENTURY—
PLUMBING THE DEPTHS

In the early decades of the nineteenth century, Palestine sank to rock bottom. The country's population hovered around two hundred thousand, possibly an all-time low.[55] A majority of the residents lived in the hill country of Judea, Samaria, and Galilee, where they were safe from

Bedouin raids and malaria. The coastal plain was sparsely populated. Jerusalem had fewer than ten thousand residents.[56]

It was soon after—in 1867—that American author Mark Twain visited Palestine. He wasn't impressed. Writing of his visit in *The Innocents Abroad*, he famously described journeys through a "desolate" and "mournful" landscape in which he "never saw a human being on the whole route" or "saw only thee persons."[57]

Palestine's Jews remained trapped in the grinding cycle of prior centuries. Violence, disease, and poverty decimated the population. Waves of immigrants returned to replenish and rebuild. Then man and nature collaborated to tear it all down again.

In 1834, Arab villagers attacked Safed's Jewish neighborhoods. Over the course of a month, they murdered, raped, and beat Safed's Jews, stole their valuables and burnt down their homes. In 1837, a major earthquake struck Galilee. The Jewish quarter of Safed—built on a steep incline—toppled over and slid down the hill, and over half of its four thousand residents were buried in the rubble.[58] In 1838, the Druze attacked Safed and pillaged what was left of the Jewish quarter. They tortured men and raped women to find out where they had hidden their few remaining valuables.[59]

Despite this series of disasters, Safed's Jews immediately returned and "rebuilt a great part of their quarter."[60] But they lived in constant fear of the next attack. In 1839, the Scottish missionaries Andrew Alexander Bonar and Robert Murray M'Cheyne noted the extent of Jewish dread: "We observed how poorly clad most of the Jews seemed to be, and were told that they had buried under ground all their valuable clothes, their money, and other precious things. It was easy to read their deep anxiety in the very expression of their countenances.... And all this in their own land!"[61]

Jerusalem shared Safed's suffering. In 1816, the Ottoman Sultan capped the total number of Jews permitted to live in Jerusalem at two thousand "on pain of death to those who exceeded that number."[62] Local rulers strictly enforced the Islamic ban on synagogue construction and repair.

Numerous travelers commented on the pathetic state of Jerusalem's Jewish community and institutions during this period. In 1833, for example, a Jewish visitor wrote this about Jerusalem's synagogues: "I found them in a most miserable and lamentable condition, since they were at the time greatly out of repair, and almost threatened to tumble in, and were useless in rainy weather, insomuch as they were roofed with nothing but old rotten boards, and our brothers could not obtain permission from 'the pious faithful' [the Muslims] to drive as much as a single nail to fasten anything in the building without first being authorized...and such a favor, not to mention to permit the making of repairs...could not be granted in order not to commit a terrible sin against Allah...."[63]

Jewish fear was palpable in Jerusalem. Visiting the holy city in 1816, English author J. S. Buckingham wrote of a group of Jews on mules who mistook him and his colleagues for Muslims. "They all dismounted and passed by us on foot. These persecuted people are held in such opprobrium here that it is forbidden to them to pass a Muslim mounted."[64]

In 1839, the British vice-consul in Jerusalem, William Tanner Young, observed, "The Jew in Jerusalem is not estimated in value much above a dog—and scarcely a day passes that I do not hear of some act of tyranny and oppression against a Jew."[65]

TURNING THE CORNER

This pathetic state of affairs finally began to improve toward mid-century. As the European powers continued to overwhelm them on the battlefield and in the marketplace, the Ottomans decided that the only way to preserve their empire was to Westernize it. As part of this strategy, they embarked on a series of legal reforms. A new legal code promulgated in 1839 gave Jews equality before the law, at least in principle. In 1855, the Ottomans abolished the jizya tax on non-Muslims. In 1856, the Ottomans passed the Edict of Toleration, which reinforced these reforms and encouraged their implementation.

The Ottomans also buckled to pressure and granted the European powers certain privileges they had been seeking in the Holy Land. Most important, the Europeans were allowed to open consulates in Jerusalem to better safeguard their citizens who visited or lived there. When the British opened their Jerusalem consulate in 1839, they decided to extend their protection to Jerusalem's persecuted Jews. For the first time in centuries, Palestine's Jews had an ally to defend them from the brutality of the tyrant and the madness of the mob.

As always, the opportunity to live safely in Palestine immediately spurred Jewish immigration. By 1840, there were five thousand Jews in Jerusalem alongside forty-five hundred Muslims and thirty-five hundred Christians. For the first time in centuries, the Jews were the largest religious community in their holiest city.[66]

As Jewish immigration continued to surge, Jerusalem grew so overcrowded that a group of Jews resorted to a drastic solution. In 1860, braving Bedouin and bandits, they built the first neighborhood outside Jerusalem's walls. As this community thrived, more Jews followed their lead. By 1882, over two thousand Jews lived in nine Jewish neighborhoods beyond the Old City's walls.[67]

By 1872, Jerusalem had eleven thousand Jews, five thousand Christians, and five thousand Muslims.[68] The Jews now constituted an outright majority of Jerusalem's population. By that time there were also Jewish majorities in Safed and Tiberias.[69] By 1895, Jerusalem's Jewish population had increased to thirty thousand out of a total of fifty-one thousand.[70]

Thus by the time the modern Zionist movement was founded in 1897, a modern wave of Jewish immigration to Palestine had already been underway for decades. Zionism was not some dramatic Jewish rediscovery of Palestine after two thousand years. Zionism is merely the latest—and the most successful—of the long list of Jewish efforts to return to their homeland dating back to their first expulsions therefrom.

CHAPTER TWO

THE PALESTINIAN CLAIM

The rights of the Arabs are derived from actual and long-standing possession....

—George Antonius, 1938[1]

I f the Jewish claim to the land is rooted mostly in history, then the Palestinian claim is based largely on demography. Simply put, the Palestinians see their right to the land flowing from the fact that they made up the majority of the people in it before the birth of the Zionist movement. As the indigenous people, they argue, they have the right to self-determination in their own land.

This is a powerful argument. After all, we live in a post-colonial era. Since World War I the international community has largely recognized the right of indigenous peoples to rule themselves. And after World War II and the fall of the Soviet Union, increasing numbers of peoples have actually been permitted to exercise this right. The number of colonies in the world—both real and de facto—has steadily declined.

Yet while this Palestinian claim has clear merit, it also has weaknesses that are often overlooked. Most universal rights—such as the right to life and liberty—are individual rights that apply to every single person. But the right to self-determination is different. Not every family, tribe,

39

and ethnic group has the right to an independent state. This right arises only once a community has developed into what we commonly call a "people" or a "nation."

Even under the most generous definition of nationhood, the Palestinians did not exist as a separate people until some point after 1967. The relative youth of the Palestinian people does not invalidate their claims. Many of the peoples who gained independence following World War II—especially those that had been colonized by Europeans—are in fact new peoples created by the new borders these colonists drew.

But the youth of the Palestinian people does place important limits upon the extent to which their claims can be used as a cudgel with which to beat Israel. The fact that the Arabic-speaking residents of what was once the British Mandate for Palestine now consider themselves to be a people separate and distinct from their Arabic-speaking cousins across multiple modern borders does not mean that their ancestors shared that view. The emergence of Palestinian nationalism was neither pre-ordained nor predictable.

Simply put, the Israelis cannot be blamed for failing to recognize a Palestinian people before the Palestinians themselves did so.

THE RIGHT OF SELF-DETERMINATION

U.S. President Woodrow Wilson was a passionate advocate of self-determination. As he led America into World War I, he made this lofty ideal one of his core wartime objectives. As he noted in a February 1918 speech to Congress, "National aspirations must be respected; peoples may now be dominated and governed only by their own consent. 'Self-determination' is not a mere phrase. It is an imperative principle of action which statesmen will henceforth ignore at their peril."[2]

When the war was won, Wilson made the long journey to Paris to personally participate in the peace talks. There he worked hard to ensure that the post-war treaties would honor this still controversial principle of self-determination.

Among the advisors Wilson brought with him to Paris was his secretary of state, Robert Lansing. As Wilson preached the right to self-determination in Paris, Lansing immediately recognized how very difficult it would be to implement. He wrote, "When the President talks of 'self-determination' what unit has he in mind? Does he mean a race, a territorial area, or a community? Without a definite unit which is practical, application of this principle is dangerous to peace and stability."[3]

Lansing further recognized an element of hypocrisy in the American position. Had the United States truly respected the right to "self-determination," he noted, it should have honored the decision of the Southern states to secede from the Union in 1861.[4]

In time, Wilson himself came to understand what his secretary of state had so quickly grasped. He later confessed to the Senate Committee on Foreign Relations, "When I gave utterance to those words ('that all nations had a right to self-determination'), I said them without the knowledge that nationalities existed, which are coming to us day after day...."[5]

Lansing was right. There is no clear, objective test for deciding when a community has evolved from an ethnic or linguistic minority to a "nation" entitled to self-determination. Quite to the contrary, the standards suggested by some of the leading proponents of self-determination have been completely subjective.

President Wilson argued that a nation was born at that point in time when a particular group of people "thinks" that it's a nation. As he elaborated, "No people can be a nation before its time, and its time has not come until the national thought and feeling have been developed and have become prevalent."[6]

The French philosopher Ernest Renan expressed a similar view when he stated that the existence of a nation is based on a "daily plebiscite." In other words, the strongest proof that a particular nation exists is the fact that a group of people believe they belong to such a nation and act accordingly. To paraphrase another French philosopher—they believe, therefore they are.

As subjective and imprecise as this definition clearly is, it is difficult to formulate a better one. The very act of seeking independence is powerful testimony to the existence of a national identity. The stronger the demand for self-rule, the stronger the national identity is likely to be.

By this subjective standard, the Palestinians are clearly a nation. Today there are millions of individuals who see themselves as Palestinians. This identity is strongly felt, and it has motivated enormous passion, sacrifice, and violence.

Yet for a people whose national rights have come to play so central a role in world affairs, the Palestinians are a surprisingly new people. The application of the same subjective test that now confirms their existence would have demonstrated that there was no such thing as a Palestinian people as recently as 1966. While Palestinian historians argue that Palestinian nationalism was born in the 1920s, they are quick to acknowledge that this nationalism was long confined to a tiny group of urban elites. It took until after the 1967 War for this new Palestinian identity to trickle down to the average Palestinian and become, in Wilson's word, "prevalent."

BEFORE WORLD WAR I: THE BIRTH OF ARAB NATIONALISM

At the start of World War I, the land currently known as Palestine was part of the Ottoman Empire. It had been part of the Ottoman Empire for four hundred years.

The Ottomans never recognized Palestine as a distinct administrative unit. They divided their vast territories into *vilayets* (provinces) that were further divided into *sanjaqs* (districts). Northern Palestine belonged to the Sanjaq of Acre, which formed part of the Vilayet of Beirut. Central Palestine belonged to Sanjaq of Nablus, which belonged to the Vilayet of Damascus. The Sanjaq of Jerusalem was an independent district under the direct control of Istanbul. To the extent that Palestine had a geographic identity beyond these administrative divisions, it was viewed as Southern Syria.

During the centuries of Ottoman rule, there was no group of people who identified themselves as Palestinians. In fact, up until the Ottoman Empire's final years, there was no group of people who identified themselves as Arabs. To the extent that they embraced any identity beyond that of their village, clan, or faith, the Arabic-speaking residents of the region saw themselves as Ottoman subjects.[7]

. The concept of nationalism—basing one's identity on one's ethnicity or language—is now so prevalent that we forget it was largely an invention of eighteenth-century Europe. And this European idea did not percolate into the Arab world until the dawn of the twentieth century. It was only then—in the early 1900s—that a tiny group of Arabic-speaking intellectuals studying in Western-run schools first began to see themselves not as Ottomans but as Arabs.

In 1938, Arab author George Antonius published *The Arab Awakening*. This was one of the first histories of Arab nationalism, and it remains a classic of the genre. Scholars have largely agreed, however, that this book suffers from a fundamental flaw: Antonius tried too hard to place the birth of Arab nationalism earlier than it actually was. In his defense, Antonius did not fabricate. He merely magnified.

Antonius dedicated the first hundred pages of his book to the development of Arab nationalism before 1908. Even he acknowledged that this was a period of "slow and almost imperceptible growth"[8] in Arab national consciousness. It makes for a tedious read.

Antonius began with a detailed description of a secret Arab society created in Lebanon in 1875. It had a total of five members. Next, he dwelled at length on a book written in the early 1900s that called for the Ottomans to return the institution of the caliphate to Arab control. The book had few readers and little impact.

That's it. Summarizing Arab nationalism prior to 1908, Antonius conceded, "Except for those two manifestations, the movement had lain prone as though in sleep."[9]

In 1907, British Arabist Gertrude Bell had summed up the situation more bluntly: "Of what value are the pan-Arabic associations and inflammatory leaflets that they issue from foreign printing presses? The answer is easy: they are worth nothing at all. There is no nation of Arabs."[10]

Six years later, on the eve of World War I, Arab nationalism remained a minuscule movement limited to "an estranged faction of the educated and urban classes."[11]

The number of pre-war Arab nationalists was tiny indeed. Historian C. Ernest Dawn has identified a total of 126 members of Arab nationalist societies before 1914.[12] Of these, the majority were Syrian or Lebanese. Twenty-two were from Palestine.[13] Another historian, Muhammad Muslih, calculates that by the end of the war, "there were at least twenty-five Palestinians confirmed as members of Arab nationalist societies."[14]

THE "ARAB REVOLT"

After World War I broke out in 1914, the combatants quickly fought to a standstill in Europe. The British began looking east, to the battle against the Ottomans, for a momentum-shifting breakthrough. In particular, the British began scouring the region for an Arab leader willing to lead a revolt against the Ottomans in the name of Arab independence.

After failed efforts to foment an Arab revolt in Syria and Iraq, the British finally found their man. In the summer of 1916, a prominent Arab leader—the Grand Sharif Hussein of Mecca—agreed to rebel against Constantinople. Hussein's actual authority was quite limited. He and his Hashemite tribe governed the western portion of the Arabian Peninsula on behalf of the Ottomans. But Hussein's descent from the Prophet

Mohammed and his role as the steward of Islam's holiest cities, Mecca and Medina, gave him a religious significance well beyond his actual power.

With the backing of the British, three of Hussein's sons attacked Ottoman garrisons in the Arabian cities of Mecca, Medina, and Taif. When initial successes were followed by devastating defeats, the British sent a young officer named T. E. Lawrence to provide training and advice. In a now famous transformation, Lawrence donned Arab clothing, mounted a camel, and became a charismatic leader of Hussein's rebels. After the war he would be immortalized on stage and screen as "Lawrence of Arabia."

This uprising against the Ottomans is typically called "the Arab Revolt." But that title greatly overstates the case. Yes, Sharif Hussein and his Hashemite tribesmen were Arabs. And yes, there were other Arabs who joined the fight. Yet the overwhelming majority of Arabic speakers remained loyal Ottoman subjects. Males of the appropriate age served in the Ottoman army, and those who remained home paid their taxes to the Ottoman regime. So long as the Ottoman Empire existed, Arab nationalism remained a fringe movement.

What was true of Arabic-speaking Ottomans in general was also true of the Arabic-speaking Ottomans living in what would later be called Palestine. Writing in August 1918, a British officer named William Ormsby-Gore noted that the Muslim population of Palestine "took little or no interest in the Arab national movement." On the contrary, he observed that Palestine's wealthy and educated classes showed "a feeling somewhat akin to hostility towards the Arab movement."[15] Lawrence himself lamented the fact that the Arabs of Palestine did not participate in the Arab Revolt.[16]

AFTER WORLD WAR I: ARAB NATIONALISM ASCENDANT

The Ottomans surrendered in October of 1918. By 1923, the Ottoman Empire had ceased to exist. This end of an empire left a vacuum in the identity of the many millions of people who had previously thought of themselves as Ottomans.

Nationalism quickly filled the void. Turkish speakers were drawn toward Turkish nationalism. Arabic speakers naturally gravitated toward Arab nationalism. As Muhammad Muslih has noted, "The collapse of the empire stamped out the ideology of Ottomanism and caused Arab nationalism to emerge as the only viable political option."[17]

The Hashemites—Sharif Hussein and his family—had led the Arab Revolt. Now the most prominent of Hussein's sons, Prince Feisal, assumed control of the post-war Arab nationalist movement. From his new base in Damascus he led the fight to ensure that his new nation would achieve the ultimate nationalist prize: an independent Arab state.

Now that the war was over, the action shifted from the battlefields of Europe and the Middle East to the negotiating tables in Paris. In 1919, Prince Feisal traveled to Paris to represent "the Arabic-speaking peoples of Asia." There Feisal fought for both Arab independence and Arab unity, insisting that "no steps be taken inconsistent with the prospect of an eventual union of these [Arabic-speaking] areas under one sovereign government."[18]

As the talks dragged on, however, Feisal's supporters back home grew restless for their independence. In March 1920, elected delegates from Syria, Lebanon, and Palestine gathered for a "Syrian Congress" in Damascus. There they declared the independence of greater Syria—including Palestine—and crowned Feisal as their king.[19]

The great powers were not moved. In April 1920, the diplomats gathered in San Remo decided to replace Britain's post-war military rule of the Middle East with a new quasi-colonial structure. With the idealistic Wilson sidelined by a major stroke, the great powers granted themselves a series of "mandates" authorizing them to govern this region while preparing its people for independence. The mandates to govern Syria and Lebanon were given to France. The mandates to govern Palestine and Mesopotamia (now Iraq) were given to Great Britain.

The Arab nationalists gathered in Damascus refused to accept French rule. But they proved no match for French firepower. On July 24, 1920, French General Henri Gouraud marched on Damascus. On July 28, Feisal fled the city. The first brief experiment in Arab independence had come to an end.

THE CREATION—AND REJECTION—
OF PALESTINE

As in the other parts of the globe they ruled, the European powers carved up the former Ottoman territories with little regard for local loyalties or preferences. The mandates imposed at San Remo created borders—and eventually identities—that had never before existed.

Palestine was one of these new creations. While "Palestine" was a name with profound historic resonance for Europeans, it had no such significance to most of the people who happened to live there. To the extent that the Arabic speakers of Palestine identified with a geographic entity smaller than the Ottoman Empire, it was with Syria. Thus their first response to British efforts to separate them into a new entity called Palestine was to resist them.

In January 1919, a group of Arab nationalists convened the First Palestinian Arab Congress in Jerusalem. There the assembled delegates adopted a resolution declaring, "We consider Palestine nothing but part of Arab Syria and it has never been separated from it in any stage. We are tied to it by national, religious, linguistic, moral, economic, and geographic bonds."[20] They therefore called for Palestine to "remain undetached from the independent Arab Syrian Government."[21]

That same year, Arab nationalists launched the first post-war newspaper in Palestine. It was called *Southern Syria*.[22]

When the Second Palestinian Arab Congress met in 1920, the delegates once again emphasized that "it never occurred to the peoples of Northern and Coastal Syria that Southern Syria [Palestine] is anything but a part of Syria." They reiterated their demand that Palestine "not be divided from Syria."[23]

When elections for the first Syrian Arab Congress were held in 1919, the Arabs of Palestine participated in the vote. When this congress was convened, a delegation of fifteen Palestinians traveled to Damascus to represent their constituents.[24] And when the Syrian Arab Congress proclaimed the independence of Syria, including Palestine, in 1920, these Palestinian delegates were among the resolution's most enthusiastic supporters.[25]

Palestine's Arab nationalists did more than vote for Syrian independence. Many moved to Damascus to help run the new country. During the heady days before and during Syria's brief independence, Damascus became a hub of nationalist activity and a gathering place for rising Arab leaders from what would later be Lebanon, Palestine, Syria, and Iraq. But of all of these, Muslih notes, "the Palestinians were perhaps the most resolute group in their pursuit of pan-Syrian unity."[26]

This embrace of Syrian identity was hardly confined to Palestine's elites. When the great powers began debating the future of the Middle East in Paris, President Wilson demanded that the delegates consider the preferences of the people who actually lived there. In order to ascertain their views, the United States sent a fact-finding mission to Syria, Lebanon, and Palestine in the summer of 1919. The "King-Crane Commission," as it came to be known, concluded that a majority of the region's people wanted to be included in an independent Syria.

PALESTINIAN NATIONALISM IS BORN

The fall of the Ottoman Empire had forced its Arabic speakers to revisit the fundamental issue of their own identity. In similar fashion, France's 1920 conquest of Feisal's short-lived Syrian kingdom triggered yet another round of reinvention.

Severed from Syria and left alone in a new entity called Palestine, the region's Arabs began to narrow their identity accordingly. Like so many of the former colonized throughout the Third World, the Arabs of Palestine may not have created or even welcomed the particular borders within which they now found themselves. But they increasingly came to define themselves by them.

This shift in identity was already apparent by late 1920. When the Third Palestinian Arab Congress met in Haifa that December, the delegates suddenly and unceremoniously dumped all talk of a united Syria.[27] As Musa Kazim al-Husseini, the Congress president and former mayor of Jerusalem phrased it, "After the most recent events in Syria, we have to change our plans completely. Southern Syria does not exist."[28] The delegates agreed to focus instead on building a "Palestinian Arab national movement."[29]

Many scholars—including leading Palestinian academics such as Rashid Khalidi—identify this 1920 congress as the birthplace of Palestinian nationalism. The record provides much to support this claim. But the record also demonstrates that Palestinian nationalism would go on to have an unusually long infancy. Like Arab nationalism before it, this new identity did not immediately capture the hearts and minds of the future Palestinians. The process by which Palestinian nationalism would trickle down to the average citizen would take decades.

THE 1948 WAR

In November 1947, the United Nations voted to partition Palestine into a Jewish state and an Arab state. The very next day, Palestinian Arab gunmen attacked their Jewish neighbors. For the next six months, Palestine's Arabs led an effort to destroy the Jewish state before it could be born.

This war to block Israel's creation could have been an authentic, albeit bloody, expression of Palestinian nationalism. It wasn't. Quite to the contrary, this effort demonstrated how very little the idea of Palestinian nationalism had spread since 1920.

Only a small minority of Palestine's Arabs volunteered to fight the Jews.[30] The large majority of those who fought did so through hundreds of local militias. These militias battled to drive Jews from their particular towns and neighborhoods. But only in "extremely rare" cases did these fighters venture beyond their immediate environs.[31] In fact most Palestinian Arabs living outside the portion of Palestine assigned to the

Jewish state—especially those living in the hill country that later became
known as the West Bank—chose to sit out the war altogether.[32]

Simply put, Palestinian Arabs were willing to fight for the sake of
their neighborhood or their village. But they were not willing to risk their
lives for a nation called "Palestine." The loyalty to country that had so
recently driven so many millions to fight in World War II did not yet exist
in this part of the Middle East.

Unable to rally a nation to action, Palestinian nationalism was
quickly eclipsed by its ambitious cousins. On May 15, 1948, the armies
of Egypt, Syria, Transjordan, and Iraq invaded the nascent Jewish state.
Lebanon joined in later. At the war's end, two of these states controlled
most of the land that the UN had set aside for an Arab state in Palestine:
Transjordan occupied the West Bank and East Jerusalem, and Egypt
occupied the Gaza Strip.

Yet there was little talk of a Palestinian state at this juncture. To the
extent they had any national identity, most of the residents of the West
Bank and Gaza were still pan-Arabs. Seeing themselves as part of one
large Arab people, they had no objection to being ruled by Arabs from
across new and largely meaningless imperial borders.

In addition, many West Bank Arabs preferred Transjordan's King
Abdullah to the violent and dictatorial Mufti of Jerusalem, Amin al-
Husseini. As Transjordan's Arab Legionnaires conquered the West Bank,
they confronted no resistance from its Arab residents. On the contrary,
they typically encountered cheering crowds showering them with rice.[33]

PALESTINIAN NATIONALISM AFTER 1948

The 1948 War impacted the Palestinians in two deep yet contradic-
tory ways. On the one hand, the shared experience of defeat and dispersion accelerated the process of national identity formation. As Rashid
Khalidi has noted, "If the Arab population of Palestine had not been sure
of their identity before 1948, the experience of defeat, dispossession, and
exile guaranteed that they knew what their identity was very soon afterwards; and they were Palestinians."[34]

At the same time, however, this crushing defeat also dampened any enthusiasm that Palestinians might have felt about their new identity. As Khalidi has also observed, "There was a hiatus in manifestations of Palestinian identity for a period after 1948. During the 1950s and early 1960s there were few indications to outside observers of the existence of an independent Palestinian identity or of Palestinian nationalism."[35]

Indeed, the Palestinian debacle of 1948 opened the door wide to rival identities. The first of these was promoted by Transjordan.

To repay the Hashemites for leading the Arab Revolt, the British created the Emirate of Transjordan in 1921 and placed Sharif Hussein's son Abdullah on its throne. This new country's territory was that portion of the British Mandate for Palestine—over seventy percent of the whole—that lay east of the Jordan River. The next year, the British secured permission from the League of Nations to exclude Transjordan from the provisions of its Mandate requiring the establishment of a Jewish national home in Palestine. With the stroke of a pen, a majority of the British Mandate for Palestine was denied to the Jewish people and given instead to one branch of one Arab family.

Yet King Abdullah was never satisfied with his sparsely populated desert kingdom. When the British withdrew from Palestine, he saw an attractive growth opportunity. During the 1948 War, Abdullah sent his troops across the Jordan River and conquered most of the area that the UN had designated for the Arab state in Palestine. In the process, Abdullah not only expanded his kingdom and its population, but he also gained control of Islam's third holiest city, Jerusalem.

Abdullah quickly annexed this new land and extended Jordanian citizenship to his new subjects. He shortened his kingdom's name to "Jordan," thereby indicating that it was no longer confined to land "across" the Jordan River. It was under Jordanian rule that this newly annexed territory came to be known by its geographic location on the "West Bank" of the Jordan River.

Most of the West Bank's leading families readily embraced their new Jordanian identity. When elections to the Jordanian Parliament were held in 1950, West Bank Arabs "flocked to the polls" despite calls for a boycott.[36] The winners served in a Jordanian Parliament of which West Bank delegates made up almost half of the total. The new Parliament voted overwhelmingly in favor of unifying Transjordan and the West Bank under Abdullah's rule.[37]

The pull of Jordanian identity did not satisfy all Palestinians. Throughout the 1950s and 1960s another rival ideology—pan-Arab nationalism—was on the rise throughout the Middle East. The pan-Arabists sought to erase what they saw as artificial colonial borders and unite all of the Arab people in one massive Arab state.

For most of this period, one outsized personality dominated the pan-Arab movement: Egyptian President Gamal Abdel Nasser. Nasser espoused a muscular nationalism aimed at uniting the Arab world to oppose imperialism in general and Israel in particular. His combination of electric rhetoric and bold action—including nationalizing the British-controlled Suez Canal—fired the imaginations of Arab nationalists throughout the Middle East.

Nasser had an ally and sometime rival in the political movement called "Ba'athism." The Ba'ath constitution, adopted in 1947, called for the creation of a single Arab state since all differences among Arabs were "accidental and unimportant" and would "disappear with the awakening of the Arab consciousness."

In 1954, Ba'athists seized control of Syria. They would later come to power in Iraq. In 1958, Nasser and the Ba'athists followed their pan-Arab ideas to their logical conclusion by merging Egypt and Syria to form the United Arab Republic.[38]

As this pan-Arab drama played out around them, the Arabs of Palestine were hardly passive bystanders. Palestinians were among Nasser's most enthusiastic supporters. They believed that this charismatic leader of the most populous Arab country was their best hope for destroying Israel. Palestinians throughout the region hung Nasser's picture on their walls[39] and waited for his imminent victory.

Other Palestinians didn't merely wait for Nasser; they joined him. In 1956, two young Palestinians named George Habash and Wadi Haddad formed the Arab Nationalist Movement to serve as the Palestinian arm of the pan-Arab effort. Both Habash and Haddad forged close ties with Nasser, for whom they exhibited "intense loyalty." Before the 1967 War, these men and their colleagues were not only popular, but "dominated" the Palestinian political scene.[40]

Even the group that would ultimately become synonymous with Palestinian nationalism—the Palestine Liberation Organization (PLO)—had pan-Arab roots. The Arab League created the PLO in 1964 as an expression of solidarity with the Arabs of Palestine. For its first four years, however, the PLO was completely controlled by Nasser.

PALESTINIAN NATIONALISM AFTER 1967

Among the rhetorical flourishes that made Nasser so popular were his repeated promises to destroy Israel. In May 1967, Nasser combined heated rhetoric with actions so provocative that he convinced Israel that he was finally making his move. That month, Nasser expelled all UN forces from the buffer zone between Egypt and Israel and massed his troops on Israel's border. Then he closed the Straits of Tiran to Israeli shipping, thereby denying Israel the use of its only Red Sea port.

Early on the morning of June 5, Israel launched a preemptive military strike against Egypt. In response, Syria, Jordan, and Iraq attacked Israel. The long promised "second round" of war against Israel had begun.

Things didn't turn out as the Arabs had hoped. In a mere six days of fighting, Israel crushed these combined Arab armies and conquered territories more than three times its original size. Israel took Sinai and Gaza from Egypt, the West Bank and East Jerusalem from Jordan, and the Golan Heights from Syria.

Egypt and Syria had been the leading proponents of pan-Arab nationalism. Their dramatic defeat shattered the powerful hold this idea had exercised
over the Arab imagination. The 1967 War represented nothing less than "the
Waterloo of pan-Arabism."[41] In the years that followed, this philosophy and
the leaders most associated with it steadily faded in power and prestige.

This pan-Arab defeat had a powerful impact on Palestine's Arabs.
Once again—as with King Feisal decades earlier—many Palestinians
had looked to a great pan-Arab leader to liberate them. And, once again,
this Arab savior had failed. When France drove Feisal out of Syria in
1920, Palestinian nationalism was born. And now, after Israel crushed
Egypt and Syria, Palestinian nationalism experienced a "rebirth."[42] After
1967, the Palestinians stopped waiting for others to save them. Increasingly, they began to take their fate into their own hands.

The 1967 War also marked the beginning of the end of Jordanian
identity as a serious competitor to Palestinian nationalism. Jordan's kings
never captured the public's imagination the way that Nasser had. Instead,
the Jordanians had to earn loyalty to their regime through the hard work
of benign administration. But once the Israeli victory severed the direct
connection between the king and his erstwhile constituents in the West
Bank and East Jerusalem, it grew increasingly difficult for Jordan to
compete for Palestinian hearts and minds.

It was after the 1967 War that Palestinian nationalism finally
eclipsed its ideological competitors. Simply put, it was after 1967 that
most people on the streets of Gaza, Ramallah, Nablus, and Hebron
stopped seeing themselves as Syrians, Jordanians, or simply Arabs. Only
then—for the first time—a majority of these individuals began to see
themselves as Palestinians.[43]

AMIN AL-HUSSEINI: THE PERSONIFICATION OF HIS PEOPLE'S SHIFTING IDENTITY

For most of the half-century from the British conquest of Jerusalem
in 1918 until the creation of the PLO in 1964, the preeminent Palestinian

leader was a man named Amin al-Husseini. In 1920, the British engineered Husseini's election to the prestigious position of Mufti of Jerusalem. From this base of power, Husseini—or "The Mufti" as he came to be commonly known—extended his authority over the Palestinian national movement to an extent that at times approached monopoly.

Yet even this man who personified Palestinian nationalism passionately embraced other Arab identities throughout most of his career. The Mufti's own shifting labels and fluid rhetoric provide powerful testimony to the general confusion that characterized the Palestinian national movement before 1967.

Amin al-Husseini was born to a prominent Jerusalem family. Early in his life Husseini was, like most of his countrymen, a loyal Ottoman. When World War I broke out, Husseini dutifully enlisted in the Ottoman army.[44]

When the Ottomans lost the war, Husseini exchanged his Ottoman identity for a Syrian one. Like so many of Palestine's young Arab nationalists, Husseini enthusiastically supported the creation of an independent Syria that would include Palestine within its borders.[45] Husseini was among the young Arab leaders who traveled to Damascus to rally around King Feisal. While there, he helped organize the Syrian Arab Congress that declared the independence of a Greater Syria including Palestine. He also served as president of Jerusalem's Arab Club, which built local support for the inclusion of Palestine in Syria.[46]

When the French conquered Syria and ousted Feisal, Husseini quickly narrowed his focus from Syria to Palestine. In the 1920s and 1930s, Husseini was a zealous advocate for an independent Palestine. Seeing Zionism as the greatest obstacle to his goal, he took the lead in fighting any British policies that advanced the Zionist agenda, namely those permitting Jewish immigration and land purchases.

When advocacy alone did not work, Husseini was quick to resort to violence. In 1920, he fomented the first post-war pogrom against Palestine's

Jews. In 1936, Husseini led Palestine's Arabs in a sustained revolt against British rule in which he made both the British military and Jewish civilians his main targets.

The British finally crushed the Arab Revolt in 1939. By this point, however, the Mufti had identified a powerful potential ally that shared his twin hatreds. The Nazis, notorious for their anti-Semitism, were now on the brink of war with Britain.

Husseini was an early and zealous champion of a Nazi-Arab alliance. Once hostilities started, he made his pitch directly to the top Nazi brass. In a January 1941 letter to Hitler, for example, Husseini stressed that with German assistance, "the Arab peoples will be ready to serve the common enemy his just deserts, and to take their place enthusiastically alongside the Axis...."[47]

Husseini also sought to demonstrate to the Nazis that he was the best man to rally the Arabs to their cause. From a strategic perspective, Palestine was marginal to the unfolding world war. But Iraq—with its vast oil supply—was a British asset the Nazis coveted. Shortly after the outbreak of war, Husseini made his way to Iraq. There he played a pivotal role in organizing the 1941 coup that temporarily ousted the country's pro-British regime.

As he emerged as one of the Nazis' most important Arab allies, Husseini's ambitions grew apace. He no longer spoke of ruling Palestine; now he wanted to rule the entire Arab world. In exchange for his continued support, Husseini demanded that the Nazis "recognize in principle the unity, independence and sovereignty of an Arab state of a Fascist nature including Iraq, Syria, Lebanon, Palestine and Transjordan."[48] He called his proposed pan-Arab entity the "Greater Arab Empire," and he naturally offered himself as its ideal leader.[49]

After moving to Berlin and developing close ties with the top Nazi officials, Hussein's ambition grew greater still. The Mufti eventually demanded a Greater Arab Empire that included these original territories as well as Saudi Arabia, Kuwait, the Gulf Emirates, Egypt, North Africa, and Sudan.[50]

As the Mufti increasingly emphasized pan-Arab nationalism, he stopped speaking of a separate Palestinian people. In his 1941 letter to Hitler, for example, Husseini referred repeatedly to the "Arab nation" and the "Arab people." He declared that his ultimate goal was the "unity and independence of the Arab states."[51]

After the Nazis were defeated, the Mufti escaped from detention in France—and a likely war crimes trial—and fled to Egypt. Now that his efforts to lead the Arab world had failed, he once again narrowed his focus to Palestine.

But even as he returned to speaking of a distinct Palestinian people, he continued to discuss them in a larger, pan-Arab context. Writing in 1953, for example, Husseini noted that, "There is no doubt that saving Palestine and redeeming it from its occupiers is a crucial need which the Arab nation cannot avoid. Palestine is the heart of the nation's lands, and it unifies the different parts of the nation. It is the single contact between the Arab territories in Asia and Africa. Its loss would erase all connections between these lands, and they too would be exposed to the most severe dangers."[52]

Toward the end of his career, the Mufti became so desperate for power and allies that he reinvented himself yet again. After the 1948 War he had strongly opposed Jordan's efforts to annex and absorb the West Bank. After the 1967 War, however, Husseini became a Jordanian nationalist who advocated the return of the West Bank to King Hussein. In March 1967, he traveled to Amman to express his full support for the "unity for the two banks of the Jordan."[53]

After Jordanian troops battled rebellious PLO forces in September 1970, Husseini mourned, "It is almost impossible to conceive of the fratricidal struggle and mutual massacre that recently took place in Jordan between residents of the same country, the same people and the same homeland."[54]

Thus the man who dominated Palestinian nationalism before 1964 was a shape shifter who repeatedly reinvented himself. In the span of one lifetime, Husseini was an Ottoman, a Syrian, a Palestinian, a pan-Arab, a Palestinian once again, and finally a Jordanian. In each case he embraced his new identity with convincing conviction. And in so doing, Husseini personified the shifting identities of his people.

When the most prominent Palestinian Arab leader is so unclear about his own identity, how exactly were the Israelis supposed to know better?

ANACHRONISM AND THE ANTI-ISRAEL NARRATIVE

Leonardo da Vinci's masterpiece *The Last Supper* is one of the world's most famous paintings. Yet this fifteenth-century portrayal of a first-century event contains some glaring historical inaccuracies. Most noted among these is the fact that it depicts Jesus and his disciples sitting together at an elevated rectangular table. But such tables only came into common usage in the Middle Ages, and even then they were largely limited to Europe. Jews in Palestine at the time of Jesus would have eaten their Passover meal at a low, round table—or possibly on the floor—while reclining on pillows.

Leonardo's tall table is a popular example of a phenomenon known as an "anachronism"—the projection of an object or idea back into the past, before it actually existed.[55] When an anachronism occurs in art, it makes for interesting trivia. When an anachronism occurs in our understanding of history, however, it can have far more dangerous implications.

The modern anti-Israel narrative is built upon an anachronism. The present existence of a Palestinian people is constantly projected back into the past. Then Israel is blamed for failing to recognize and accommodate a nation not yet born.

As we've seen, however, history makes a mockery of this charge. Yes, Arabic-speaking people have lived in Palestine for centuries. And yes, they were the majority in Palestine when the Jews began their latest wave of return in the late 1800s. But no one can fault the early Zionists for failing to predict that these Arabic speakers would one day come to see themselves as a separate people needing their own independent state. It was first necessary that the Palestinians—and their leaders—recognize themselves.

Yet exposing this anachronism does not clear Israel of all of the charges against it. Even before Palestine's Arabs had a national identity giving rise to corresponding national rights, they were of course human beings entitled to full human and civil rights. International law had yet to codify these rights. And the Ottomans fell well short of honoring them. But Israel's founders always held themselves to a higher standard.

Thus while we cannot fault the Zionists for failing to honor national rights that did not yet exist, we most certainly can and should hold them accountable for any failure to respect the human and civil rights of their Arabic-speaking neighbors. This inquiry is especially relevant in light of repeated claims that the Zionists ignored the very existence of these Arabs, stole their land, and then ethnically cleansed them from the country. It is to this human and civil rights record that we now turn.

CHAPTER THREE

THE JEWS COME HOME

Palestine is not an unpopulated country.... By no means and under no circumstances are the rights of these inhabitants to be infringed upon—it is neither desirable nor conceivable that the present inhabitants be ousted from the land. That is not the mission of Zionism.

—David Ben Gurion, 1918[1]

Columbia University Professor Rashid Khalidi is among the most prominent Palestinian Americans. He's also a leading expert on the history of the Palestinian people. Khalidi's 1997 book *Palestinian Identity* is among the most influential works yet written on the rise of Palestinian nationalism.

When *Palestinian Identity* turns its focus to the modern Zionists who built the State of Israel, Khalidi accuses them of a grave oversight: "In the early years of the Zionist movement, many of its European supporters—and others—believed that Palestine was empty and sparsely cultivated. This view was widely propagated by some of the movement's leading thinkers and writers, such as Herzl, Bialik, and Mandelstamm, with Herzl never even mentioning the Arabs in his famous work, *The Jewish State*. It was summed up in the widely-propagated Zionist slogan, 'A land without a people for a people without a land.'"[2]

Khalidi's accusation has become a core component of the anti-Israel narrative. The Jews, we're told, simply failed to recognize that over the centuries of their exile other people had moved into the land to which they sought to return. By ignoring the existence—or the humanity—of this population, the Zionists pursued a program that would inevitably lead to their displacement or death.

This allegation could not be more serious. And it could not be more mistaken. The fact is that "a land without a people for a people without a land" was never a Zionist slogan. The saying was originated by Christian enthusiasts of a Jewish return to Palestine well before the birth of the modern Zionist movement. The only Zionist leader of any significance to use this slogan was the British author Israel Zangwill.[3] And although Zangwill invoked it in 1901, he quickly conceded that he was wrong to have done so. By 1904 Zangwill had publically repudiated this formulation.

More important, this was never a Zionist slogan because this was never a Zionist belief. No serious Zionist ever suggested that Palestine was uninhabited. They all recognized and wrote about the Arabic speakers who lived there. The Zionists simply believed that there was plenty of room in the land to accommodate these existing residents, their descendants, *and* millions of Jews. Far from harming these existing communities, they maintained, Jewish immigration would bring them multiple blessings.

If the Zionists nurtured an illusion, it was that they and their blessings would be welcome.

HERZL'S INCLUSIVE VISION

For Europe, the nineteenth century was the era of nationalism. People throughout the continent began seeing themselves as members of distinct "peoples" or "nations" bound together by language, culture, history, and geography. As these new national identities grew, so did the animosity toward what was now seen as "foreign" rule by kings or emperors from other nations. This resentment eventually burst forth in a series of nationalist revolutions against the reigning empires of the day. In the early decades of the 1800s, the Serbs and Greeks rebelled against

Ottoman rule. In the middle of the century, Czechs, Slovaks, Italians, and others fought for their independence from the Habsburg Empire.

Europe's Jews were hardly immune to this wave of nationalism. But their efforts to seek inclusion within the new nations emerging around them were repeatedly rebuffed. The Jews shared geography, and typically language, with their neighbors. But most new nations defined themselves in narrower terms, stressing shared blood and an ancient mystical connection between a people and their local landscape. Religion often featured prominently as well. Thus as European nationalism grew, the Jews were increasingly classified as foreigners and perceived as enemies in the lands they had inhabited for centuries.

Rejected by these new European nations, it was only a matter of time until the Jews looked homeward. After all, the Jewish people possess one of the oldest nationalisms on earth. For over three millennia the Jews have seen themselves as a distinct people bound by blood, language, faith, and ties to a particular land in which their nation was birthed. The Jews did not need nineteenth-century nationalism to forge their national identity. Their challenge was simply to translate their ancient aspirations into modern terms. The man who accomplished this task was a Viennese journalist named Theodor Herzl.

Herzl was Jewish, but for most of his life he didn't define himself as such. He was, quite to the contrary, a most dedicated secular European. Herzl loved Vienna's symphonies, operas, and coffee houses. He admired the precision of the German language. And he dreamed that one day he could be accepted as a full Austro-Hungarian instead of being marginalized as a Jew. Writing years later, he summarized this longing so common to Europe's Jews with the words: "If we could only be left in peace...."[4]

Herzl's dreams were dashed in 1894 when he traveled to Paris to cover the trial of Alfred Dreyfus, a Jewish captain in the French army falsely accused of spying for Germany. In France, the very birthplace of the Enlightenment, Herzl witnessed angry mobs marching in the streets chanting "death to the Jews." The following year, Herzl's beloved Vienna elected the virulently anti-Semitic politician Karl Lueger as its new mayor. These events drove Herzl to a life-changing conclusion: "I think we shall not be left in peace."[5]

By the end of 1895, Herzl had written a short book called *The Jewish State*, in which he argued for creating an independent Jewish state and provided a practical program for doing so. This book and Herzl's prodigious efforts launched the modern Jewish nationalist movement known as "Zionism."

Rashid Khalidi's critique is technically correct: Herzl does not use the word "Arabs" anywhere in *The Jewish State*. But as Khalidi surely knows, when Herzl wrote this book there were no more than a handful of people anywhere in the world who would have used that term to describe the Arabic speakers of the Ottoman Empire. And, as anyone who reads the book can see, Herzl was not yet certain whether the Jewish state should be built in Palestine, Argentina, or elsewhere. But Herzl was quite clear that wherever the Jewish state was built, "We could offer the present possessors of the land enormous advantages."[6]

While *The Jewish State* remains Herzl's most famous book, it was not the only one he wrote. Herzl also published a novel in 1902 known by its German title *Altneuland* ("The Old New Land"). Herzl used his second book to color in the broad outlines of his first and set forth his vision for society in the future Jewish homeland. If *The Jewish State* reflects Herzl's head, then *Altneuland* gives us a window into Herzl's heart.

Altneuland is a lousy novel. It is utopian and preachy to the point of distraction. Yet there's one area in which Herzl's book is profoundly prescient. Writing over a century ago, Herzl described a Jewish state that is perfectly multicultural and tolerant even when judged by the most rigorous of modern standards. At a time when Europe was experiencing violent spasms of ethnic nationalism and America was still racially segregated, Herzl imagined a multi-racial society in which citizens were judged not by the color of their skin but by the content of their contributions.

The Jewish state Herzl envisioned in *Altneuland* is built in Palestine. Yet the cities of Herzl's "New Society" are still dominated by Muslim minarets. The best neighborhoods in these cities contain Arab houses "in the Moorish style" built right next to modern Jewish homes. The book's hero passionately battles to maintain full civil rights for all. The villain is a politician who wants to relegate non-Jews to second-class citizenship.

Altneuland's noble protagonist is David Litwack, a poor Jewish boy from Vienna who grew to be a wise and generous leader in his restored homeland. Litwack's best friend and traveling companion is an Arab citizen named Reschid Bey. At one point, a foreign visitor asks Bey a tough question: "Were not the older inhabitants of Palestine ruined by the Jewish immigration? And didn't they have to leave the country? I mean, generally speaking. That individuals here and there were the gainers proves nothing."[7]

When Herzl placed this question in the visitor's mouth, he anticipates Khalidi's critique of Zionism a full ninety-five years before the fact. And in the answer he has his Arab character speak, Herzl predicted the Zionist response. Reschid Bey replies, "What a question! It was a great blessing for all of us. Naturally, the land-owners gained most because they were able to sell to the Jewish society at high prices, or to wait for still higher ones.... Those who had nothing stood to lose nothing, and could only gain. And they did gain: Opportunities to work, means of livelihood, prosperity.... When the swamps were drained, the canals built, and the eucalyptus trees planted to drain, and 'cure' the marshy soil, the natives...were the first to be employed, and were paid well for their work!"[8]

Later, Reschid Bey waxes poetic on the contributions made by Jewish immigration to his country: "The Jews have enriched us. Why should we be angry with them? They dwell among us like brothers. Why should we not love them? I have never had a better friend among my co-religionists than David Litwack here.... He prays in a different house to the God who is above us all. But our houses of worship stand side by side, and I always believe that our prayers, when they rise, mingle somewhere up above, and then continue on their way together until they appear before Our Father."[9]

Looking back at Herzl's vision, one can certainly find faults. Writing in 1902, he failed to predict the emergence of Arab nationalism and the Palestinian Arab nationalism that would grow out of it. But, as we've seen, Arab nationalism was a minuscule movement at that time. And a distinctive Palestinian nationalism was not yet even a twinkle in the eyes of the first Arab nationalists. Herzl also failed to predict the emergence of a militant Islam that would so violently reject his vision of religious harmony.

But while Herzl may have failed to foresee Arab trends, he successfully set Jewish priorities. Herzl's followers did not dismiss his tolerant vision. On the contrary, they embraced his values and sought to implement them in the face of an often bitter reality.

Precisely as Herzl predicted through his character Reschid Bey, the Zionists returning to their ancient land would not expel those already living there. They would instead enrich their new neighbors by purchasing their land "at high prices." They would provide them with "opportunities to work" and "prosperity" by draining the swamps and planting trees—eucalyptus and others—by the millions. And the Zionists would insist upon the full equality of their non-Jewish neighbors within their new society.

Altneuland may have been a poor novel. But it proved to be an uplifting guide to Zionist action.

HERZL'S LOYAL DISCIPLES

Theodor Herzl died in 1904. From that point until the creation of the State of Israel in 1948, the Zionist movement was dominated by two men. A Russian-born chemist named Chaim Weizmann assumed the role of Zionism's ambassador-at-large. He would go on to become Israel's first president. And a Polish-born laborer named David Ben Gurion led the Jewish community living in Palestine. He would become Israel's first prime minister. These two leaders often disagreed, and they fought many bitter battles. But when it came to Herzl's inclusive vision for Palestine's Arabs, both were the most loyal of disciples.

CHAIM WEIZMANN

Chaim Weizmann stressed the theme of Arab inclusion and equality throughout his long career. And he did so with a bluntness not at all typical for this courtly diplomat.

In a 1919 address to a Zionist Conference in London, for example, Weizmann stated that when it came to returning to Palestine, "We cannot afford to drive out other people. We who have been driven out ourselves cannot drive out others. We shall be the last people to drive off the Fellah [Arab peasant] from his land; we shall establish normal relations between us and them. The Arabs will live among us; they won't suffer; they will live among us as Jews do here in England. This is our attitude towards the Arabs. Any other attitude is criminal, childish, impolitic, stupid."[10]

Decades later, Weizmann was still emphasizing this same theme. On November 29, 1947, the United Nations voted in favor of partitioning Palestine into two states, one Jewish and one Arab. The next morning, Arab gunmen launched a civil war against their Jewish neighbors in an effort to destroy the nascent Jewish state. Yet writing that same day, Weizmann chose to stress one theme above all others: the need for full equality between the Arab and Jewish citizens of the future Jewish state: "There must not be one law for the Jew and another for the Arabs. We must stand firm by the ancient principle enunciated in our Torah: 'One law and one manner shall be for you and for the stranger that sojourneth with you.' In saying this, I do not assume that there are tendencies towards inequality or discrimination. It is merely a timely warning which is particularly necessary because we shall have a very large Arab minority."[11]

DAVID BEN GURION

Like Weizmann, David Ben Gurion embraced Herzl's tolerant vision from the start. Ben Gurion always viewed the Arabs living in Palestine as "an organic, inextricable part of Palestine" who were "embedded in the country, where it toils and where it will stay."[12]

In 1936, when he fully recognized the imminent danger facing Europe's Jews, Ben Gurion continued to insist that Jewish immigration never be so large as to displace Palestine's Arabs. When he met with Arab nationalist author George Antonius that year, he told him, "I want to settle in Palestine that number of Jews for whom it would be possible to create new possibilities of existence without ousting the Arabs or reducing their ability to support themselves. That was the only restriction we accepted, and we accepted it willingly and from conviction, for both moral and political reasons."[13]

As we'll see, Ben Gurion would eventually reconsider this commitment. But he would do so only under drastically changed circumstances. It would take prolonged Arab violence and the existential threat of a multi-front Arab invasion to force Ben Gurion to abandon his lifelong opposition to displacing any of Palestine's Arabs.

Ben Gurion's commitment to Palestine's Arabs was rooted in a philosophy of rights that guided his actions throughout his life. Ben Gurion believed that Palestine's Arabs derived their rights to the land from the fact that they lived on it. But if Arab rights flowed from their presence on the land, then—Ben Gurion insisted—the Arabs did not have the right to exclude Jews from land on which they did not live. What the Arabs lacked, Ben Gurion stated, was the "right to close the country to us."[14]

As he noted in 1918, "The true aim and the real capacity of Zionism are not to conquer what has already been conquered, but to settle in those places where the present inhabitants of the land have not established themselves and are unable to do so. The preponderant part of the country's land is unoccupied and uncultivated.... It is on these vacant lands that the Jewish people demands the right to establish its homeland."[15]

In 1924, Ben Gurion reiterated this theme in a speech to his fellow labor Zionists: "We demand the same national autonomy for the Arabs as we demand for ourselves. But we do not accept their right *to rule over the land*, to the extent that the land has not been built up by them and it awaits its builders. They do not have the right to forbid it being built, to forbid the resurrection of its ruins, the development of its resources, the expansion of its cultivated areas, the advancement of its culture, the increase of its laboring settlements."[16]

In 1937, Ben Gurion still clung to this vision. He wrote to his son Amos that it was essential that the Negev desert ultimately be part of a Jewish state: "Because we cannot stand to see large areas of unsettled land capable of absorbing thousands of Jews remain empty, or to see Jews not return to their country because the Arabs say that there is not enough room for them and us."[17]

Ben Gurion recognized that most of these uninhabited areas were either malarial marshes or desert. But this never discouraged him. He was certain that these wastelands could be reclaimed.

Ben Gurion's faith in the country's future was based on his knowledge of its past. He often noted that Palestine had sustained four million people at the time of the Second Temple. If modern methods were employed, he reasoned, as many as six million people could earn their livelihoods from farming this reclaimed land.[18] The introduction of modern industry would enable the land to sustain "an untold number."[19]

Ben Gurion's confidence in Palestine's potential was also the product of his firsthand experience. He had immigrated in 1906. After arriving at the port of Jaffa, he set out on foot for Petach Tikvah, the oldest Jewish farming settlement in the country. Ben Gurion later described what happened next: "At Petach Tikvah, I literally starved.... Every day, hundreds of Arabs would walk into the fields and vineyards to begin the chores.... The young Jews would gather near the synagogue hoping a farmer would come by. If one did, he would feel each candidate's arm to determine whether there was sufficient muscle for the work.... It took me ten days to get my first assignment. Then it was the lesser task of carting wheelbarrows of manure for spreading in the orange groves."[20]

While unpleasant, Ben Gurion's time in Petach Tikvah taught him just how easily Palestine's land could be coaxed into supporting a far larger population. Petach Tikvah had been founded in 1878 on land from which twenty poor Arab families had scratched out a livelihood. By the time Ben Gurion arrived in 1906, the community was supporting two thousand families—both Jews and Arabs—at a much higher standard of living.[21] In fact, more Arabs than Jews were now earning their livelihood from this land.

After leaving Petach Tikvah, Ben Gurion wandered from village to village looking for work. "My clothing was inadequate and so was my diet. I quickly succumbed to malaria."[22] A doctor urged Ben Gurion to return to Europe since "staying in Palestine meant death."[23] Ben Gurion wasn't alone in his suffering. Sixty percent of the first generation of Jewish farmers contracted malaria as they drained the swamps and reclaimed the lands that this disease had rendered so sparsely populated.[24]

As he literally walked his way across Palestine, Ben Gurion was able to observe the land in great detail. In 1908, Ben Gurion hiked from Haifa down to Jaffa, thereby traversing that portion of the coastal plain that is now Israel's most densely populated region. He later recalled what he saw: "Walking through the barren plain, seeing only an occasional tribe of nomadic Bedouins…and a few poverty-stricken Arab villages…. There was nothing here. It was literally a forgotten corner of the Turkish Empire and of the globe."[25]

Ben Gurion had seen the emptiness. And he had witnessed what could be built in it. And he discerned the dark clouds gathering over the millions of Jews trapped in Europe. It is easy to understand Ben Gurion's driving passion for bringing these doomed people to build up these desolate places.

David Ben Gurion was elected Israel's first prime minister in 1948. He was still serving in this capacity in 1953 when he drove by a group of young people toiling in the burning sun of the Negev Desert. When he asked what they were doing, the workers explained that they were building a new kibbutz (collective farming community).

A few weeks later, Ben Gurion shocked the Israeli public. He announced that he was resigning his office. He had decided to move to the Negev to help these young pioneers develop the desert. Within weeks, the newspapers were publishing photos of the former prime minister tending to the kibbutz's sheep.

Ben Gurion would eventually return to politics. But he continued to make his home in this Negev kibbutz—called Sde Boker—until his death and burial there in 1973.

Thus even in retirement, Ben Gurion clung to his early conviction that Israel's future lay not in displacing Palestine's Arabs but in reclaiming Palestine's waste places. And the largest of these empty places was the Negev Desert. This desert made up almost sixty percent of Israel's land mass but was home to only a tiny percentage of its inhabitants. As Ben Gurion noted, "That I decided to live in the Negev represents a continuation of the ideas I have followed throughout my life and namely the concept that the principal way the Jews can re-claim their ancient land is not by argument or invoking historical precedent but by their labor, that is, by creating an enduring, fruitful home for themselves where previously there was nothing."[26]

In 1970, just a few years before his death, Ben Gurion remained as enthusiastic as ever about the Negev's potential. "We can easily accommodate five million people here," he exclaimed. "Yes, five million!"[27]

JABOTINSKY AND THE "EXTREMIST WING OF ZIONISM"

Weizmann and Ben Gurion were pragmatists. Since Britain ruled Palestine, they both saw British goodwill as a precondition to their ultimate success. These leaders, therefore, chose to accommodate the British even when they dealt major blows to Zionist aspirations.

In the early 1920s, for example, the British significantly narrowed the borders of a potential Jewish state by creating a new entity—the

Emirate of Transjordan—in the eastern two-thirds of the British Mandate for Palestine. The British also refused to allow Palestine's Jews to bear arms in their own defense even after Arab rioters had killed scores of them. Yet their objections to these policies notwithstanding, Ben Gurion, Weizmann, and the Zionist Organization they led continued their steady collaboration with the British.

Not all Zionists were so quick to concede these losses. The undisputed leader of these rebels—known as the "Revisionists"—was a fiery writer and orator named Vladimir "Ze'ev" Jabotinsky. Among other areas of disagreement, Jabotinsky was a territorial maximalist who continued to demand that Jews be permitted to settle in all of the British Mandate for Palestine including Transjordan. He was also a militarist, urging the British to create a Jewish militia to defend Palestine's Jews at home and a Jewish Legion to enable Palestine's Jews to fulfill their responsibilities to the British Empire abroad.

But when it came to the human and civil rights of Palestine's Arabs, Jabotinsky was in complete agreement with the inclusive vision of Herzl, Weizmann, and Ben Gurion. Thus even the "so-called extremist wing of Zionism" (Jabotinsky's term) recognized the need to share the land with the Arabs already living there.

Throughout his career, Jabotinsky stressed that "there will always be two nations in Palestine."[28] He never saw this reality as a problem. Echoing Ben Gurion, Jabotinsky repeatedly argued that "Palestine can offer a solution to our immigration problem without expelling any Arabs or harming them in any way."[29] As he phrased it to Britain's Peel Commission in 1937, "the idea is that Palestine on both sides of the Jordan should hold the Arabs, their progeny, *and* many millions of Jews."[30]

Writing in 1941, before the Nazis had launched their Final Solution, Jabotinsky stressed once again that rescuing Europe's Jews would not require displacing Palestine's Arabs:

> The transformation of Palestine can be effected to the full without dislodging the Palestinian Arabs. All current affirmations to the contrary are utterly incorrect. A territory of over

100,000 square kilometers settled at the average density of France would hold over 8 million inhabitants; at the density of Switzerland over 10 million; at the density of Germany or Italy about 14 million. It [Palestine] now holds, counting Arabs and Transjordanians and all, just over one million and a half inhabitants. There is margin enough left for Palestine to absorb the better part of East Central Europe's ghetto—the better part of five million souls—without approaching even the moderate density of France. Unless the Arabs choose to go away of their own accord, there is no need for them to emigrate.[31]

In 1934, the executive committee of Jabotinsky's Revisionist Zionist Alliance composed a draft constitution for the future Jewish state. A section called "Civic Equality" states that "the principle of equal rights for all citizens of any race, creed, language or class shall be enacted without limitation throughout all sectors of the country's public life."[32]

The next paragraph jumps from the general to the surprisingly specific. The draft stipulates that "In every Cabinet where the Prime Minister is a Jew, the vice-premiership shall be offered to an Arab, and vice-versa." The next section ensures, "Proportional sharing by Jews and Arabs both in the charges and in the benefits of the State shall be the rule with regard to Parliamentary elections, civil and military service, and budgetary grants."[33]

Thus even the Zionist movement's often maligned right wing envisioned a Jewish state much like Herzl's in *Altneuland*. It would be a state with a vibrant Arab minority. It would be a state in which Jews and Arabs would live together as full equals. And it would be a state in which an Arab child could grow up to be prime minister.

ZIONISM IN ACTION

These Zionist pronouncements about equality and coexistence are all well and good. But Israel's critics are quick to dismiss them as meaningless. Never mind that these declarations were offered freely, clearly, and repeatedly. Forget that they were typically issued to fellow Zionists in Hebrew and not merely to outsiders in English. Under the cover of such lofty rhetoric, we are told, the Zionists presided over massive Jewish immigration which most certainly did uproot Palestine's Arabs.

This claim—that returning Jews displaced indigenous Arabs—has become a central plank of the anti-Israel narrative. It is often identified as the root cause of the ongoing conflict. And it is completely false.

When Jews began to immigrate to Palestine in large numbers, Palestine's Arab population did not shrink—it soared. And lest there be any confusion about causation, it's important to note that Palestine's Arab population grew fastest in those parts of the country to which the Jews were moving.

In other words, those who claim that Jewish immigration to Palestine displaced Palestine's Arabs have it exactly backward. What Ben Gurion experienced as a young man in Petach Tikvah was repeated on an even greater scale throughout the country as a whole. The lands the Jews reclaimed and developed supported not only returning Jews, but also far more Arabs than ever before. Arabs streamed into these Jewish areas from other parts of Palestine and from neighboring Arab countries. Once there, they enjoyed a standard of living far higher than any of their neighbors in Palestine or beyond.

ARAB POPULATION GROWTH

The peak years of Jewish immigration to Palestine before the birth of the State of Israel were from 1920 to 1937. During this period, Palestine's Arab population rose from approximately 600,000 to 950,000. This is a growth rate of over 50 percent in only seventeen years, a statistic Britain's Peel Commission called "remarkable."[34]

This rapid Arab population growth continued for another decade, up until the outbreak of war in 1947. A study based on British census data from 1922 to 1947 concluded that Palestine's permanent Arab population increased from 554,500 to 1,207,600 during this period. This represents an increase of approximately 120 percent in only twenty-five years.[35]

Even more noteworthy than the explosive rate of Arab population growth in general is its regional concentration. The Arab population grew at its fastest rates in those parts of Palestine to which Jews were immigrating. Between 1922 and 1947, the Arab population of Haifa grew by 290 percent. During the same period, the Arab population of Jaffa grew by 158 percent.[36]

The Arab population grew at a far slower pace in those parts of Palestine untouched by Jewish immigration. In Nablus, the Arab population grew by only 56 percent during these years. In Bethlehem it grew by a mere 37 percent.[37]

These growth patterns governed not only the cities but also the rural areas bordering these cities. Thus between 1922 and 1947 the rural Arab population increased 212 percent in the Jaffa district, but only 72 percent in the Nablus district.[38]

The direct connection between Jewish immigration and Arab population growth was clear to all objective observers. In 1937, for example, the Peel Commission recognized that "The general beneficent effect of Jewish immigration on Arab welfare is illustrated by the fact that the increase in the Arab population is most marked in urban areas affected by Jewish development."[39]

Just as there is no dispute as to the fact of this Arab population growth, there is also no dispute about its causes. This upsurge was the product of three factors: (1) Arab immigration into Palestine from neighboring countries, (2) Arab in-migration to Palestine's Jewish areas from its predominantly Arab areas, and (3) decreases in Arab infant mortality and increases in Arab in life expectancy resulting from improved living conditions and health care.

The only ongoing debate concerns the relative importance of these three factors. Some, such as author Joan Peters, have argued that Arab immigration into Palestine played a significant role in the overall Arab population growth. And while Peters has been criticized for alleged flaws in her scholarship, she is hardly alone in making this argument. Israeli historian Arieh Avneri has noted that "During the period of peak Jewish immigration, tens of thousands of Arabs immigrated to Palestine legally. Tens of thousands more immigrated illegally. During the period of the mandate, the country had absorbed an estimated 100,000 legal and illegal Arab immigrants and their offspring."[40]

The Peel Commission concluded that "no accurate estimate can be made of the number of Arabs who have come into Palestine from neighboring Arab lands and settled there."[41] The commissioners nevertheless "reckon[ed]" that roughly one-tenth of total Arab population growth was the result of such immigration. Thus even the Peel Commission— which was eager to downplay Arab immigration, especially of the illegal variety—acknowledged that tens of thousands of Arabs had immigrated into Palestine during these years.

Finally, all observers agree that Jewish contributions to Palestine's environment and health care contributed to Arab population growth. The Jews drained the swamps and eradicated malaria. They built clinics and hospitals that served all of Palestine's residents, Arab and Jew alike. Thus throughout these years of Jewish immigration, Palestine's Arabs enjoyed a steady increase in their life expectancy while their mortality rates plummeted.

ARAB ECONOMIC PROGRESS

While Palestine's Arab population grew, Arab standards of living soared. Arab-owned citrus groves and vegetable farms proliferated. Arab-owned factories and Arab industrial workers multiplied. Arab wages and savings rapidly increased.

But just like the population growth, these Arab economic advances were largely limited to Jewish areas. The further Palestine's Arabs lived from Jewish centers, the less such numbers improved. And nothing even close to such advances occurred in neighboring Arab countries, including those also ruled by Britain.[42]

As Britain's Peel Commission acknowledged in 1937, "Broadly speaking, the Arabs have shared to a considerable degree in the material benefits which Jewish immigration has brought to Palestine."[43] It further noted that these benefits were experienced across the economic spectrum. Not only did wealthy Arabs make large sums by selling their land to Jews at inflated prices, but "the fellaheen [Arab peasants] are on the whole better off than they were in 1920."[44]

Zionist dreamers such as Herzl, Weizmann, and Ben Gurion had argued that they could bring hundreds of thousands of Jewish immigrants into Palestine without displacing the Arabs already living there. They had further claimed that they could do this while bringing the blessings of increased wealth and improved health to Palestine's Arabs. As it turned out, this loftiest of Zionist rhetoric was supported by the most impressive of results.

THE MYTH OF THE LANDLESS ARABS

This dramatic growth in Arab population and prosperity during the peak years of Jewish immigration to Palestine are facts that no serious observer disputes. Such overwhelming evidence makes it difficult to argue that Jewish immigration to Palestine displaced Arabs. But these inconvenient facts don't prevent Israel's detractors from trying to argue exactly that.

Rather than deny this growth, Israel's critics prefer to divert our attention from it. They typically do this by narrowing the focus from this overwhelming trend to some of the exceptions thereto. In particular, much has been made of the claim that when Jews purchased land in Palestine they evicted the Arabs who were already living there, thereby "dispossessing" them and rendering them "landless."

For starters, let's focus on the operative verb. Prior to the 1948 War, Palestine's Jews *purchased* every square inch of land on which they lived.

They bought this land from Arab landowners. And they typically bought this land at wildly inflated prices.

It is difficult to claim that a man who sells his land for an enormous profit has somehow been "dispossessed" of it. Israel's critics therefore seek to narrow our focus further still. They stress that some of the land sold to Jews was being cultivated by tenant farmers. A tenant farmer, by definition, doesn't own the land he farms. He merely rents it from the owner. When Jewish purchasers stopped renting their land to these Arab tenants, the tenants were forced to seek their livelihoods elsewhere. Eureka! These tenant farmers are the displaced Arabs we've been looking for.

Yet even this claim disintegrates upon deeper examination. After all, most societies permit the private ownership of land and recognize that landowners have broad discretion over how their property is used. A landowner can choose to rent agricultural land to tenant farmers much as he might choose to rent residential apartments to tenant dwellers. And once such leases have expired, he can choose to renew them—or not—at his discretion.

An owner's decision to stop renting real estate is certainly disruptive to his tenants. But unless one favors extreme curbs on the rights of property owners, it's perfectly moral. And unless the government has stepped in to provide special protection to tenants, it's also perfectly legal.

In their centuries of rule, the Ottomans never provided special protection to tenant farmers. When an owner sold his land, the tenants could be—and often were—evicted.[45]

After the British conquered Palestine in 1918, Arabs opposed to Jewish land purchases began complaining to the new authorities about the plight of the displaced tenant farmers. The British responded with a series of measures to protect Palestine's tenant farmers that went far beyond the norm in free market economies.

In 1920, the British issued the Land Transfer Ordinance. This law called upon government officials to review the sale of any land in Palestine being cultivated by tenant farmers. These officials were instructed to block such sales unless they were satisfied that each tenant would retain "sufficient land in the district or elsewhere for the maintenance of himself and his family."[46]

The law proved easy to circumvent. At the time, the "overwhelming preponderance" of tenant farmers preferred monetary compensation to land grants.[47] Thus an Arab landlord wanting to sell his land free of any encumbrances could simply pay his tenants to leave before the sale.[48] In 1929, the British bowed to this reality and recognized the payment of monetary compensation as a legal alternative to providing tenants with "maintenance" tracts to farm.[49]

In 1933, this policy was reversed yet again. Ignoring the tenant farmers' actual preferences, the British prohibited the payment of cash compensation to vacating tenants. Thereafter, the only legal way to remove tenants from land they had farmed for a year or more was to provide them with alternative land "whose adequacy was determined by a governmental board."[50]

But even these new restrictions were no obstacle to creative Arab sellers determined to cash in on historic high prices. In 1936, the outbreak of the Arab Revolt ended these futile efforts to force tenant farmers to remain on their rented lands.

Ultimately, the Zionists were able to buy land in Palestine because both Arab owners and Arab tenant farmers overwhelmingly preferred cash to land. Given the economic conditions at the time, this preference made perfect sense.

Throughout the peak years of Jewish immigration, agricultural work was a losing proposition. From 1926 to 1936, Palestine suffered from cattle plagues, recurring droughts, field mice, and locusts. These circumstances caused a series of successively poor harvests. While lower yields typically bring higher prices, the laws of supply and demand did not rescue the farmers of this era. A worldwide economic depression actually caused a drastic decline in agricultural prices just as harvests were hitting historic lows.[51]

In this environment, it's little wonder that owners and tenants alike were eager to take what they viewed as "exorbitant amounts of money"[52] from Jewish buyers. Most chose to use these funds to begin new lives in Palestine's rapidly growing cities.[53] Like every developing nation in history, Palestine experienced a major migration from rural to urban areas. Ultimately, there was little the British could do to combat these overwhelming market forces.

Unable to stop these land sales, Britain decided that it needed to provide direct assistance to those who had been rendered landless by them. In March 1931, the British announced the creation of the Palestine Development Department, an agency with one central task: to find and resettle any Arabs rendered landless by Jewish land purchases.

The Development Department solicited claims from Palestine's landless Arabs. By 1935, approximately 3,700 such claims had been submitted. Of these, fewer than a quarter were recognized as legitimate. The department ultimately concluded that 899 Arab families had been rendered "landless" by Jewish land purchases. These landless Arabs were all offered alternative land elsewhere in Palestine.[54]

Thus the Jewish land purchases that brought so much growth and prosperity to so many hundreds of thousands of Jews and Arabs ended up displacing 899 Arab families from land they rented. All of these so-called landless Arabs were offered alternative land elsewhere. Yet most ultimately shunned farming in favor of far more promising opportunities in the cities.

The plight of Palestine's landless Arabs turns out to be just another myth. Rarely has so much moral outrage been expended over so few who suffered so little.

THE REAL PROBLEM

The Zionists lived up to their lofty rhetoric regarding Palestine's Arabs. They had said that they would not displace the Arabs, and they didn't. They had said that they would improve their standard of living, and they did.

Yet Palestine's Arabs continued to oppose Jewish immigration into Palestine. In fact, their opposition to Jewish immigration seemed to grow in direct proportion to the improvement in their economic status that this immigration produced. As the Peel Commission observed in 1937, "Though the Arabs have benefitted by the development of the country owing to Jewish immigration, this has had no conciliatory effect. On the contrary... with almost mathematical precision the betterment of the economic situation in Palestine meant the deterioration of the political situation."[55]

In seeking to explain this surprising fact, the Peel Commission paraphrased a common Arab complaint: "You say we are better off: you say my house has been enriched by the strangers who have entered it. But it is my house, and I did not invite the strangers in, or ask them to enrich it, and I do not care how poor or bare it is if only I am master in it."[56]

Over the course of the 1920s and the 1930s, Palestine's Arabic speakers had undergone a significant transformation. They no longer considered themselves Ottoman subjects, happy to live under foreign rule. Nor did they view themselves as members of a tribe, village, or clan for whom material progress was sufficient. These Arabic speakers had developed a national consciousness. They had come to view themselves as Arabs and, in some cases, as Palestinian Arabs. And like so many emerging nations around the world, Palestine's Arabs wanted to rule themselves.

The Zionists had respected Arab human and civil rights. They had made good on their promise of prosperity. But the Zionist project did not offer Palestine's Arabs a path to fulfill their national aspirations. The development of Palestinian Arab nationalism exceeded the limits of Herzl's prescience. His vision had finally been overtaken by events.

CHAPTER FOUR

ZIONISM ENCOUNTERS ARAB NATIONALISM

The Arabs of Palestine could not have it both ways. If they considered themselves to be part of the Arab world, they must take the larger view, in which Arab national aspirations had been in general satisfied and would not be threatened by a relatively small Jewish State....

—David Ben Gurion, 1939[1]

On June 18, 1913, a group of Arab nationalists gathered in the great hall of the French Geographical Society in Paris for an event that has come to be known as the First Arab Congress. These delegates passed a series of resolutions requesting that the Ottoman Empire grant its Arabic-speaking subjects greater political and cultural autonomy. They stopped well short of seeking independence. Yet to many observers, this conference marked the moment when the idea of Arab nationalism crystallized into a movement.

This First Arab Congress had only twenty-three official delegates. Among these were eleven Muslims, eleven Christians, and one Jew.[2] The Jewish delegate was Sami Hochberg, the publisher of a Constantinople-based newspaper called *Le Jeune Turc*. Hochberg was also a Zionist leader who had already met with some of the first Arab nationalists in Cairo and Beirut. He had made great progress in persuading these leaders that the two nationalist movements—Jewish and Arab—were natural allies. Hochberg came to Paris with high hopes of formalizing this nascent partnership.

Ultimately, the Arab Congress did not address the issue of Zionism. But the Congress president, Abd al-Hamid Zahrawi, agreed to issue a public statement of support. Referring to "Syrians"—the land later known as Palestine was universally seen as part of Syria at the time—Zahrawi declared, "All of us [the Arabs], both Muslims and Christians, have the best of feelings toward the Jews. When we spoke in our resolutions about the rights and obligations of the Syrians, this covered the Jews as well. Because they are our brothers in race and we regard them as Syrians who were forced to leave the country at one time but whose hearts always beat together with ours, we are certain that our Jewish brothers the world over will know how to help us so that our common interests may succeed and our common country will develop both materially and morally."[3]

Upon his return to Constantinople, Hochberg lobbied a number of senior Ottoman officials on behalf of his new Arab allies. According to the president of the Arab Committee in Constantinople, Abd al-Karim Al-Khalil, Hochberg's efforts, "made a great contribution to the Arab cause."[4]

The early Zionists neither ignored nor denied the rise of Arab nationalism. Quite to the contrary, Zionist leaders were already studying and debating the first Arab nationalist texts well before the overwhelming majority of Arabic speakers even knew what an "Arab" was. As their neighbors began embracing Arab nationalism in increasing numbers, the Zionists not only recognized the movement, they offered it their support.

As naive as it may seem in hindsight, most Zionists saw no inherent conflict between Jewish nationalism and Arab nationalism. They actually viewed Arab nationalists as potential allies in liberating the Middle East from Ottoman and then European rule. This Zionist optimism

flowed from the fact that Arab nationalism began as a "pan-Arab" movement. The first generation of Arab nationalists stressed that all Arabic
speakers belonged to one indivisible Arab people. Their dream was to
unite these Arabs within one great Arab state.

As a result, both the Zionists and the Arab nationalists viewed Palestine as just a small portion of a far larger Arab whole. As keen students
of European nationalism, the Zionists understood that rival claims had
forced almost every nation on the continent to accept borders that fell
short of their maximum territorial demands. They therefore saw no
moral or practical reason why a massive Arab state should not live peacefully alongside a Jewish state created on a small sliver of the vast lands
the Arabs claimed.

This view was perhaps best expressed by Revisionist Zionist leader
Vladimir Jabotinsky. Jabotinsky fully acknowledged his hope that Jewish immigration would one day render the Arabs of Palestine a minority.
But he denied that such minority status would be the disaster some suggested. As he explained to Britain's Peel Commission in 1937,

> It is not a hardship on any race, any nation, possessing so
> many National States now and so many more National States
> in the future. One fraction, one branch of that race, and not
> a big one, will have to live in someone else's State: Well, that
> is the case with all the mightiest nations of the world. I could
> hardly mention one of the big nations, having their States,
> mighty and powerful, who had not one branch living in some-
> one else's State. That is only normal and there is no "hard-
> ship" attached to that.
>
> So when we hear the Arab claim confronted with the Jew-
> ish claim; I fully understand that any minority would prefer
> to be a majority, it is quite understandable that the Arabs of
> Palestine would also prefer to be the Arab State No. 4, No. 5
> or No. 6—that I quite understand; but when the Arab claim
> is confronted with our Jewish demand to be saved, it is like
> the claims of appetite versus the claims of starvation.[5]

Jabotinsky grossly underestimated Arab nationalism's ultimate success. Today, the Arab League boasts not six but twenty-two member states (including the Palestinian Authority). These states control over five million square miles of territory stretching from Morocco eastward across North Africa and Asia to Iraq.

Ben Gurion shared this view. He described the Arabs of Palestine as "one droplet of the Arab people," for whom Palestine was only one "small parcel of a tremendous, giant territory settled by Arabs,"[6] which stretched "from the Mediterranean coast to the Persian Gulf and from the Taurus Mountains to the Atlantic Ocean."[7] He therefore concluded that "the economic and cultural existence of the Arab nation, its national independence and sovereignty, do not depend upon Palestine."[8]

Yet for the Jewish people, Ben Gurion stressed, Palestine "was everything, *and there was nothing else.*"[9] For the Jews, "only in Palestine can independent life, a national economy, and an autonomous culture be established. Only here can we realize our sovereign independence and freedom."[10]

Even the League of Nations Permanent Mandates Commission recognized this distinction when it declared in 1937, "It should also be remembered that the collective suffering of Arabs and Jews are not comparable, since vast spaces in the Near East, formerly the abode of a numerous population and the home of a brilliant civilization, are open to the former, whereas the world is increasingly being closed to settlement by the latter."[11]

This perspective motivated the early Zionist leaders to seek an alliance with their Arab counterparts. As Jews who wanted independence in their ancient land, they fully identified with Arabs who shared the same goal. And as Semites who wanted to build a prosperous Middle East free from foreign control, they had every reason to hope for a robust partnership with Arab leaders who presumably wanted the same.

ARAB NATIONALISM AND ZIONISM: EARLY ALLIANCES

In the summer of 1918 the Arab Revolt against the Ottoman Empire was at its height. Having conquered the port city of Aqaba in present-day

Jordan, the Arab forces were encamped in the hills to the city's north. From this base Colonel T. E. Lawrence led the rebels on frequent night raids to destroy segments of the Hejaz railway, a vital Ottoman supply and communications artery.

One night that June, a most unlikely delegation approached the Arab camp. Although coming from nearby Jerusalem, they had spent the prior ten days traveling by train, boat, car, camel, and foot to circumvent the Ottoman Army. They were tired and dirty from their long journey.

From a distance, the group's Semitic-looking leader would have appeared to be an Arab dignitary of some significance, especially when wearing his Arab headdress. But this man was not an Arab. He was the Jewish leader of the Zionist movement. And as Chaim Weizmann entered the Arab camp, he was neither captured nor killed. He was welcomed as an honored guest.

The next morning Emir Feisal, the commander in chief of the Arab Army, received Weizmann in his tent. For over two hours these leaders of their respective nationalist movements shared tea and conversation. Weizmann stressed familiar Zionist themes. He told Feisal that the Zionists were natural allies who could help the Arabs build their future state. And, when it came to Palestine, Weizmann emphasized that "there was a great deal of room in the country if intensive development were applied, and that the lot of the Arabs would be greatly improved through our work there."[12]

These talks were long on pleasantries but short on specifics. Weizmann recalled that Feisal was "in full agreement" with his views and stated that Arabs and Jews needed to work "in harmony" to build the Middle East following the war.[13] These vague promises would soon be put to the test.

When Weizmann and Feisal next met, on January 3, 1919, their circumstances had changed for the better. In the intervening months, the allies had won the war. Instead of Feisal's dusty desert camp, the two now met in London's plush Carlton Hotel. And instead of hypotheticals, they now discussed the details of building a new Middle East in the aftermath of the Ottoman surrender.

This second meeting was, by all accounts, every bit as cordial as the first. And this time the two leaders signed an agreement summarizing the substance of their talks. Looking back over the blood-drenched years that followed, the Feisal-Weizmann agreement stands as a tragic testament to what could have been.

In its preamble, the agreement stresses the "racial kinship" and "ancient bonds" existing between the Arab and Jewish peoples. Envisioning the creation of two states—a massive pan-Arab state next to a separate Palestine—the agreement affirms that "the surest means of working out the consummation of their [the Arabs' and the Jews'] national aspirations is through the closest possible collaboration in the development of the Arab State and Palestine."[14]

The agreement then narrows its focus to some very significant specifics, namely that "All necessary measures shall be taken to encourage and stimulate immigration of Jews into Palestine on a large scale, and as quickly as possible to settle Jewish immigrants upon the land through closer settlement and intensive cultivation of the soil. In taking such measures the Arab peasant and tenant farmers shall be protected in their rights, and shall be assisted in forwarding their economic development."[15]

And such Arab-Jewish cooperation would not stop at Palestine's borders. The two leaders further agreed that "The Zionist Organization will use its best efforts to assist the Arab State in providing the means for developing the natural resources and economic possibilities thereof."[16]

A couple of months later, Feisal returned to the theme of Arab-Jewish kinship and cooperation with even greater zeal. In a letter to Felix Frankfurter, a prominent American jurist and Zionist, he wrote,

> We feel that the Arabs and Jews are cousins in race, having suffered similar oppressions at the hands of powers stronger than themselves, and by a happy coincidence have been able

to take the first step towards the attainment of their national ideas together.

We Arabs, especially the educated among us, look with the deepest sympathy on the Zionist movement.... We will wish the Jews a most hearty welcome home.

We are working together for a reformed and revived Near East, and our two movements complete one another. The Jewish movement is national and not imperialistic. Our movement is national and not imperialistic; and there is room in Syria for us both. Indeed, I think that neither can be a real success without the other.[17]

Feisal was not the only Arab nationalist who saw Zionism as a potential ally for the Arab cause. Colonel T. E. Lawrence—Lawrence of Arabia—shared this view.

With the possible exception of Feisal himself, Lawrence was the most outspoken and effective Arab nationalist of the World War I era. During the war, he organized and led the Arab forces into battle against the Ottomans. After the war was won, he brought his zeal for the Arab cause home to Britain's foreign policy establishment and Europe's negotiating tables. Lawrence had rallied the Arabs to action with the promise of independence after the war. He was determined to deliver on his pledge.

Yet Lawrence of Arabia was also a Zionist. Like Feisal, Lawrence never regarded Zionism as some sort of foreign invasion. He recognized Zionism as an effort by the Jews to "return once more to the Orient from which they came." He saw the Jews and Arabs as people of "kindred origin."[18] Lawrence even boasted of having invented the slogan "Arabia for the Arabs, Judea for the Jews, Armenia for the Armenians."[19]

Beyond believing Zionism to be inherently just, Lawrence also viewed it as a valuable resource that could benefit his beloved Arabs. Lawrence had visited Palestine in 1909 while still a student at Oxford. Like so many other European visitors during this era, he was appalled by the desolation and poverty he witnessed. But he also saw some impressive exceptions to this rule. As he wrote in a letter to his mother, "Palestine was a decent country then [in Roman Times], and could so easily be made so again. The sooner the Jews farm it all the better: their colonies are bright spots in a desert."[20]

Lawrence was convinced that the Zionists could help the Arabs develop not only Palestine but the entire region. In 1920, for example, Lawrence wrote the following of the Zionists, "The success of their scheme will involve inevitably the raising of the present Arab population to their own material level, only a little after themselves in point of time, and the consequences might be of the highest importance for the future of the Arab world. It might well prove a source of technical supply rendering them independent of industrial Europe."[21]

According to Chaim Weizmann, with whom he developed a close friendship, Lawrence believed that cooperation between Arabs and Jews was "of the most importance" to the Arab cause since the "Arab redemption was likely to come about through Jewish redemption."[22]

Lawrence reiterated his support for Zionism in 1930. "I back it," he told Professor Lewis Namier, "not because of the Jews, but because a regenerated Palestine is going to raise the whole moral and material status of its Middle East neighbors."[23]

BEN GURION'S "SEMITIC FEDERATION"

Like Weizmann, Ben Gurion did not ignore the rise of Arab nationalism. The future prime minister was a keen student of the Arab national movement from its earliest days.

As Arab nationalism continued to grow throughout the 1920s and 1930s, Ben Gurion realized that he needed to update the initial Zionist formula. It would no longer be sufficient to offer Palestine's Arabs full civil rights and economic prosperity in a future Jewish state. For both moral and practical reasons, the Jews also needed to find some way to reconcile their own national aspirations with those of their Arab neighbors.

Ben Gurion ultimately formulated a new policy. He proposed that a future Jewish state enter into a union with its Arab neighbors to form a larger "Semitic Federation." Thus even if Jewish immigration one day rendered the Arabs a minority within Palestine, these Arabs would still be part of the overwhelming Arab majority in the Federation as a whole. This majority position would protect Palestine's Arabs from the dangers and indignities to which minority status had subjected the Jews for so long.[24]

Like Weizmann before him, Ben Gurion also offered to put Zionist clout and expertise at the disposal of the Arabs. As Ben Gurion phrased it, "If the Arabs agreed to our return to our land, we would help them with our political, financial and moral support to bring about the rebirth and unity of the Arab people."[25]

Ben Gurion recognized that he could never forge an alliance between Zionism and Arab nationalism by negotiating with Arabs who lacked credibility among their own people. Thus he set out to promote his plan to the most powerful—and most militant—Palestinian Arab leader of his day: Amin al-Husseini, the Mufti of Jerusalem.[26]

On March 20, 1934, Ben Gurion met with a Husseini ally named Musa Alami. At the time, Alami was serving as the attorney general of the British Mandatory government. According to Ben Gurion, Alami "had a reputation as a nationalist and a man not to be bought by money or by office."[27]

As the two talked, Alami quickly confirmed Ben Gurion's belief that Palestine's Arab leaders were now nationalists—and that their nationalism would conflict with the Zionists' vision for Palestine. Ben Gurion later wrote, "The prevailing assumption in the Zionist movement then was that we were bringing a blessing to the Arabs of the country and that they therefore had no reason to oppose us. In the first talk I had with Musa Alami...that assumption was shattered. Musa Alami told me that he would prefer the land to remain poor and desolate even for another hundred years, until the Arabs themselves were capable of developing it and making it flower, and I felt that as a patriotic Arab he had every right to this view."[28]

Ben Gurion responded to Alami's complaint by sharing his proposal for a Semitic Federation. He later wrote that Alami expressed sincere interest in the proposal and promised to communicate its substance directly to the Mufti.[29] While he awaited the Mufti's response, Ben Gurion tried to build momentum for his plan by reaching out to additional Arab leaders.

Among those Ben Gurion met with in the following months was Awni Abd al-Hadi, the Palestinian leader of the pan-Arab Istiqlal Party. Ben Gurion repeated his pitch, emphasizing that the Jews did not want to displace a single Arab, but sought only to develop the uncultivated and unpopulated "surplus" of land in Palestine. He again offered a robust partnership to help the Arabs achieve independence, prosperity, and unity. According to Ben Gurion, Abd al-Hadi became enthusiastic on hearing this last point, exclaiming, "If by your help we achieve our unity, I'll agree not only to four million, but to five or six million Jews in Palestine."[30]

Abd al-Hadi may well have been sincere. As a devoted pan-Arab, he never restricted his national aspirations to Palestine alone. As late as 1937, he told the Peel Commission, "There is no such country [as Palestine].... Palestine is a term the Zionists invented.... Our country was for centuries part of Syria."[31]

On August 14, 1934, Ben Gurion traveled to Musa Alami's village outside of Jerusalem to resume their talks. The two met again on August 27 and 31 at Alami's Jerusalem apartment.

As promised, Alami had met with the Mufti and shared Ben Gurion's plan with him. Alami reported that the Mufti had listened to the details with "great interest" and "had no objection" to the plan, provided that any final agreement ensured the religious, economic, and political interests of the Arabs of Palestine.[32] There was just one catch. Before the Mufti would publicly endorse Ben Gurion's proposal, he wanted the Zionists to prepare Arab public opinion for such a compromise.[33]

Alami and Ben Gurion agreed to a set of next steps. Ben Gurion was already scheduled to travel to London the following month. On his way home, he would stop in Geneva to meet with two influential Arab nationalists—Shakib Arslan and Ihsan al-Jabri—whom the Mufti respected. Provided these leaders agreed to the plan, Ben Gurion would meet directly with the Mufti upon his return.[34]

The Geneva meeting took place on September 23, 1934. Ben Gurion left Switzerland believing that the talks had gone well. Speaking to a Jewish delegation in Warsaw shortly thereafter, an optimistic Ben Gurion explained, "It is my duty to point out that there is no historic contradiction between Zionism and the Arabs. Greater Zionism will find a common language with the greater Arab movement."[35]

Ben Gurion's high hopes were crushed as soon as he returned to his Jerusalem office. Waiting for him on his desk was a copy of the latest issue of *La Nation Arabe*, the nationalist journal published by Arslan and Jabri. The two leaders had written a distorted and dismissive account of their supposedly secret meeting with Ben Gurion. There would be no meeting with the Mufti.[36]

Ben Gurion was not one to give up easily. In 1936, he sought out yet another of the Mufti's confidants, Arab historian George Antonius. In a series of three meetings, Ben Gurion once again presented his peace plan.

When the topic of Jewish immigration came up, Ben Gurion used the example of Tel Aviv to demonstrate how Jews could immigrate to Palestine without displacing the Arabs already living there: "I told Antonius that if, thirty years before, we had discussed how many Jews could come to Jaffa, which then had a population of 20,000 or 30,000, he would undoubtedly have said: only 15,000. We had already brought

130,000, but this had not been at the expense of the Arabs in Jaffa, but thanks to our new creative enterprise in Tel Aviv.... We had established a new Jewish city in a desolate place."[37]

According to Ben Gurion, he and Antonius were close to an agreement and had scheduled a fourth meeting. But before this meeting date arrived, Antonius fled Palestine for Turkey during a British crackdown on Arab nationalists. "After that," Ben Gurion wrote, "I did not see him again."[38]

Ben Gurion would later conclude that the apparent interest that the Mufti and his colleagues had expressed in his plan amounted to nothing more than "machinations." He realized that "In the very days when they purportedly sought a way to peace they organized acts of murder and terror in the country."[39] Indeed, 1936 was the year that the Mufti and his allies started the violent Arab Revolt that targeted and killed so many of Palestine's Jews.

The deal that Ben Gurion sought required moderate Arab partners willing to compromise on their maximum territorial demands. But with each passing year, Arab nationalism developed along more absolute lines that rendered such compromises unpopular and, eventually, fatal.

ARAB NATIONALISM GROWS EXTREME

As nationalism has grown and spread during the course of the past two centuries, it has sometimes metastasized into more extreme forms. The super-nationalists thus produced refuse to accept the compromises that are inevitably required when an abstract ideology is implemented in a complex reality. These radicals revive claims to neighboring territories that their people once ruled but that have since fallen under foreign control. They likewise rail against the fact that some branches of their peoples must live as minorities in the nation states of others. Their all-consuming goal is to expand their state's borders until they include all such land and people within them.

This expansionist urge is so common that there's a word for it: irredentism. This English word has Italian roots. In the late nineteenth century, Italian nationalists agitated to expand Italy's borders to include all of the neighboring territories with significant historic or linguistic ties to Italy. They proposed seizing the island of Corsica and the city of Nice from France. They also sought much of the Dalmatian coast in present-day Croatia. These ambitious men founded a movement that came to be known as *Italia Irredenta* (Unredeemed Italy) to pursue their dream of uniting all Italians within one great Italian state.

Italian irredentism was no fringe movement. Italy's primary motivation for joining World War I was to conquer these coveted borderlands. When the post-war peace treaties failed to give Italy all it had sought, the Fascists seized on the ensuing outrage to fuel their rise to power. Mussolini then embarked on an even more ambitious campaign to redeem the lands Italy had been denied, as well as additional territories further afield.

Yet while the Italians may have pioneered irredentism, the Germans were the ones who set Europe ablaze in pursuit of it. The peace treaties that followed World War I lopped off sizable territories from Germany and, in the process, left millions of ethnic Germans as minorities in neighboring states. To cite just one example, Germany lost the Sudetenland to the new state of Czechoslovakia despite the fact that over ninety percent of its residents were German.

For hardcore German nationalists, these new borders were an unacceptable mutilation of their motherland. Like their Fascist cousins, the Nazis embraced these irredentist complaints and made them the centerpiece of their populist platform. When Hitler rose to power, he turned Nazi irredentism into German foreign policy. The Nazi expansion that sparked World War II was largely an effort to reclaim these German lands and liberate these German minorities.

Like the large majority of nationalists pressing their claims in Paris after World War I, both Feisal and Lawrence were moderates. They never expected that the Arab state they sought would extend to *all* of the territories in which Arabs happened to live. Their flexibility left the door open for compromise and collaboration with neighboring peoples asserting competing claims, including Jews, Armenians, Assyrians, and Kurds.

Tragically, this moderation did not last for long. Like the Germans and the Italians, the Arabs began to demand what no nation had been given in Paris: the complete satisfaction of their maximum nationalist claims. In other words, Arab nationalism gave way to Arab irredentism. Feisal was eclipsed by Amin al-Husseini. Talk of shared roots and destinies was replaced by threats of expulsion and jihad. And those Arabs who pursued compromise were not hailed as pragmatists but threatened as traitors.

In time, even Feisal was forced to renounce his former moderation. In 1931, Feisal was king of Iraq and desperate to prove his nationalist bona fides to his increasingly radical subjects. When asked about the Feisal-Weizmann agreement, his aides issued the following statement, "His Majesty does not remember having written anything of that kind with his knowledge."[40]

ARAB NATIONALISM SPLINTERS

Had Arab nationalism remained a unified, pan-national movement, it would likely be recognized as among the world's most successful nationalist movements. After all, Arabs now rule over almost all of the vast lands they claim. As a result, the overwhelming majority of Arab people now live under Arab rule. The "unredeemed" land about which they complain most bitterly—the former British Mandate for Palestine—is less than one percent of the landmass of the Arab League member states.

Under such circumstances, Arab demands for the complete satisfaction of their maximum national claims—whether applied in Palestine or elsewhere—would likely generate little sympathy. The international community has grown skeptical of such irredentist claims after a century in which they fueled two world wars and countless smaller conflicts. Germany learned to live with much of the land it sought forever beyond its borders. Italy has done likewise. When the Russians asserted their claims to Crimea and other parts of Ukraine in 2014, they found few supporters.

But Arab nationalism did not remain unified; it splintered. Separated into new states by colonial borders, each branch of the large Arab family began to develop its own narrow nationalism within the larger pan-Arab tent. Syrians came to see themselves as both Syrians and Arabs. Egyptians developed an Egyptian identity alongside their Arab one. To varying degrees, the same can be said of the inhabitants of the other twenty member states of the Arab League.

This trend toward the development of a second, local identity was perhaps most pronounced among the Arabs of Palestine. The borders of the British Mandate for Palestine had subjected these Arabs to a unique fate. It was to their land that Jews immigrated in large numbers. And it was in their land that these Jews eventually created their state. In time, the Arabs of Palestine came to see themselves as a distinct people, the Palestinians, with unique national aspirations that could no longer be satisfied by Arab independence next door.

In so splintering, Arab nationalism has taken a unique path. No other major nation has broken apart and spawned so many smaller national groups, each demanding its own independent state. The Sudeten Germans were German nationalists who sought unification with Germany. They never saw themselves as a separate Sudeten German people requiring an independent Sudetenland. The ethnic Russians of Crimea are Russian nationalists who sought annexation to Russia. They never claimed to be a new Crimean Russian people needing a separate Crimean state.

One of the reasons that Arab nationalism has been so difficult to accommodate is that it has been a moving target.

It took decades for this separate Palestinian nationalism to take root. The Arab League and the United Nations did not officially recognize the existence of a Palestinian people until the early 1970s. Before that time, Palestine's Arabs were an indecisive national customer, trying on, rejecting, and then recalling a series of shifting identities.

But as they wrestled with their identity, Palestine's Arabs were hardly indifferent to the events unfolding around them. Jews were arriving in Palestine in increasing numbers, buying land and building communities. Things were changing rapidly, and many of Palestine's Arabs did not want things changed.

At the human level, many of the interactions between Palestine's Arabs and Jews were warm and even inspiring. At the political level, however, the men who led Palestine's Arabs responded to Jewish immigration with a toxic mixture of rejection and violence. Their brutal reply to Zionist progress would produce the first mass casualties of this conflict. And their refusal to recognize any Jewish rights in the land would birth the extremism that drives the conflict down to the present day.

CHAPTER FIVE

PALESTINE'S ARABS RESPOND

There is no place in Palestine for two races. The Jews left Palestine 2,000 years ago. Let them go to other parts of the world where there are wide vacant places.

—Amin al-Husseini, 1936[1]

Ben Gurion, Weizmann, and the Zionists they led believed that the land to which they were returning was the home of two peoples: the Jews coming home and the Arabs already living there. They saw no inherent tension between these two claims. As the Jews returned, they argued, they would develop the economy sufficiently to support themselves as well as their Arab neighbors.

Ben Gurion and his colleagues went so far as to agree that if Jewish immigration ever surpassed Palestine's "economic absorptive capacity"—thereby causing Arab unemployment—then Jewish immigration would have to be restricted until the economy caught up. Ben Gurion summarized this commitment to Palestine's Arabs in 1928 when he stated, "our sense of morality forbids us to deny the right of a single Arab child, even though by such denial we might attain all that we seek."[2]

This may sound like self-serving hype. But the demographic statistics provide eloquent testimony to the fact that Ben Gurion and his colleagues succeeded in honoring this pledge. It would take an Arab invasion and the very real prospect of Jewish annihilation to force the Zionists to revisit this core commitment.

The man who led the Palestinian Arabs during this period—Amin al-Husseini, the Mufti of Jerusalem—had a less generous approach. He believed that Palestine was only big enough to hold one people: his own. Husseini stated unequivocally, "There is no place in Palestine for two races." Or, as he phrased it elsewhere, "Just as it is impossible to put two swords into the same sheath, it is impossible to squeeze two peoples into one small country."[3]

For Husseini, the Zionist claim to Palestine had launched a zero-sum battle in which every Jewish gain somehow constituted an equivalent Arab loss. The Mufti's philosophy led him to view Jewish children quite differently than Ben Gurion viewed Arab children. Far from respecting their rights, the Mufti tried to kill Jewish children before they could reach Palestine.

By late 1942, reliable reports of the Nazi Final Solution began reaching the West. In response, a number of initiatives were launched to rescue Jewish children from Nazi-occupied Europe. Among these were efforts to save four thousand children from Bulgaria, eighteen hundred children from Romania, and nine hundred children from Hungary. In each case, Husseini learned of these plans. And each time, he aggressively petitioned his friends at the highest levels of the Nazi government to block them.[4]

Husseini was never ashamed of his role in foiling these rescues. Quite to the contrary, he bragged about it. In his 1968 memoirs, the Mufti wrote of this rescue effort, "I objected to this attempt, and wrote to Ribbentrop, to Himmler and to Hitler...until I succeeded in frustrating the attempt."[5] To back up his boast, the Mufti included copies of these letters in his memoirs, along with the supportive responses he received.[6] A year before his death, the Mufti was still gloating over his triumph. "My letters," he wrote, "had positive and useful results for the Palestinian problem."[7]

When he wrote his letters to the Nazi leadership, the Mufti had already been briefed on the Final Solution and visited Nazi death camps. He knew what would become of these Jewish children if they failed to escape Nazi-occupied Europe. And this knowledge caused him neither pause nor regret, but only pride.

Since the birth of modern Zionism, the Arabic speakers of Palestine have had a series of successive identities, including Ottoman, Arab, Syrian, Jordanian, and Palestinian. Yet while their identity has shifted, Palestine's Arabs never wavered in their official response to the claims of their Jewish neighbors. There were certainly internal debates, disagreements, and dissenters. But those who won these struggles and led Palestine's Arabs were, like Amin al-Husseini, the ones who insisted that their conflict with the Jews was a zero-sum game that would ultimately result in displacement and disaster for one of these two peoples. As this dark vision drove Palestine's Arabs to increasing rejectionism and violence, it ultimately became a self-fulfilling prophecy bringing tragedy to the Palestinians themselves.

UNDER THE OTTOMANS

In August 1882, a group of 228 Romanian Jews set off for Palestine by boat across the Black Sea. As the ship approached its destination, these pioneers found ominous signs posted at the Ottoman ports proclaiming: "Jewish immigrants are forbidden to cross the coast of Syria and in all circumstances forbidden to live in Palestine. This ban is permanently binding."[8]

Barred from landing at Haifa and Jaffa, this ship of Jews sailed up and down the coast as conditions on board steadily deteriorated. Finally, the authorities granted permission for them to dock at Jaffa. But corrupt local officials arrested the passengers and held them until they had raised enough money to pay the requested bribes.[9]

Before embarking for Palestine, these Jews had purchased land fifteen miles south of Haifa. When they finally reached their new home, they saw little to encourage them: "The newly arrived settlers found a few tired oxen and horses, one or two wooden Arab plows, remnants of some mud-and-wattle huts, a few sacks of grain, and an accumulation of centuries of stones.[10]

The worst was yet to come. The immigrants soon realized that "shifts of wind brought thick swarms of mosquitoes from the swamps along the coast."[11] And these mosquitoes carried malaria.

Like most Jews who returned to Palestine over the centuries, this first wave of modern immigrants did not receive a warm welcome home. The Ottomans who ruled Palestine severely restricted Jewish immigration to their ancient land. Ben Gurion later recalled, "Under the Turks there had been a law in Palestine which provided that a Jew entering the country could remain there only for three months. The Jews had been compelled to break that law for the sake of a higher law. I myself was one of those who had remained in the country illegally."[12]

The Ottomans likewise limited the rights of Jews to purchase land in Palestine. These constraints were so severe that some of the most successful Jewish communities of this era had only enough land to accommodate one son in each family. The others were forced to move to new communities or leave Palestine altogether.[13]

As Ben Gurion's ability to overstay his visa reveals, these Ottoman restrictions were not always actively enforced. And even when they were, a large enough bribe could almost always convince the authorities to turn a blind eye. Thus many thousands of Jews were able to enter the country during the closing decades of Ottoman rule. By 1914, there were over eighty thousand Jews in Palestine.[14]

It didn't take long for Palestine's Arabs to notice an increasing number of Jews strolling city streets and farming land near their villages. And it didn't take long for some of their leaders to demand that the Ottoman authorities block this Jewish immigration and curtail the rights of those who had already returned.

On June 24, 1891, Palestine's Arabs launched their first official protest against the modern wave of Jewish return. A telegram was sent from Jerusalem asking the Ottoman grand vizier to prohibit Jews from entering Palestine and purchasing land there. It is widely believed that this telegram was written by Arab merchants and craftsmen eager to eliminate their Jewish competition.[15] Similar efforts followed. In response, the Ottoman governor of Jerusalem issued a new edict forbidding the sale of land to Jews.

When the Ottomans repealed this restriction in 1897, a group of local Arab leaders immediately objected. They formed a commission chaired by the Mufti of Jerusalem, Mohammed Tahir al-Husseini (the father of the next, more infamous Mufti), which lobbied to reinstate the ban. This commission ultimately succeeded in blocking Jewish land purchases for another few years.[16]

After the Young Turks seized power in 1908, they enacted a series of political reforms that made it far safer for Ottoman subjects to criticize their government. Palestine's Arabs took advantage of these new liberties to escalate their opposition to Jewish immigration and land purchases. In 1909, an Arab delegate from Jaffa was the first to speak out against Zionism in the Ottoman Parliament. He demanded that the port of Jaffa be closed to Jewish immigrants.[17] In May 1910, Arab notables in both Haifa and Nazareth wrote to the Ottoman government protesting Jewish land purchases.[18]

These efforts intensified in 1911. That year, Arab delegates to the Ottoman Parliament from Jerusalem and Damascus made a series of speeches warning about Zionism and demanding a ban on Jewish immigration and land purchases.[19] Five hundred Arab leaders from Jaffa and Jerusalem signed a petition supporting such a ban. In response, the governor of Jerusalem was directed to once again prohibit the sale of land to Jews, including Jews who were Ottoman subjects.[20]

UNDER THE BRITISH

Toward the close of World War I, British troops conquered Palestine from the Ottomans. The League of Nations later granted Britain a formal "mandate" to rule Palestine. The mandate's text obligated the British to "secure the establishment of the Jewish national home" in this territory. Accordingly, they eliminated all prior restrictions on Jewish immigration and land purchases.

For the first time in centuries, a friendly government had opened the gates of Palestine to the Jews. Palestine's Arab leaders responded by immediately seeking to slam them shut. Some Arabs fought against Jewish immigration and land purchases through politics and diplomacy. Others chose violence. During the mandate years, Arab militants sometimes targeted British officials and facilities. But they often preferred to direct their fire at a far softer target: Jewish civilians. There is, of course, a word for targeting civilians with violence to achieve a political goal. It's called terrorism.

THE RIOTS OF 1920 AND 1921

On March 7, 1920, the Syrian Arab Congress declared Syrian independence under the reign of King Feisal. Less than a month later, on April 4, tens of thousands of Arabs streamed into Jerusalem for the annual Nebi Musa festival. This religious celebration provided a perfect opportunity for Palestine's Arab nationalists to send a strong message to their British overlords. They took to the streets carrying photos of King Feisal and demanding that the British cede Palestine—which they called "Southern Syria"—to the new monarch.

When the procession reached Jerusalem's Arab Club, a number of nationalist leaders appeared on the balcony to address the crowd below. Speaker after speaker demanded independence and unity with Syria. They also called for violence against the Jews. Observers recalled hearing the crowd chant, "Slaughter the Jews,"[21] "We will drink the blood of the Jews,"[22] and "Palestine is our land, the Jews are our dogs."[23] In Arabic, this last phrase forms a rhyming couplet.

Thus incited, Arabs wielding knives, clubs, and stones burst into the Jewish quarter. They ransacked Jewish homes and looted Jewish stores.

They raided synagogues and yeshivas and ripped up Torah scrolls.[24] And they attacked any Jews they found. By the time the riots finally ended several days later, 5 Jews had been killed and 211 had been wounded.[25] Many of the female victims had been raped.[26]

The British police quickly concluded that a young nationalist leader (and future Mufti), Amin al-Husseini, was responsible for the violence. A court found Husseini guilty of inciting the riots and sentenced him to ten years in prison. He evaded jail by fleeing to Damascus.[27]

A year later, on May 1, 1921, Palestine's Arabs launched another round of violence against their Jewish neighbors. This time the Arabs of Jaffa went on the attack. Author Tom Segev describes what followed: "Arab men broke into Jewish buildings and murdered the occupants; women came afterward and looted. Bearing clubs, knives, swords, and in some cases pistols, Arabs attacked Jewish pedestrians and destroyed Jewish homes and stores. They beat and killed Jews, children included, in their homes; in some cases they split the victims' skulls open."[28]

The attacks quickly spread from Jaffa to neighboring villages and beyond. On the morning of May 5, two to three thousand Arab villagers and Bedouin attacked the Jewish town of Petach Tikvah. This time, however, the British intervened. British infantry, aided by armored cars and air support, turned back the Arab assault.[29]

Two more attacks followed the next day. Several thousand Arabs from Ramle attacked the neighboring Jewish town of Rehovot, shouting, "Slaughter the Jews." Rehovot's residents successfully repelled the offensive. Further north, hundreds of Arabs from Tulkarem and its surrounding villages attacked the Jewish town of Hadera. Here the British intervened with infantry and air power to rout the invaders.[30]

By the time the British had quelled the 1921 riots, 47 Jews had been killed and another 146 had been wounded.[31]

The British were still new to Palestine. The way in which they reacted to these first instances of Arab aggression would set the tone for the coming decades of conflict. But while British soldiers had fought this Arab violence, British administrators chose to reward it.

The first British decision following this bloody season was to empower its author. The British pardoned Amin al-Husseini for his role in inciting the 1920 Jerusalem riots. Then they engineered his election to the position of Grand Mufti of Jerusalem. From his new post as Palestine's top Muslim official, Husseini aggressively crushed his opposition and consolidated his power. Husseini—now known simply as "the Mufti"—would dominate the Palestinian national movement until the 1960s.

The British were also quick to buckle to the terrorists' demands. While the violence in Jaffa was still ongoing, the British turned away ships carrying some three hundred Jewish immigrants fleeing pogroms in Russia.[32] On May 14, 1921—a mere two weeks after the Jaffa massacre—the British temporarily suspended all Jewish immigration into Palestine. In a June 3 speech, British High Commissioner Herbert Samuel imposed a permanent limit on Jewish immigration, ordering that it not exceed Palestine's ability to absorb the newcomers or otherwise prejudice "the interests of the present population."[33]

The British later formalized these concessions in a government document known as a "white paper." The White Paper of 1922 established that Jewish immigration "cannot be so great in volume as to exceed whatever may be the economic capacity of the country at the time to absorb new arrivals. It is essential to ensure that the immigrants should not be a burden upon the people of Palestine as a whole, and that they should not deprive any section of the present population of their employment."[34]

This policy was based on two mistaken premises. As we've seen, Jewish immigration did not produce Arab unemployment; it actually fueled unprecedented job growth for both Jews and Arabs. Thus limiting Jewish immigration would only harm Arab economic prospects.

More important, Palestine's Arabs were not slaughtering their Jewish neighbors because they were unhappy with their job prospects. There was a deeper rage driving this violence. Thus the solution offered—limiting but not eliminating Jewish immigration—was bound to be insufficient. And now that some violence had reduced Jewish immigration, hopes were raised that more violence might stop it altogether.

THE 1929 RIOTS

The Western Wall in Jerusalem is Judaism's holiest site. This massive stone edifice was never part of the Jewish Temple. It's merely a portion of the retaining wall that surrounded the plaza on which the Temple once stood. But after the Muslims conquered Jerusalem and claimed the Temple Mount as their own, this outer wall was as close as most Jews would ever get to their ancient sanctuary. Whenever circumstances permitted, Jews flocked to it.

During the centuries they ruled Jerusalem, the Ottomans severely restricted Jewish worship at the Western Wall. Jews had to pray quietly, so as not to disturb the Muslims worshiping on the Temple Mount above. And Jews were not permitted to make any physical changes—even temporary ones—to the portion of the wall allotted to them. This meant that they could not place a barrier between male and female worshippers as required by Jewish law. This also meant that they couldn't bring benches or chairs to the site so that they might sit down while they prayed. When the British conquered Jerusalem in 1918, they decided to maintain this discriminatory status quo.

On September 23, 1928—the eve of Yom Kippur—a large group of Jews gathered at the Western Wall to pray. Some brought a portable partition made of wooden frames covered with cloth to separate the male and female worshippers. Nearby Muslim officials were quick to notice the partition and complain. The British ordered the Jews to remove it by morning. When they failed to do so, British police disrupted Yom Kippur worship to carry it away themselves.[35]

That was it. The Jews had mounted a symbolic challenge to their second-class status, and they had failed. Yet Amin al-Husseini saw an opportunity in this incident. With characteristic hyperbole, he warned the Muslim world that the Jews had launched an effort to destroy the

Temple Mount mosques in order to rebuild their Temple.[36] He offered himself—the Mufti of Jerusalem—as the one leader who could prevent this tragedy.

Within a month, Husseini convened an emergency conference in Jerusalem. Over seven hundred Muslim leaders from Palestine and beyond joined him to address the Jewish threat to the holy mosques.[37] Throughout the year that followed, Husseini used this imaginary crisis to raise his profile abroad and consolidate his power at home. All the while, he continued to inflame passions against the Jews.

On August 23, 1929, this steady agitation finally boiled over into violence. That day thousands of Arabs streamed into Jerusalem from surrounding villages. Many carried knives and sticks. After morning prayers on the Temple Mount they poured out of the mosques and began attacking Jews in Jerusalem's Old City. The riots quickly spread to other Jewish neighborhoods in Jerusalem and beyond.[38] For one terrible, blood-drenched week Arabs attacked Jews in villages, towns, and cities throughout Palestine.

On August 24, the Arabs of Hebron attacked their Jewish neighbors. Violent mobs burst into Jewish homes and fell upon anyone they found inside. The commander of Britain's police force in Hebron, Raymond Cafferata, later testified about what he saw when he entered a Jewish home in the midst of the massacre: "On hearing screams in a room I went up a sort of tunnel passage and saw an Arab in the act of cutting off a child's head with a sword. He had already hit him and was having another cut.... Behind him was a Jewish woman smothered in blood with a man I recognized as [an Arab] police constable...standing over the woman with a dagger in his hand."[39]

A Polish Jew who was visiting Hebron that day hid behind a book-case. When he emerged, he found a pile of bodies and a "sea of blood." He noted of the dead and dying that "almost all had knife and hatchet wounds in their heads.... A few bodies had been slashed and their entrails had come out."[40] According to other survivors, two of Hebron's senior rabbis had been castrated together with five of their students.[41]

By the time the Hebron massacre was over, sixty-seven Jews had been killed and dozens more wounded.[42] Two days later, the surviving Jews of Hebron were evacuated. Hebron, the second holiest city in Judaism, was now Jew-free.

On August 29, the violence spread to the ancient Jewish community of Safed. The Arabs of Safed and surrounding villages invaded the city's Jewish quarter. Residents—including many children—were attacked with knives. Women were raped. Homes and stores were looted and set ablaze. The violence in Safed ultimately took the lives of eighteen Jews and left approximately eighty more injured.[43]

Similar attacks were launched against the Jewish communities of Tel Aviv, Haifa, Hadera, and a number of rural villages. Although timely British intervention saved the Jews of these localities, it did not always save their homes. When several thousand Arabs attacked Kibbutz Hulda, for example, the British evacuated its residents to safety. But everything that they had built was burned to the ground.[44]

By the time the 1929 riots were over, the Arabs of Palestine had murdered 133 Jews and injured over 300 more. In addition to the Jewish community of Hebron, six Jewish farming cooperatives had been largely destroyed.[45] As the Peel Commission would later note, "There was little retaliation by the Jews."[46]

While they were slow to stop the violence, the British were quick to send a commission to investigate its causes. Actually, they sent two commissions. The first, the Shaw Commission, arrived in Palestine in October 1929 and issued its report in early 1930. The Shaw Report essentially blamed this spasm of Arab violence on the Jews. More specifically, it concluded that the riots had been triggered by "excessive" Jewish immigration into Palestine. The Report recommended that Jewish immigration be suspended until a second study could propose new policies to remedy this problem.

In May 1930, Sir John Hope-Simpson arrived in Palestine to conduct this immigration study. Ignoring the explosive population and economic growth over the years of Jewish immigration, Hope-Simpson reached some surprisingly pessimistic conclusions regarding Palestine's ability to absorb immigrants. Deciding that there was not enough land available for agricultural settlement, Hope-Simpson recommended against further Jewish immigration to the agricultural sector. Concluding that there were not enough jobs for Arab factory workers, he also proposed strict limits on Jewish immigration to the industrial sector.

Following these recommendations, the British issued another white paper: the Passfield White Paper of 1930. The severe limits on Jewish immigration that this document recommended would have effectively rendered the Jews a permanent minority in Palestine. Arab violence had once again paid off with a significant political victory.

Having lost the battle in Palestine, the Zionists took the fight to London. Zionist activists and their allies lobbied Britain's government to repeal the Passfield White Paper. In 1931, British Prime Minister Ramsay MacDonald cancelled the White Paper's most severe restrictions. This Zionist victory kept the doors of Palestine open to Jewish immigration at a critical juncture. But this reprieve would not last for long.

THE ARAB REVOLT

On January 30, 1933, Adolf Hitler was appointed Chancellor of Germany. Jews in Germany and beyond quickly recognized that the Nazi leader was not just another politician stooping to anti-Semitic rhetoric. Hitler was clearly determined to practice the anti-Semitism he so vigorously preached. For millions of Jews, escaping Europe became an increasingly urgent priority.

As their panic increased and the number of countries willing to accept them declined, Europe's Jews flooded into Palestine. In 1932, only 9,553 Jews moved to Palestine. In 1933, the year Hitler came to power, the number of Jews arriving in Palestine jumped to 30,327. In 1934, this number rose to 42,359. And in 1935, Jewish immigration to Palestine peaked at 61,854.

This influx of Jewish refugees drove Arab outrage to new heights. In an unprecedented demonstration of unity, Husseini joined with Palestine's other prominent Arab leaders to demand an end to Jewish immigration. On April 22, 1936, the umbrella group they formed—the Arab Higher Committee (AHC)—announced a general strike. Palestine's Arabs were ordered to close their stores and stay home from work "until the British Government changes its present policy in a fundamental manner, the beginning of which is the stoppage of Jewish immigration."[47]

But even during the strike the AHC did not renounce violence. Quite to the contrary, it threatened to launch an armed revolt if its demands were not met by May 15.[48] When the British offered to severely curtail—but not stop—Jewish immigration, the AHC announced that its ultimatum had not been satisfied.

On Saturday night, May 16, a Jewish crowd had gathered at the Edison Cinema in West Jerusalem to see a new movie called *The Song of Happiness*. As they exited after the film, an Arab gunman opened fire. Three Jews were killed.[49] The Arab Revolt had begun.

Since they were revolting against British rule, Palestine's Arabs naturally directed much of their fire against British officials and institutions. But from its start the Arab Revolt was also a terrorist campaign that targeted Jewish civilians and their property. The rebels' slogan summarized their dual goals: "The English to the sea and the Jews to the graves."[50]

By the end of the year, Arab rebels had murdered 80 Jews and wounded another 308. In addition, the Jewish Agency reported the destruction of 80,000 citrus trees, 62,000 fruit trees, 64,000 forest trees, and 16,500 dunams (approximately 900 square meters) of crops.[51]

The British responded to this wave of violence with their standard remedy. In November of 1936, yet another Royal commission—this time under the leadership of Lord Peel—arrived in Palestine to explore the causes of the violence and propose a solution. The Arab Higher Committee agreed to suspend its attacks pending the Commission's review.

On July 7, 1937, the Peel Commission published a 404-page report of its findings and recommendations. The Peel Report concluded that the Arab Revolt was the result of a "conflict between Arab and Jewish Nationalism." It further recognized that this conflict was irreconcilable. There was simply no way that the British could forge a common "Palestinian" identity out of two rival national movements that each sought sovereignty in Palestine.

Given this intractable divide, the Commission recommended a radical solution: partition. It suggested that the British Mandate for Palestine be divided into two states, one Jewish and one Arab. Yet the proposed portions were far from equal. The Jews were offered a tiny strip of land—less than twenty percent of the territory of Palestine—made up mostly of the northern coastal plain and parts of Galilee. Despite its Jewish majority, Jerusalem was to remain under British control. The Arabs were to be given everything else, almost seventy-five percent of the total.

This offer—this tiny rump of a state—was far from the Jewish ideal. Yet for the Zionists, the offer of Jewish independence anywhere in their homeland was too significant to ignore. The top Zionist leaders, David Ben Gurion and Chaim Weizmann, strongly supported the compromise and went to work trying to convince their colleagues to do likewise. Weizmann argued that the Jews would be "fools" to reject the offer of a state, even if the territory on offer "were the size of a table cloth."[52]

By 1937, most Zionist leaders recognized that Europe's Jews were in grave peril. An independent state, even one limited to a tiny territory, still offered them an opportunity to rescue their European brethren. When the Twentieth Zionist Congress met in Zurich that August, a two-to-one majority accepted the partition proposal while also recommending that their leaders try to negotiate a better deal.

The Arab response was less nuanced. Husseini's Arab Higher Committee called for an emergency Arab summit to address the Peel plan. On September 8, 1937, over one hundred delegates from Palestine and its Arab neighbors met in the town of Bloudan, Syria. These assembled delegates unanimously rejected the partition proposal. Iraqi Prime Minister Hikmat Sulayman went so far as to declare, "Any person venturing to agree to act as Head of such a [partitioned Palestinian Arab] State would be regarded as an outcast throughout the Arab world, and would incur the wrath of Moslems all over the East."[53]

Far from being prepared to share sovereignty over the land, the leader of Palestine's Arabs wasn't even prepared to let most Jews continue living there. When the Mufti testified before the Peel Commission, Lord Peel asked him if he believed that Palestine could "assimilate and digest the 400,000 Jews now in the county." Husseini replied with one word: "No." Peel then asked him if this meant that some of the Jews already in the land would have to be expelled. Husseini answered: "We must leave all things for the future." When Peel asked him if these Jews would be safe under Arab rule, Husseini replied ominously, "That would depend on the Arab government."[54]

Tragically, Palestine's Arabs did not object to partition in words alone. In late September 1937, they resumed the revolt that had prompted the appointment of the Peel Commission in the first place.

The renewed revolt continued to target Jewish civilians. That October, for example, Arabs raided the Jewish neighborhood of Tiberias and murdered nineteen people, including eleven children. A British truck driver who arrived shortly after the massacre described the scene as "one of the worst sights I ever saw in my life." He couldn't forget the charred bodies of many of the children and the fact that "the naked bodies of the women exposed evidence that the knives had been used in the most ghastly way."[55]

The rebels also increasingly murdered their fellow Arabs, especially those who had expressed support for partition or otherwise questioned the Mufti's authority. In 1937, Arab rebels launched a total of 438 attacks. Of these, 109 were against British military and police and 143 were against Jewish settlements. Most of the remainder targeted "Arab houses." These numbers increased across the board in 1938.[56]

Now that political concessions had failed to end the revolt, the British finally decided to defeat it by force. They sent twenty-five thousand soldiers and policemen to Palestine and placed them under the command of an aggressive young major general named Bernard Montgomery.[57] Palestine's Jews and even some of Husseini's Arab opponents joined the British in fighting back against the rebels. By May of 1939, the British had crushed the Arab Revolt.

But even in victory the British quickly returned to the well-worn path of appeasement. At this juncture, another European war appeared all but inevitable. The British government was growing increasingly preoccupied with securing Arab allies who could provide access to oil and strategic territories in the coming conflict. Given Arab opposition to the creation of a Jewish state in Palestine—even one confined to less than twenty percent of its territory—the British simply dropped the idea.

THE 1939 WHITE PAPER

On May 17, 1939, the British government—now under Prime Minister Neville Chamberlain—issued yet another white paper for Palestine. This document constituted Britain's official abandonment of all prior commitments to the Jews. The 1939 White Paper not only rejected the Peel recommendation to partition Palestine into two states, but it effectively repudiated the League of Nations mandate to create a Jewish national home in Palestine.

The White Paper restricted Jewish immigration to Palestine to a total of seventy-five thousand over the five-year period 1940–44. It further stipulated that no Jewish immigration would be permitted after 1944 unless first approved by Palestine's Arabs. These restrictions guaranteed that the Arabs would remain the majority in Palestine.

The White Paper further pledged that Britain would grant independence to Palestine within ten years. Thus, within a decade, Palestine's Arab majority would be in control of yet another Arab state.

Winston Churchill criticized the 1939 White Paper as a "surrender to Arab violence" and "another Munich."[58] Chamberlain himself more or less conceded Churchill's point when he acknowledged that "We are now compelled to consider the Palestine problem mainly from the point of view of its effect on the international situation.... If we must offend one side, let us offend the Jews rather than the Arabs."[59]

The British defeated the Mufti's Arab Revolt. Then they capitulated to all of the Mufti's core demands. Yet the Mufti was still not satisfied. He wanted an immediate end to Jewish immigration and instant independence. And, by 1939, he saw a much faster way to accomplish these goals. When the British refused to buckle to his demands, Husseini offered his allegiance to the Nazis.

It was during World War II that Husseini demonstrated the true depths of his depravity. And it was during this war that Husseini took his zero-sum view of the conflict with the Jews to its ultimate, ghastly conclusion.

WORLD WAR II

Amin al-Husseini was not shy in his pursuit of the Nazis. As early as 1933, less than two months after Hitler's rise to power, Husseini requested an audience with the German consul general in Jerusalem. The consul general reported back to Berlin that, "The Mufti made expressly clear that Muslims within and without Palestine salute the new government of Germany and hope for the spread of fascist anti-democratic governments elsewhere. Contemporary Jewish influence on economics and within politics is damaging everywhere and should be combated."[60]

Husseini would eventually prove the sincerity of these words. After re-launching the Arab Revolt in 1937, he fled Palestine for Lebanon. In 1939, he made his way to Iraq. There he played a central role in orchestrating the 1941 coup that ousted Iraq's pro-British government and placed Nazi sympathizer Rashid Ali in power.[61]

It took less than a month for British forces to overpower Rashid Ali's loyalists and restore their allies to power. But all did not end well. When a group of Iraqi Jews went out to greet their returning leaders, they were attacked by an Arab mob wielding knives and axes. Then soldiers, police, and individuals still loyal to Rashid Ali descended upon Baghdad's Jewish neighborhoods determined to do their worst.

The massacre began on June 1, 1941, and continued well into the following day. The official statistics listed 110 Jewish dead, including 28 women, and hundreds more injured.[62] Jewish leaders claimed that the real casualty figures were far higher. In addition, over 3,000 Jewish homes and 586 Jewish shops and warehouses were looted.[63] The Iraqi committee of inquiry that investigated the slaughter listed the Mufti as one of its key instigators.[64]

As British forces were defeating his Iraqi allies, Husseini escaped justice once again. This time, he fled across the border into Iran. From there, he continued to his ultimate destination: Nazi Germany. The Mufti arrived in Berlin on November 6, 1941. On November 28, he was received by Hitler for a private meeting.

Now ensconced in Berlin and receiving a generous monthly retainer, the Mufti threw himself into his new role as the Nazis' most prominent Arab ally. In May 1942, he began broadcasting Nazi propaganda in Arabic. Day after day he made the Nazi case to his fellow Arabs, often stressing what he saw as the shared goals of Nazism and Islam. He infamously summarized this anti-Semitic imperative with the mantra: "Kill the Jews. Kill them wherever you find them. This pleases God, history, and religion. This serves your honor. God is with you!"[65]

But Husseini did more than merely talk. He enthusiastically took the lead in recruiting Arab volunteers to fight alongside the Nazis. His efforts ultimately helped to deliver thousands of fresh troops to the Nazi war machine. With Husseini's assistance, the Nazis were able to form two Tunisian battalions, one Moroccan battalion, and one Algerian battalion.[66]

As the war dragged on and the Nazis grew more desperate for troops, Himmler decided to create an entire SS division of ten thousand Muslim soldiers from Bosnia and Albania. But many Balkan Muslim leaders opposed the Nazis, and they were able to slow the pace of recruitment. Himmler responded by sending the Mufti to take the lead in persuading these Muslims to enlist. The Mufti ultimately raised not one, but three full divisions of Balkan Muslim soldiers for Nazi Germany.[67]

In December 1941, Husseini met with Adolf Eichmann, who shared with him the first plans for the Nazi Final Solution.[68] At his war crimes trial, Eichmann's assistant Dieter Wisliceny testified that Husseini was deeply impressed with what he learned. Before leaving, Wisliceny noted, Husseini asked Eichmann to send an expert to Jerusalem to help him murder Palestine's Jews once the war was won.[69]

While waiting for his chance to kill Palestine's Jews, Husseini did his best to convince both Italy and Germany to extend the Final Solution to those Arab countries they already occupied. Eventually, the Italians agreed to intern all Libyan Jews under the age of forty-five, and 562 of them died in forced labor camps.[70] The Nazis agreed to send Walter Rauff, the Nazi officer who had developed the mobile gassing van, to Tunisia. Under his supervision, twenty-five hundred Tunisian Jews died in a network of slave labor camps.[71] Had Hitler's Afrika Korps not been stopped in time, Cairo's ancient Jewish community would have been Rauff's next victims.[72]

In June 1943, Husseini is believed to have visited Auschwitz with Eichmann.[73] Shortly thereafter, Husseini met with Himmler in the nearby Ukrainian town of Zhitomir. In his memoirs, Husseini revealed that during this meeting Himmler informed him that "Up to now we have liquidated about three million of them [Jews]."[74] Yet the Mufti continued to do his best to prevent any Jews—including children—from escaping Europe.

Beyond merely seeking to extend Hitler's Holocaust to the Middle East, Husseini may well have played a role in persuading Hitler to murder Europe's Jews in the first place.

Up until 1941, Hitler did not plan to kill the Jews in the lands he occupied; he merely wanted to expel them. At the same time, however, Hitler was aggressively courting Husseini as an ally who could deliver critical Arab and Muslim support to the Nazis. In January 1941, Husseini sent a letter to Hitler offering him an alliance provided certain conditions were met. One of his core demands was that Hitler prohibit Jewish emigration from the territory he controlled.[75]

In October 1941, as his first meeting with Husseini approached, Hitler officially outlawed the emigration of Jews from German-occupied territories.[76] On November 28, 1941, Hitler held a ninety-minute meeting with Husseini in his Berlin headquarters. That same day—only a few hours later—Hitler ordered SS General Reinhard Heydrich to convene a conference to initiate the "final solution of the Jewish question."[77]

The very next day, Heydrich sent invitations to thirteen high-ranking Nazi officials asking that they join him for a meeting in the Berlin suburb of Wannsee. The "Wannsee Conference" would go down in history as the meeting at which the Holocaust was initiated. On December 4—well in advance of the conference—Eichmann personally briefed Husseini on the proposed Final Solution.[78]

This timing may represent nothing more than startling coincidence. Hitler might have eventually chosen the path of genocide no matter what the demands and counsel of his new Arab ally. But there is something about Hitler's interactions with Husseini that seems to have affirmed his hate, pushed his hand, and moved him closer to the most horrific of actions.

As the Nazi regime crumbled around him, Husseini was captured and imprisoned by French troops. For once, it seemed, he would be held to account for his crimes.

Yet Husseini had sympathizers everywhere, including among his French captors. He soon escaped France and the war crimes trial that awaited him and made his way to Egypt. Once safely back in the Middle East, Husseini resumed his day-to-day leadership of Palestine's Arabs.

Husseini's return came at a critical juncture. In 1947, the United Nations proposed the partition of Palestine into two states, one Jewish and one Arab. The Jews once again accepted the compromise. From his headquarters in Egypt, Husseini was able to ensure that Palestine's Arabs not only rejected partition, but did so in the most violent of ways.

KILLING THE OPPOSITION

Amin al-Husseini dominated the Palestinian Arab national movement from its formation until well into the 1960s. It was Husseini who, through the force of his personality and arms, imposed his all-or-nothing approach to the conflict with the Jews upon his people. It was Husseini, therefore, who ensured that his people ultimately ended up with nothing.

It would be a gross injustice, however, to assume that Husseini spoke for all of Palestine's Arabs. In fact it's doubtful he spoke for even a majority of them. Only a fraction of Palestine's Arabs participated in the violence of 1920, 1921, and 1936–39. And only a small minority volunteered to serve in the Palestinian militias that fought to prevent the birth of a Jewish state in 1947.[79]

Indeed, there was another side to almost every atrocity perpetrated by Husseini and his collaborators. In both the 1920 Nebi Musa riots and the 1921 Jaffa riots, many Jews escaped the violence by hiding in the homes of their Arab neighbors. In the 1929 Hebron massacre, over two-thirds of Hebron's Jews survived because they found refuge in twenty-eight Arab homes.[80] According to witnesses, "Had it not been for a few Arab families not a Jewish soul would have remained in Hebron."[81]

Husseini also faced political opposition. From the start of his career, Husseini competed for control of Palestine's Arabs with a series of more moderate Arab parties and leaders, including the Muslim National Associations, the farmers' parties, the Semitic Union, the Palestine Labor League, the National Defense Party, the peace units, the Nashashibi family, and King Abdullah of Transjordan. This is not to say that these rivals were enthusiastic Zionists; most were not. Nor did they need to be. Accommodation—not admiration—was the only requirement for peace.

The problem with Palestine's Arab moderates was not that they didn't exist. The problem was that they didn't win. Husseini repeatedly defeated these rivals for power and was thus able to determine the path Palestine's Arabs ultimately took. And for Husseini, there was only one acceptable path: the complete rejection of Jewish rights in Palestine.

In vanquishing his political opponents, Husseini typically shunned the arts of persuasion and politics. He preferred murder. Simply put, every leader who emerged as a serious challenger to Husseini's rule ended up dead.

In the 1920s a group of moderate Arabs formed an organization called the Muslim National Associations (MNA) as a counterweight to the Husseini-controlled Muslim-Christian Associations.[82] The two leaders of this effort were Haifa Mayor Hassan Bey Shukri and Sheikh Musa Hadeib from a village outside Hebron.

These Arab leaders believed in coexistence, and they recognized the benefits that Jews were bringing to their country. In a 1921 telegram to the British government, for example, they enthusiastically expressed their support for Jewish immigration:

We do not consider the Jewish people as an enemy whose wish is to crush us. On the contrary. We consider the Jews as a brotherly people sharing our joys and troubles and helping us in the construction of our common country. We are certain that without Jewish immigration and financial assistance there will be no future development of our country as may be judged from the fact that the towns inhabited in part by Jews such as Jerusalem, Jaffa, Haifa, and Tiberias are making steady progress while Nablus, Acre, and Nazareth where no Jews reside are steadily declining.[83]

In October 1929, Sheikh Musa Hadeib was assassinated in Jerusalem for "collaborating" with the Zionists.[84]

On May 11, 1936, explosives were planted at Mayor Shukri's home. He escaped without injury. Several months later, an Arab gunman fired four shots at Shukri as he entered Haifa's City Hall. All four bullets missed their mark. After this second assassination attempt, Shukri fled to Beirut. When he returned from exile, a third attempt was made on his life.[85]

Throughout the British Mandate, a prominent Jerusalem family, the Nashashibis, were the main rivals to Husseini and his clan. The British appointed Raghib Nashashibi as mayor of Jerusalem in 1920. In the mid-1930s, Raghib and his nephew, Fakhri Nashashibi, formed the National Defense Party as an alternative to the Husseini-dominated political institutions.

The Nashashibis were not Zionists. They opposed Jewish immigration and land purchases and would have preferred a purely Arab Palestine. But unlike the Husseinis, the Nashashibis recognized that Zionism could not be defeated by force and that some sort of compromise would have to be reached. As the Peel Commission was finalizing its partition proposal in the spring of 1937, the Nashashibis expressed interest in it.

Husseini and his allies let it be known that any Arab who supported partition would be labeled a traitor. And they backed up their threat with firepower.[86] That June, bullets were fired at the home of a prominent Nashashibi ally in Bethlehem, wounding his wife and daughter. A bomb was thrown at another Nashashibi activist in Jerusalem. And a gunman tried to assassinate Fakhri Nashashibi. The only reason the younger Nashashibi survived is because he raised his hand to scratch himself just as the shot was fired. The bullet aimed for his head lodged in his arm instead.[87]

Even though its targets survived, this violence achieved its goal. The Nashashibis never publicly endorsed the Peel plan. They eventually came out against it. According to one of the Zionists' Arab informants, "The opposition, which was prepared to agree to partition, had to go along with the opponents of partition after they learned of the decision to murder everyone who supported that opinion, even if they were among the greatest [leaders]."[88]

In the fall of 1938, the Nashashibis finally decided to fight back. They openly broke with Husseini and formed a rival military organization—known as "the peace units"—under the command of Fakhri Nashashibi. With help from both the British and Palestine's Jews, the peace units made an important contribution to ending the Arab Revolt.

In November 1941, the British asked Fakhri Nashashibi to travel to Iraq to help them counteract Amin al-Husseini's pro-Nazi agitation there. On November 9, Nashashibi was assassinated outside his Baghdad hotel. The murderer, Ahmad Nusseibeh, told investigators that he had acted on the orders of the Husseini clan.[89]

Almost everyone who attended Nashashibi's funeral in Jerusalem was Jewish or British. Most Arabs feared that the mere act of honoring Husseini's fallen enemy would place them on his hit list.[90]

After the State of Israel was born in 1948, King Abdullah of Transjordan conquered the West Bank and granted citizenship to its residents.

The king thus became the Mufti's chief rival for leadership of Palestine's Arabs. He also was rumored to be pursuing a separate peace with Israel.

On July 20, 1951, Abdullah decided to attend Friday prayers at Jerusalem's Al-Aqsa Mosque. He was shot dead as he approached the entrance. The assassin was a young Husseini loyalist who had fought in one of Husseini's militias during the 1948 War.[91]

Husseini didn't kill only those who challenged his leadership. He also murdered anyone who dared to violate his policies, especially men he deemed guilty of "treason."[92] Throughout the Arab Revolt, however, Husseini continually broadened the definition of "treason." In time, even business dealings with Jews—including going to a Jewish doctor or employing a Jewish waitress—were added to the list of treasonous acts punishable by death.[93]

For Husseini and his colleagues, killing such traitors was an even higher priority than killing Jews. Toward the end of the revolt, the rebel leadership offered one hundred Palestinian pounds for the murder of Arab opposition leaders and commanders of the anti-Husseini peace units. They paid twenty-five pounds for lesser Arab traitors. Murdering a Jew earned the killer a mere ten pounds.[94]

By the time the Arab Revolt was over, the rebels had killed over nine hundred of their fellow Arabs who had in some way challenged Husseini's rule or dissented from his dictates.[95] Any hopes for peace and coexistence died along with them.

CHAPTER SIX

1948: Palestine's
Arabs Attack

The first Arab-Israeli war, of 1948, was launched by the Palestinian Arabs, who rejected the UN partition resolution and embarked on hostilities aimed at preventing the birth of Israel. That war and not design, Jewish or Arab, gave birth to the Palestinian refugee problem.

—Benny Morris, 2004[1]

Among all of the lies that have been told about Israel, few rival those surrounding its desperate struggle for survival in 1948. The conventional anti-Israel narrative asserts that after the UN voted to create a Jewish state in Palestine, the Jews decided to expel the proposed state's substantial Arab minority. Thus Israel was the aggressor whose ethnic cleansing demanded an Arab response.

This is how Palestinian Authority President Mahmoud Abbas described these events in a 2011 *New York Times* op-ed: "Shortly thereafter [after the UN vote], Zionist forces expelled Palestinian Arabs to ensure a decisive Jewish majority in the future state of Israel, and Arab armies intervened. War and further expulsions ensued."[2]

In this telling, Palestine's Arabs were the passive victims of forces beyond their control. It's as if they were swept away by a tornado or swallowed by an earthquake. What they suffered was, in their preferred term, a *nakba*, the Arabic word for catastrophe.

125

There is much truth to the Palestinian claim of loss and displacement. Many innocent Palestinian Arabs did die in this war. And hundreds of thousands more did become refugees. But this nakba narrative glosses over one critical issue: causation. The fact is that this Palestinian tragedy was the direct result of Palestinian action.

Palestine's Arabs started the 1948 War. Their explicit goal was to prevent the UN-authorized Jewish state from ever coming into existence. When the Palestinians proved unable to vanquish the Jews on their own, five Arab nations invaded Israel in an effort to finish the job. The large majority of Arab refugees were individuals who fled this war that their leaders launched and their neighbors escalated.

Palestine's Jews tried desperately to rise above the ugly facts of modern warfare. At first, they limited themselves to purely defensive measures. When they later went on the offensive, they restricted their troops to "hitting the guilty"—striking those who had been involved in attacking them. Strict orders were issued not to attack any village that had remained peaceful or to harm any Arab who did not have blood on his hands.

While admirable, such rigid rules of engagement almost cost the Jews the war. As defeat loomed, Palestine's Jews recognized that they needed to descend from their high moral perch and fight like any other army. They finally decided to make decisions based on military strategy and necessity. And as they took the strategic initiative, the Jews finally began winning victories on the ground.

Among the tragedies of modern warfare is that the circle of suffering extends well beyond the combatants. The decision by Palestine's Jews to seize strategic strongholds—often Arab towns and villages controlled by Arab forces—guaranteed that there would be civilian death and suffering. But these realities of war do not erase the vast moral gap between aggressor and defender. They do not lift the awesome burden from the shoulders of Palestine's Arab leaders for what they wrought upon Palestine's people, both Arabs and Jews.

The 1948 War was certainly not the first time that a nation has launched a war of annihilation against its neighbor. But it may well be the first time that the invaders expressed such indignation when their neighbors dared to fight back. Most aggressors throughout most of human history have at least had the decency not to cry "victim" when they lose.

PRELUDE TO WAR

With the end of World War II, the Jewish people confronted a disastrous new reality. Six million Jews had been slaughtered by the Nazis and their allies. Hundreds of thousands of survivors languished in displaced persons camps with nowhere to go. Britain, still stubbornly enforcing its 1939 White Paper, was blocking these Jews from returning to their ancient homeland.

But the Holocaust did not deal the crushing blow to Jewish aspirations that the Mufti and his allies had hoped. Instead, it had two opposite and unintended effects. This tragedy proved to the world the truth of the basic Zionist premise that the Jewish people need a state of their own. And this near-death experience caused the Jews of Palestine to lose their epic patience. Before World War II, the Arabs had rebelled against British rule in Palestine. After the war, the Jews were the ones to revolt against the British.

The British emerged from World War II both physically and economically exhausted. British leaders quickly recognized that they could no longer maintain an empire upon which the sun never set. Confronted by the humanitarian crisis of the Holocaust survivors, the persistence of the Jewish revolt, and the outrage of the world, they decided to punt. In 1947, Britain asked the United Nations to decide the future of Palestine.

Like the British before them, the United Nations sent a commission to Palestine to study the conflict and recommend a solution. Ultimately, a majority of the United Nations Special Committee on Palestine (UNSCOP) reached the same conclusion as the Peel Commission a decade earlier. They decided that both the Jews and the Arabs of Palestine had valid yet irreconcilable claims to sovereignty in Palestine. Thus they recommended that this land be partitioned into two states, one Jewish and one Arab, so that both claims could be satisfied.

The United Nations was more generous to Palestine's Jews than the Peel Commission had been. This time the Jews were offered fifty-six percent of Palestine—although a majority of this was desert. Palestine's Arabs were offered forty-two percent, but with much less desert. A small bloc surrounding Jerusalem and Bethlehem was to be placed under international control.

On November 29, 1947, the United Nations General Assembly voted by a two-thirds majority to adopt the UNSCOP partition plan. The world had decided to create a Jewish state.

The Jewish state approved by the UN was far from the Jewish ideal. The Jews would be getting merely half of an already truncated Palestine. The half on offer included neither the ancient Jewish capital of Jerusalem nor the biblical heartland of Judea and Samaria. It was smaller than the state of New Jersey.

Yet despite this heartbreaking reality, Palestine's Jews immediately accepted partition. They and the vast majority of Jews around the world were prepared to make painful compromises to regain the sovereignty that had eluded them for so long. They did not dwell on what they had been denied.

The Arabs said "No." Amin al-Husseini, the Palestinian Arab Higher Committee, and the Arab League were all quick to condemn the UN vote. Their objection had nothing to do with the size or the borders of the proposed Jewish state. What they rejected, quite explicitly, was the creation of any Jewish state in Palestine no matter what its size or shape. Both the Arabs of Palestine and their Arab neighbors threatened to take up arms to prevent the UN vote from being implemented. They did not wait long to demonstrate that this threat was not idle.

CIVIL WAR: PALESTINE'S ARABS ATTACK

As soon as the UN votes were tallied, the Jews of Palestine burst into spontaneous celebration. They poured out onto the streets of their cities and danced until sunrise. Remembering that night years later, David Ben Gurion wrote, "I could not dance, I could not sing that night. I looked at them so happy dancing and I could only think that they were all going to war."[3]

Ben Gurion's grim prediction quickly came true. As night gave way to morning, a group of Jewish revelers boarded a bus in Netanya. As the bus approached the village of Faja, three Arab gunmen opened fire on it with submachine guns. When the driver swerved to avoid the shots, he lost control of the bus and it tumbled down a ditch. The gunmen approached the overturned bus and continued shooting. They ultimately killed five passengers and seriously wounded five more. Then they left to attack another bus, where they killed two more passengers.[4]

Thus it began. Later that morning, Arab snipers began firing on Tel Aviv and the Jewish neighborhoods of Jerusalem and Haifa. The following day brought another round of bombings, shootings, and stabbings.[5] In the twelve days following the UN vote, eighty Jews were killed and many more were wounded.[6]

In the course of the month that followed, the conflict quickly escalated from terrorism to guerrilla war. Hundreds of Palestinian Arab militias attacked Jewish villages, neighborhoods, and transportation. By the end of the year, another 140 Jews had been killed.[7]

For the Israelis, the fighting thus thrust upon them would be their War of Independence; the trial by fire through which they established in fact what the UN had authorized in law. For the Arabs of Palestine, this would be their nakba—the catastrophe through which their society was destroyed and their population scattered. Those seeking a more neutral term simply call these events the 1948 War.

These names all refer broadly to what were really two separate wars. The first was largely a civil war between Palestine's Arabs and Palestine's Jews. This war began the day after the November 29, 1947, UN vote. It effectively ended with the start of the second war.

The second war was international. It began with the May 15, 1948, invasion of Israel by the armies of four Arab nations—Egypt, Transjordan, Syria, and Iraq—in an effort to succeed where their Palestinian cousins had failed. A fifth Arab nation, Lebanon, later joined the fighting. This second war ended with the signing of a series of armistice agreements in early 1949.

Israel paid a steep price for the independence it ultimately won. By war's end, one of every one hundred Jews in Palestine was dead, and two out of every hundred Jews were injured.[8] Palestine's Arabs were hardly the only ones to suffer as a result of this Arab aggression.

THE CIVIL WAR PHASE ONE: ISRAEL PLAYS DEFENSE

During the civil war, Palestine's Jews faced an Arab force made up of hundreds of local militias, buttressed by thousands of volunteers from neighboring Arab states.[9] Approximately half of the eight hundred Arab towns and villages in Palestine sent their men into the battle against the nascent Jewish state. The remaining Arab villages—mostly located in the territory that later became known as the West Bank—did not participate in the fighting.[10] Because these villages did not attack the Jews, the Jews had no reason to attack them. Thus the Arab population of the West Bank experienced little fighting, little flight, and no expulsions.

Palestine's Arabs launched the civil war the morning after the UN vote. And they held the strategic initiative for the following four months, until the end of March 1948. During this period they attacked Jewish targets at the time and place of their choosing. Thus they controlled both the size and the pace of the conflict.

During these first four months, the major Jewish militia—known as the *Haganah*—maintained a largely defensive posture. For reasons both moral and strategic, the Haganah limited itself to two types of actions. From the start, the Haganah defended Jewish communities from Arab attacks. When this restraint seemed to encourage only more attacks, the Haganah decided that it would also "hit the guilty." This meant retaliating against the gunmen who attacked them and the infrastructure that supported them, including "houses serving as concentration points, supply depots, and training sites."[11]

Yet even on these retaliatory raids, Haganah soldiers were given strict instructions to spare noncombatants in hostile villages and to avoid peaceful villages altogether.[12] As Ben Gurion phrased it, his troops must "under no circumstances hurt any Arabs who maintain the peace."[13]

These limited objectives were captured in a Haganah circular distributed to the troops in January 1948: "The moral principle—that has never ceased to guide us—as well as the imperative of political expediency command us to do our utmost to avoid killing ordinary civilians and to always hit the criminals themselves, the bearers of arms, and the perpetrators of attacks."[14]

The Haganah also communicated this policy to those Arabs who had not yet joined the fight. A Haganah flyer widely distributed in Arab neighborhoods and villages that winter included the following plea: "We therefore implore you to deny them [Arab attackers] the use of your villages, homes, and fields for the establishments of centers, shelters, or bases so as to spare us the need to enter your villages—in self-defense—and harm you and your property."[15]

During this first phase of the war, the Haganah conquered no Arab territory. And only two Arab villages—both hostile—were destroyed.[16] Toward the end of this period, Ismail Safwat—the commander of the Arab Liberation Army fighting Israel in the north—acknowledged that "the Jews have constantly endeavored to narrow the theater of operations" and "have not attacked a single Arab village unless provoked by it."[17]

THE MOUNTING DANGER

The Haganah's initial strategy may have been moral, but the passage of time also showed it to be suicidal. Simply put, the Jews were losing the war. And a loss in this war meant national and quite likely physical annihilation.

By the end of March, Palestine's Arabs had killed over 900 Jews and wounded an additional 1,858.[18] And while they had not conquered a single Jewish town or neighborhood, they were winning what came to be known as the "war of the roads." Palestine's Arab villages were typically built on hilltops. These villages thus controlled the high ground overlooking most of the country's critical transportation arteries, including the only road linking Tel Aviv to Jerusalem. From these strategic strongholds it was easy for Arab forces to ambush and destroy Jewish convoys passing below them.

The Arabs were using their control of the roads to blockade—and slowly starve—the isolated Jewish communities of Judea, Galilee, and the Negev. Most significantly, they maintained a tight siege of Jerusalem's Jewish neighborhoods and their one hundred thousand residents. In late March, Jerusalem's top Haganah official warned Ben Gurion that unless the Arab blockade was broken, "Jerusalem will not hold out even until May 15."[19]

As Jerusalem's Jews starved, the Haganah made increasingly desperate efforts to break the Arab blockade with convoys of food and essential supplies. Most of the Haganah's "armored vehicles"—typically trucks with scraps of metal welded onto their sides—were sent to participate in these convoys. Most of the Palmach—the Haganah's elite fighters—were ordered to drive and guard the trucks.

Yet even the best of soldiers could not overcome so serious a strategic deficit. In the last week of March, for example, 136 supply trucks set out for Jerusalem. Only forty-one reached their destination.[20] By the end of the month, the Haganah had lost almost all of its armored vehicles and hundreds of its best troops in this futile effort to feed Jerusalem's Jews.

As difficult as the war of the roads became, the Haganah knew that it would soon face a far greater challenge. The British Mandate—and with it Britain's military presence in Palestine—was due to end on May 15. The Arab nations surrounding Israel had repeatedly threatened to launch a multi-front invasion of the Jewish state the moment the Mandate ended.

The Haganah's top generals disagreed about whether they would be able to prevail against these combined Arab armies. But they all understood that they had no chance of repelling these attacks if they had to confront the Arab armies on their borders while simultaneously battling hundreds of Palestinian militias in their rear.

Finally, beyond these military challenges, the nascent Jewish state was also facing an imminent diplomatic demise. Many sympathetic Western countries had worried from the start that the Jews would prove unable to defend themselves from their Arab neighbors. The Jews were terribly outnumbered and outgunned, and the stereotype of the passive Jewish victim had yet to be supplanted by the legend of the brave Israeli warrior. The mounting Jewish death toll only reinforced the worst of Western fears.

The nations that had voted to create a Jewish state were now the ones that felt most responsible for stopping the impending massacre. The United States was the first to waver. On March 19, Warren Austin, the U.S. representative to the UN, called for the partition plan to be abandoned and for Palestine to be placed under a UN trusteeship. Although President Truman sidelined this proposal, pressure for its passage grew every time a Jewish neighborhood was bombed or a Jewish convoy destroyed. Arab violence was paying diplomatic dividends.

THE CIVIL WAR PHASE TWO: ISRAEL SEIZES THE INITIATIVE

By the end of March 1948, these combined threats had converged to push Palestine's Jews to the brink of disaster. If they didn't win the war of the roads, Jerusalem would be lost. If they didn't win the ongoing civil war, they would never survive the looming international war. And if they didn't score some quick military victories, the United Nations might abort the Jewish state before the Arabs ever had the chance to destroy it.

On March 31, David Ben Gurion called his top generals to his apartment and huddled with them late into the night. It was at this meeting that the Jewish leadership made the decision to change tactics. Going forward, they would no longer merely respond to Arab attacks; they would seize the strategic initiative. And in seizing the initiative, they would consider strategic factors—geography, supply routes, and the like—every bit as much as the history of relations with each Arab village. In other words, the Haganah would begin behaving like any other army in the history of warfare.

Armed with this new strategy, Palestine's Jews tried once again to break the siege of Jerusalem. This time they didn't send yet another convoy of trucks through a gauntlet of Arab villages firing mortars and bullets down on them. The Haganah was now free to attack the villages from which this fire had come. Their first target was the village of Kastel, which dominated the final approach to Jerusalem.

The Haganah conquered Kastel on April 2. But five days later the Arabs launched a successful counter-attack in which they won back the village and killed dozens of Haganah troops. On April 9, the Haganah took Kastel for the second time.

The original order for the attack on Kastel had forbidden Haganah troops from destroying its buildings. The April 8 directive to recapture Kastel specified that the village be razed.[21] The Israelis had learned the hard way that so long as a conquered village stood, they would have to leave troops behind to prevent its recapture. But with the Arab invasion only six weeks away, the Israelis had no such troops to spare.

Kastel was the first major Arab village conquered by the Haganah. It was also the first major Arab village destroyed by the Haganah. And no more Haganah men fell fighting for Kastel.

Fresh from their victory at Kastel, Haganah forces quickly implemented their new proactive strategy across the country. They set forth to decisively defeat the hundreds of Palestinian militias they had been fighting. This meant conquering the villages that sent and supported these militias. And this meant destroying those villages believed likely to resume hostilities once the Haganah left. Destroying villages required expelling village residents. The Haganah had finally accepted the brutal logic of war.

Throughout this period, the impending May 15 multi-front Arab invasion was the ticking clock that dictated the pace and intensity of Haganah operations. Haganah communiqués issued during this time constantly count down the number of days left before May 15. Some refer to the necessity of establishing "territorial continuity" before the expected invasion. Others address the need to "block the way for [Arab] armor." Still others focus on the need to "deny the enemy a base for future operations." There are repeated references to eliminating the threat of Arabs striking "from behind" or "from the rear" while Haganah troops were confronting the invaders on their borders.

As Haganah soldiers conquered certain strategic villages and expelled their residents, it was clear to all concerned why they were doing so. The secretary general of the Arab League, Azzam Pasha, complained that the Jews "were driving out the inhabitants on or near roads by which Arab regular forces could enter the country.... The Arab armies would have the greatest difficulty in even entering Palestine after May 15th."[22]

Azzam Pasha was correct. And that was precisely the point.

THE FLIGHT FROM HAIFA

The Haganah was on the offensive. The Jews were now involved in the dirty business of defeating and sometimes destroying villages. But Jewish decision-making was driven strictly by strategic—not racial—imperatives. The goal was to win the war and survive, not to drive the Arabs from Israel, Thus peaceful Arab towns and villages were still largely left alone. And in many cases, Palestine's Jews went to surprising lengths to persuade their Arab neighbors to stay and build the country together with them.

The events that transpired in the city of Haifa provide a dramatic example of this ethos in action. Haifa's pre-war population was almost evenly divided between Jews and Arabs, and its Arab community was the second largest in Palestine. Shortly after the UN partition vote, Haifa's Jewish mayor, Shabtai Levy, approached Haifa's Arab leaders and urged them to sign a citywide ceasefire. His offer was rejected.[23]

In April, Britain began a phased withdrawal of its troops from positions across Palestine in preparation for the May 15 departure. On April 21, Britain removed its forces from important buffer zones in Haifa. With no ceasefire in place, Jewish and Arab forces rushed to seize these strategic positions. The fighting quickly escalated into an all-out struggle for control of the city. Within twenty-four hours, Jewish forces had prevailed.

As the fighting raged, thousands of Haifa's Arabs made their way to the city's port and fled by boat. But far from seeking to accelerate their flight, Haifa's Jews made repeated efforts to stop it. They even went so far as to launch a public campaign—through media alerts and leaflet drops—urging fleeing Arabs to return home and resume "regular work in peace and security."[24]

These efforts did not go unnoticed by British officials in Haifa. For example, a report issued by the British military confirms that "The Jews have been making strenuous efforts to check the stream of refugees, in several cases resorting to actual intervention by the Haganah. Appeals have been made on the radio and in the press, urging Arabs to remain in the town."[25]

In the early morning of April 22, Haifa's remaining Arab leaders met with Mayor Levy and Haganah representatives to discuss surrender terms. The Haganah demanded that all foreign Arab fighters leave the city. But they promised the local Arabs a future "as equal and free citizens of Haifa."[26]

The Arab leaders asked for time to consider these terms. According to Britain's top official in northern Palestine, Major General Hugh Stockwell, they returned that evening and informed the mayor that "They were not in a position to sign the truce, as they had no control over the

Arab military elements in the town and that, in all sincerity, they could not fulfill the terms of the truce even if they were to sign. They then said as an alternative that the Arab population wished to evacuate Haifa...man, woman and child."[27]

With tears in his eyes, Mayor Levy spoke "very passionately...and begged [the Arabs] to reconsider." But the Arab leaders responded that they "had no choice."[28]

Many of Haifa's Arabs fled out of fear of the fighting and doubts about their future in a Jewish state. But the instructions coming from their own leaders certainly contributed to the extent of the flight. The Arab Higher Committee repeatedly ordered Haifa's Arabs to leave town. Even more ominously, they suggested that any Arabs who stayed and submitted to Jewish rule would be branded as "traitors."[29] And traitors did not live very long.

Major General Stockwell criticized the Arab decision to evacuate Haifa. "You have made a foolish decision," he told Haifa's Arab leaders. "After all, it was you who began the fighting, and the Jews have won."[30] General Stockwell's words about Haifa's Arabs could apply just as easily to Palestine's Arabs as a whole.

THE FLIGHT FROM JAFFA

A few days later, a similar scenario played out in Palestine's largest Arab city, Jaffa. Since the start of the war, Jaffa had been the source of repeated Arab attacks on the neighboring Jewish city of Tel Aviv. On the night of April 22, Jaffa's Arabs renewed their shelling of Tel Aviv.[31] On April 25, a Jewish militia called the Irgun attacked Jaffa. As the Irgun advanced and began the return fire of mortars, Jaffa's port filled with Arabs desperate to flee.

Determined not to allow a repeat of the events in Haifa, the British intervened and forced the parties to accept a cease-fire. But this pause in the fighting did not slow the Arab flight. On the contrary, the exodus actually accelerated when Arab reinforcements—mostly Iraqi—streamed into Jaffa during the cease-fire and went on a spree of rape and robbery.[32]

On May 13, Jewish forces accepted the surrender of Jaffa's remaining Arab leaders. On May 14, the Haganah seized the almost empty town.

Upon receiving the city's surrender, the Haganah announced, "This is not a time to rejoice. The city of Jaffa is almost empty. We promised the residents a peaceful and dignified life and it is incumbent upon each and every one of us to uphold this commitment; this is a matter of honor and the hard moral core of our army."[33]

Visiting Jaffa shortly thereafter, Ben Gurion was dumbfounded. "I couldn't understand," he later wrote. "Why did the inhabitants...leave?"[34]

DEIR YASSIN

It was during this second, proactive phase of the war—on April 9, 1948—that Jewish militias attacked the Arab village of Deir Yassin. In the course of the attack, as many as 110 of the town's approximately 700 residents were killed, including many women and children.[35] From that day forward, "Deir Yassin" has been the rallying cry of all who accuse Israel of war crimes and atrocities.

Almost everything that happened that day has been the subject of multiple conflicting claims. Fighters from the two Jewish militias that carried out the attack—the Irgun and the Lehi—have insisted that they behaved reasonably. They argue that Deir Yassin was an important military target and that any civilians who died there were the unintentional victims of difficult house-to-house fighting. Arab survivors, as well as some Jewish observers, have claimed otherwise. They contend that Deir Yassin was a peaceful village with little strategic value and that the dead were largely victims of an intentional massacre.

As time has passed and more documents have been released, historians have been able to piece together a more objective account. The fact is that Deir Yassin did occupy a strategic position overlooking the Jerusalem–Tel Aviv road. But Deir Yassin had signed a non-aggression pact with the neighboring Jewish village of Givat Shaul.[36] By most accounts, Deir Yassin was honoring this agreement and had repeatedly barred Arab fighters from the village.[37] Thus the decision to attack Deir Yassin was both morally and strategically questionable.

As they launched their operation, the Irgun and Lehi were willing to give up the element of surprise in order to warn the village's residents to flee. As they advanced toward Deir Yassin, they brought a truck with a bullhorn mounted on top to announce the impending attack. But the truck got stuck in a ditch on the village's outskirts and ended up issuing the warning from further away than planned.[38] While at least one Deir Yassin resident recalled clearly hearing the announcement, others claimed that they did not.[39] Whether because of the warning or the fighting, however, most of the village's population—including most of the able-bodied males—did in fact flee.[40] Those intent on perpetrating massacres neither give warnings nor permit flight.

As Jewish forces reached Deir Yassin, they encountered unexpectedly strong resistance in the form of sniper fire from houses.[41] By the end of the battle, over one-quarter of the Jewish attack force had been killed or wounded, including the operation's commander.[42] Thus the decision to fight house to house was legitimate.

In their fear and anger, however, these inexperienced Irgun and Lehi fighters employed excessive force. In some cases, hand grenades were thrown into houses. In other cases, houses were dynamited.[43] As historian Benny Morris explains, "The weight of the evidence suggests that the dissidents did not go in with the intention of committing a massacre but lost their heads during the protracted combat."[44]

Finally, there is the question of how the triumphant Jewish forces treated the residents of Deir Yassin after the battle was won. Widely publicized claims of wholesale slaughter, the rape of female prisoners, and the murder of pregnant women have all been disproven.[45] The Irgun and Lehi transported most of the survivors to East Jerusalem and released them.[46] Yet there is credible evidence that some of Deir Yassin's residents—both combatants and civilians—were killed after the fighting had ended.[47] Such murders are war crimes, pure and simple.

Palestine's mainstream Jewish leadership was quick to denounce the attack on Deir Yassin. The Haganah, the Jewish Agency, and the Jewish community's two chief rabbis all issued public condemnations. Ben Gurion wrote a letter of apology to King Abdullah regretting the "atrocity."[48] The Haganah soon forced the heretofore independent Irgun and Lehi militias to come under its command. It was the Haganah's code of ethics—not that of the dissidents—that would ultimately govern Israel's soldiers in the field.

Whatever happened in Deir Yassin, word quickly spread that the Jews had perpetrated a terrible massacre there. Many of these accounts were intentionally exaggerated in an effort to rally the Arab world against Palestine's Jews. But this publicity had a major unintended consequence. As the atrocity grew ever bloodier in the telling, it fueled the mounting communal panic. Arab flight from Palestine accelerated.

These claims of atrocities also provoked an immediate and terrible revenge. The very next day, Arab militias attacked a ten-vehicle convoy bound for Hadassah Hospital. Two buses filled with Jewish doctors, nurses, and students were unable to escape the onslaught. When the guards ran out of ammunition, the Arab attackers approached the buses and set them on fire.

By the end of the day, seventy-eight people—mostly medical personnel—had been murdered. Many were burned alive. Almost all of the victims had provided essential health care to both Jews and Arabs alike. Among the dead was an ophthalmologist named Chaim Yassky whose pioneering work on the eye disease trachoma had saved the eyesight of tens of thousands of Arabs.[49] The Arabs gave no warnings, no opportunities to flee, and no apologies.

No account of the 1948 War is complete without a discussion of Deir Yassin and the Jewish atrocities that this name has come to represent. But the existence of such exceptions must not blind us to the larger rule. From the start, Palestine's Jews battled against Arab opponents who intentionally targeted Jewish civilians. The fact that the Jews chose to hold themselves to a higher moral standard is laudable. The fact that they largely succeeded in meeting this higher standard is remarkable. The fact that some Jews may have chosen to follow the Arabs down the moral rabbit hole to terrorism is unusual only in how very rare it was.

THE PAN-ARAB INVASION

The British Mandate for Palestine was scheduled to end on May 15, 1948. On the morning of May 14, messengers delivered invitations to the members of the provisional Jewish legislature—the State Council— requesting their presence at the Tel Aviv Museum that afternoon. At the appointed time, David Ben Gurion read Israel's Declaration of Independence aloud to the gathered crowd. The Council members signed the document. The State of Israel was born.

That very day, Egyptian aircraft bombed Tel Aviv. That night, the armies of Egypt, Transjordan, Syria, and Iraq invaded Israel. Lebanon soon joined the attack. Saudi Arabia, Yemen, and Sudan sent troops to participate in the fighting. Arab volunteers streamed in from as far away as Morocco.

These Arab invaders openly and repeatedly declared their intention to do what the Palestinian militias had failed to do: destroy the Jewish state. As Arab League Secretary General Azzam Pasha so infamously phrased it: "This will be a war of extermination and momentous massacre which will be spoken of like the Mongolian massacre and the Crusades...."[50]

The Israelis facing this onslaught had every reason to fear the worst. The Israel Defense Forces—formed from the union of the Haganah, the Irgun, and the Lehi—were small in number, poorly trained, and pathetically equipped. According to some estimates, the Israelis had only one gun for every three soldiers. Israel had no real air force. And Israel's only artillery was a homemade device—the "Davidka"—that made a loud sound but did little actual damage.

The Arab invaders enjoyed clear quantitative and qualitative advantages. They had the ability to mobilize an invasion force many times larger than any defensive force the Israelis could muster. They could equip these soldiers with guns, ammunition, and artillery that dwarfed the Jewish supply. Egypt, Iraq, and Syria had air forces. Egypt and Syria had tanks. Transjordan's Arab Legion was British trained, British armed, and British commanded; it was by all accounts the best army in the Middle East.

Israel's top brass had grave doubts about their ability to survive this Arab offensive. On May 12—three days before the invasion—Ben Gurion summoned his chief commander, Yigael Yadin, to advise him of Israel's chances. Yadin's response could not have been encouraging: "I'd say that at the moment, our chances are about even. If I wanted to be more honest, I'd say that the other side has a significant edge."[51]

An August 1947 CIA report was equally pessimistic. It predicted that if war broke out between Israel and the surrounding Arab states, the Arabs would win.[52]

Israel's first major battle with an Arab army confirmed the worst of these fears. On May 12, Transjordan's Arab Legion jumped the gun on the official end of the British Mandate and joined local Palestinian militias in attacking Kibbutz Kfar Etzion on the outskirts of Jerusalem. On May 13, following a devastating artillery bombardment, the Arab Legion's armored cars penetrated the kibbutz perimeter. The surviving kibbutz fighters surrendered.

The victorious Arabs herded over one hundred kibbutz defenders into an open square and disarmed them. Then some of the Arabs opened fire on the prisoners. As their frenzy mounted, the Arabs pursued and killed fleeing captives and mutilated the bodies of those already dead. Before this bloody day was over, all but 4 of the 134 disarmed defenders of Kibbutz Kfar Etzion had been murdered.[53]

In the days that followed, Transjordan's Arab Legion and its Palestinian allies conquered three additional Jewish communities near Kfar Etzion. They destroyed all of them. Many of the residents were killed. The remainder were expelled.

The Israelis suffered yet another major defeat in one of the first battles to follow Israel's Declaration of Independence. On May 19, Transjordan's Arab Legion attacked the Jewish Quarter of Jerusalem's Old City. They systematically blew up each building they captured, including the ancient Hurva Synagogue. On May 28, the Jewish Quarter's defenders surrendered. Transjordan expelled every last Jew from the Old City.

These early incidents set the pattern for what was to follow. During the course of the 1948 War, the Transjordanian, Syrian, and Egyptian armies conquered twelve additional Jewish communities. They destroyed every single one of them. Any residents who survived the fighting were either murdered or expelled.[54] When the Arabs won a battle, the expulsion of Jews from their homes was not an extreme measure; it was as good as it got.

ISRAEL TURNS THE TIDE

After declaring its independence, Israel immediately opened its doors to the hundreds of thousands of Holocaust survivors who had been languishing in Europe's displaced persons camps. Upon their arrival in Israel, those who were physically able were immediately drafted into the army. Approximately one-third of Israel's dead in the 1948 War were Holocaust survivors.

In addition to people, Israel also began receiving arms. In the early months of the conflict, the international community had imposed an arms embargo on both the well-armed Arabs and the poorly armed Jews. The United States strictly maintained this embargo throughout the war. But the Soviet Union eventually permitted Czechoslovakia to sell arms to Palestine's Jews. By the time Israel declared its independence, shipments of Czech arms—including planes and artillery—were steadily improving Israel's combat capabilities.

Thus reinforced with men and materiel, the Israel Defense Forces began to turn the tide against the Arab invaders. These battles were often louder and bloodier than those of the civil war. They therefore triggered an even larger Arab exodus. Israel also continued to make more direct contributions to the refugee crisis by expelling the residents of hostile towns and villages.

THE EXPULSIONS FROM RAMLE
AND LYDDA

By far the largest of these Israeli expulsions occurred in the neighboring towns of Ramle and Lydda. This was the only time Israel expelled a substantial urban population. The approximately fifty thousand people forced from these two towns account for almost ten percent of the war's Arab refugees.

Lydda and Ramle are located in Israel's strategic heartland. They sit astride the Tel Aviv–Jerusalem road that was so critical to the survival of Jewish Jerusalem. They border what was and remains the country's only international airport. And, most important, these towns are only ten miles outside of Tel Aviv.

In mid-May 1948, Transjordan's Arab Legion seized Lydda and Ramle. From this point on, Israel's leaders feared that these towns would serve as the forward base from which Transjordan would attack Tel Aviv. By July, the conquest of Lydda and Ramle had become one of Ben Gurion's top strategic priorities.

On July 9, two Israeli brigades surrounded the towns. An aerial bombardment followed. On July 11, the Israelis launched a ground offensive. A battalion approaching Lydda from the east encountered sustained machine-gun fire and spent much of the day pinned down in an olive grove before battling its way into town.[55] Another battalion—led by future general Moshe Dayan—broke through heavy resistance and sped through Lydda, shooting up militia outposts and, by some reports, "spraying machine-gun fire at anything that moved."[56]

By the end of the day, most of Ramle and Lydda were in Israel's hands. The Arab Legion had largely withdrawn.[57] Only a small group of Arab Legionnaires and Palestinian militiamen were still holding out at Lydda's police station.[58]

At this point, both towns offered to surrender. The Israelis agreed to accept their surrender—and to permit peaceful residents to remain—provided that all combatants relinquished their weapons within twenty-four hours.[59] But when Lydda's mayor went to the police station to convince the remaining fighters to lay down their arms, they murdered him in a hail of bullets. No weapons were turned in. The battle for Lydda was still on.[60]

The next day, July 12, two or three Transjordanian armored cars entered Lydda on what appeared to be a reconnaissance mission.[61] A firefight erupted. Believing that the Transjordanians had come to liberate them, many of Lydda's residents began firing at the Israelis from their windows and roofs. Grenades were thrown. Five Israeli guards outside the Dahmash mosque were killed and their bodies mutilated.

Israeli commanders feared the worst. They and their approximately 350 soldiers were occupying a town of 20,000 Arabs. It now appeared that the Transjordanians were launching a counterattack and that Lydda's Arabs were rising up to help them. Israeli forces were ordered to aggressively suppress the sniping before the resistance spread.[62] By the end of the day, Lydda was quiet.

Yet the Israelis still faced a perilous situation. Transjordanian troops were massing east of Lydda, threatening to counterattack at any moment.[63] The day's events had highlighted the likelihood that any such counterattack would be accompanied by a mass uprising. The Israeli commanders decided that they couldn't leave an armed and hostile population in their rear as they left to confront the Transjordanians in the east. On July 13, those residents of Ramle and Lydda who had not yet fled were forcibly expelled.[64]

As with Deir Yassin, there is a general consensus that the Israelis committed war crimes in Lydda. Upwards of three hundred of Lydda's residents were killed in the fighting, including many unarmed civilians. By their own testimony, it's clear that some Israeli soldiers overreacted to perceived dangers and failed to distinguish between civilians and combatants. There are even reports that some soldiers intentionally shot wounded prisoners and civilians.[65] Then came Israel's largest and most brutal expulsion. The town's residents—including the very old and the very young—were forced to walk over ten miles in the July heat without sufficient water or food. "Quite a few"[66] and possibly "dozens"[67] died on the way.

Even in the heat of this battle, many Israelis argued against expelling the Arabs of Lydda and Ramle. Among these dissenters were future Prime Minister Moshe Sharett and Minority Affairs Minister Bechor Shitrit. Future Prime Minister Yitzhak Rabin, who ordered the expulsions, noted, "Psychologically, this was one of the most difficult actions we undertook."[68]

Israel's most celebrated poet, Natan Alterman, condemned Israel's behavior in Lydda in a poem called "On This." David Ben Gurion ordered that the poem be distributed to every soldier in the army.[69] Before the war was over, three separate investigations into IDF excesses were conducted and strict new rules on the treatment of civilians were issued.[70]

From the safe distance of Israel's ultimate victory, many more Israelis have come to view the expulsions from Lydda and Ramle as the nation's moral nadir. This soul searching over Israel's actions in these two towns—which continues down to the present day—is a healthy sign of a moral society. But once again this focus on Israel's behavior tends to obscure the broader context in which these actions were taken. As a result, difficult decisions made in the midst of terrible circumstances are often portrayed as acts of pure aggression.

It is therefore important to remember that the 1947 United Nations Partition plan had actually assigned both Lydda and Ramle to the proposed Arab state. Had the Palestinian Arabs not rejected partition in November 1947, there would not have been a war. Had the Arab states not invaded Israel in May 1948, Lydda would not have become such a significant strategic objective. Had Lydda not resisted, there would have been no reason to conquer the town by force. And had Lydda actually surrendered instead of resuming hostilities at the first sign of a

Transjordanian counterattack, there would have been no need to expel its residents.

Ben Gurion summed up his government's thinking at the time: "We did not start the war. They made the war. Jaffa waged war on us, Haifa waged war on us, Beisan waged war on us. And I do not want them again to make war. That would not be just but foolish.... Do we have to make the war, which is already fought in inhuman conditions, even more difficult for us? Will it be easier for us if, while fighting the Arab Legion in Nablus, we will also have to fight Arabs near Tel Aviv?"[71]

It is difficult to imagine that many statesmen facing similar circumstances would dispute this logic.

Over the course of the months that followed, the Israeli army continued to grow in numbers, arms, experience, and strength. In time, the Israelis drove the Syrians and Lebanese out of the north. After losing Jerusalem's Jewish Quarter, they stopped the Transjordanian advance from the east. And, lastly, they were able to push the Egyptians out of the south.

The 1948 War formally ended with the signing of armistice agreements between Israel and her four immediate neighbors during the early months of 1949. Only Iraq refused to sign one. At the war's end, Transjordan and Egypt occupied most of the land that the UN partition plan had set aside for an Arab state in Palestine.

THE ARAB REFUGEES

By the time the war was over, between six and eight hundred thousand Palestinian Arabs had left their homes in what became Israel. They were now refugees in the parts of Palestine ruled by Transjordan and Egypt as well as in neighboring Arab countries.

For decades to follow, Israel and her supporters offered a simple explanation for this exodus. These Palestinian Arabs left their homes, we were told, because they were ordered to do so by their own leaders. Under this narrative, Arab generals forced Arab civilians out of harm's way so that Arab armies could safely drive the Jews into the sea.

But recent research, mostly by Israeli scholars, has debunked this simplistic account. One scholar in particular, Benny Morris, earned the enmity of many of his fellow Israelis by uncovering and publishing a number of hidden truths about Israel's War of Independence. It was Morris who first documented the multiple instances in which the Israelis did in fact expel Arabs from their homes.

Ironically, Morris's scholarship, which debunked a pro-Israel oversimplification of history, is now being twisted to support an anti-Israel oversimplification. Israel's detractors have long argued that the Israelis expelled Palestine's Arabs in order to ethnically cleanse the new Jewish state. Those making this claim now cite Morris as their source.

Yet Morris's work lends itself to no such argument. He demonstrates quite clearly that while Israeli expulsions did take place, they were motivated by military necessity, not racial animosity. And his research further shows that these Israeli expulsions produced only a minority of the refugees. Many Arabs were in fact ordered to leave their homes by Arab leaders and commanders. And the large majority of Arab refugees fled on their own initiative—because they were afraid of a war being fought in their towns, villages, and neighborhoods.

The voluntary nature of the Arab exodus from Palestine is highlighted by the fact that it began well before the outbreak of hostilities. Many of Palestine's Arabs had friends, relatives, and even homes in neighboring Arab countries. As war grew increasingly likely toward the end of 1947, thousands of those with the means to do so simply removed themselves from harm's way.

This flight continued apace during the first four months of the war. During this period the Haganah maintained a purely defensive posture. Jewish forces were not destroying Arab villages or expelling their inhabitants. Yet the Arabs of Palestine nevertheless fled in droves. By the end of March 1948, between seventy-five and a hundred thousand Arabs had already left the territory that would become Israel.[72]

Most of Palestine's wealthy and middle-class Arab families fled during these early months. So too did most of the leaders of the Mufti's Arab Higher Committee.[73] Those who didn't leave often sent away their wives, children, and elderly family members.

The departure of the middle class brought Palestine's Arab economy to a standstill. Factories, businesses, and stores closed. Prices and unemployment soared. By the end of April, every last Arab bank in Palestine had shut its doors. As the Arab economy deteriorated, the Arab exodus accelerated.[74] Between April 1 and the May 15 Arab invasion, the number of Arab refugees grew to approximately three hundred thousand.

Israel's decision to seize the strategic initiative in April 1948 certainly contributed to this second wave of refugees. Just as in the first wave, however, most of those who left during this period did so by choice. As we've seen, Israel's capture of Haifa and Jaffa sparked a spontaneous Arab exodus from both towns. Once the Arabs had left these cities, most of the Arabs living in the surrounding villages followed.[75]

Starting in April, Haganah field commanders had the authority to expel Arabs and destroy villages that resisted or might otherwise threaten Israel. Yet, as Benny Morris has observed, throughout this second phase of the civil war, "Relatively few commanders faced the moral dilemma of having to carry out the expulsion clauses. Townspeople and villages usually left their homes before or during battle, and Haganah commanders rarely had to decide about, or issue, expulsion orders."[76]

The May 15 Arab invasion unleashed a third and final wave of refugees. During this phase, Israel engaged in its largest expulsions, including those from Lydda and Ramle. Yet even at this late date, Israeli policy was driven by strategy, not race. Villages that fought the Israelis were typically the ones to be destroyed. Villages that offered no such resistance were almost always left in peace.

Simply put, the Arab tragedy of 1948 was the direct result of the Arab aggression of 1948. Like every army, Israel's was certainly guilty of mistakes and excesses. Yet most of this Arab suffering flowed from only one Israeli action: the decision to fight back and survive.

The ultimate rebuttal to the claim that Israel ethnically cleansed the Arabs living within its borders is the fact that a hundred and fifty thousand Arabs still lived in Israel after the war was over. This total includes those Arabs who chose not to flee Haifa and Jaffa. It includes the residents of most of the Arab villages that decided not to take up arms against Israel. It even includes hundreds of Arabs who returned to Lydda and Ramla in the days following their expulsion.

These Arabs and their descendants now number over 1.7 million people. Israel's actual Arab population thus long ago surpassed Israel's pre-war Arab population. As a result, one in every five Israeli citizens is Arab. Galilee—where many Arab villages peacefully accepted or even requested inclusion within Israel—is majority Arab.[77]

CHAPTER SEVEN

ISRAEL ENCOUNTERS PALESTINIAN NATIONALISM

We have to compromise in the name of peace, to give up parts of our promised land in which every hill and every valley is saturated with Jewish history and in which our heroes are buried. We have to relinquish our dream to leave room for the dream of others so that all of us can enjoy a better future.

—Israeli Prime Minister Ehud Olmert, 2006[1]

In March 1969, Golda Meir became Israel's fourth prime minister. Shortly thereafter, she gave an interview to London's *Sunday Times*. In the course of a wide-ranging conversation, Meir shared her understanding of Palestinian history: "There were no such thing as Palestinians. When was there an independent Palestinian people with a Palestinian state? It was either southern Syria before the First World War, and then it was a Palestine including Jordan. It was not as though there was a Palestinian people in Palestine considering itself as a Palestinian people and we came and threw them out and took their country away from them. They did not exist."[2]

To this day, Israel's critics delight in trotting out this quote. Here, they claim, is the prime minister of Israel denying the very existence of the Palestinian people.

But Meir was saying nothing of the sort. It is important to note her use of the past tense—there "were" no such thing as Palestinians. In

151

other words, Meir was commenting on history, not current events. And the historical claim she made was absolutely correct.

What is truly surprising about this quote is not Meir's understanding of the past but her apparent willingness to reevaluate the present. Meir gave this interview a mere two years after the 1967 War. She spoke at a time when a separate Palestinian identity was just starting to emerge as the preference of the majority of Palestine's Arabs. Yet Meir seemed to be adjusting in real time to the shifting identity of her neighbors.

After the 1967 War, Palestine's Arabs increasingly emphasized their unique Palestinian identity over their shared Arab identity. As they came to see themselves as a separate people distinct from their Arab neighbors, the Palestinians argued that their national aspirations could no longer be satisfied in adjacent Arab states. They therefore stopped discussing Palestine in the context of the irredentist Arab claim to rule every last inch of the vast lands on which Arabs lived. They spoke instead of seeking for the Palestinian people that most basic of rights, the right to self-determination.

The rise of Palestinian nationalism effectively narrowed the zone of potential Arab-Israeli compromise to Palestine itself. The only way that both Jewish and Palestinian nationalism could be satisfied would be for these two peoples claiming the same land to divide it between them—a two-state solution. Yet while the names of the parties may have changed, this concept was hardly new. Palestine's Jews had already demonstrated their willingness to split this land with their Arab neighbors in 1937 and again in 1947. The Arabs of Palestine had rejected both of these compromises. Instead of agreeing to split the land with the Jews they strove to destroy the Jewish state.

All of this could have changed in 1968. That year, Yasser Arafat took over the Palestine Liberation Organization and replaced the Mufti as the leader of the Palestinian national movement. Tragically, however, Arafat and his colleagues chose to follow in the failed footsteps of their forefathers. The PLO explicitly rejected recognition of Israel, negotiations with Israel, and compromise with Israel. Instead, they became terrorist pioneers who dedicated their full energies to finding innovative ways to murder Israelis.

It would take over two decades for the PLO to revisit their rejectionism and agree to negotiate with Israel. As soon as the PLO so much as mouthed the word "peace," Israel jumped at the chance to negotiate with these recently reformed terrorists. Tragically, time would prove that terrorism is a hard habit to break.

The Jewish people have a history extending back over three thousand years. There are few peoples on earth who can document a longer existence as a distinct national group with a unique culture, language, and passionate connection to a specific strip of earth. Yet most Jews have been quick to recognize one of the newest peoples on the planet: the Palestinians. Given this vast age gap, Israel's rapid recognition of Palestinian national claims is stunning in its generosity.

THE WORLD AND THE PALESTINIANS

If in 1969 Golda Meir was not yet certain that there was such a thing as a Palestinian people, she was far from alone. At this juncture, neither the United Nations nor the Arab League recognized the existence of such a people. In fact, it's far from clear that a majority of Palestine's Arabs would have characterized themselves as Palestinians at the time.

Barely two decades earlier, in 1947, the United Nations General Assembly had voted to partition Palestine into two states. The text of the partition resolution stipulates that "Independent Arab and Jewish States…shall come into existence in Palestine." Throughout the remainder of the resolution, the terms "Arab State" and "Jewish State" are used to describe the entities that will come into being, and the terms "Arab" and "Jew" are used to describe the individuals who will inhabit these entities.

As this language makes clear, all of the parties involved in drafting the 1947 partition resolution believed they were creating yet another

Arab state, not the first Palestinian state. No one thought to call this proposed entity a "Palestinian state" because almost no one viewed the Arabs of Palestine as a separate "Palestinian" people. All concerned— including the Arab and Muslim nations that so vehemently opposed this resolution—saw these individuals as Arabs living in a small corner of the Arab world called Palestine.

Yet this proposed Arab state never came into existence. Instead of accepting their own state, the Arabs of Palestine fought alongside their Arab neighbors to destroy the Jewish state. In the course of the war that followed, Transjordan conquered the West Bank and Egypt conquered Gaza. The large majority of the land allocated for the Arab state in Palestine was now occupied by other Arab states. For the next two decades, there was little talk of an Arab state in Palestine or a separate Palestinian people.

In the 1967 War, Israel seized the West Bank from Jordan and the Gaza Strip from Egypt. The United Nations Security Council responded by passing Resolution 242, which urged the parties to respect the territorial integrity and independence of "every State" involved. This resolution refers to the people who would later become the Palestinians only once, when it calls on the parties to achieve "a just settlement of the refugee problem." Two years later, in 1969, the United Nations was still referring to the Palestinians as "Palestine Arab Refugees."

The year 1974 was a watershed in the emergence of a separate Palestinian identity. That year, the Arab League met in Rabat, Morocco, and unanimously passed a resolution that for the first time recognized the Palestinian right to "self-determination" and to "establish an independent national authority." The Arab League also recognized the PLO as the "sole legitimate representative of the Palestinian people." While Jordan reluctantly consented to these resolutions, it did not officially relinquish its claim to the West Bank until 1988.

Now that the Arabs had decided that the Palestinians constituted a separate people, the United Nations quickly followed suit. On November 13, 1974, Yasser Arafat infamously addressed the UN General Assembly with a pistol on his hip. On November 22, the General Assembly passed

Resolution 3236 recognizing the existence of the Palestinian people and their right to "self-determination," "national independence," and "sovereignty."

THE 1967 WAR: ANOTHER LOST OPPORTUNITY

Far from being slow to recognize the Palestinians as a new people, the Israelis were actually the first major player in the Middle East to explore Palestinian autonomy and independence. The Israelis acted well before the Arab League and the United Nations had accepted the Palestinians as a separate people. In fact, the Israelis acted before the Palestinians themselves had fully come to terms with their own emerging identity. In retrospect, the Israelis acted prematurely.

Less than ten days after the end of the 1967 War—on June 19, 1967—the Israeli cabinet met to debate the future of the vast new territories they now controlled. These victorious leaders made some surprising decisions. They voted to authorize the government to return Sinai to Egypt and the Golan Heights to Syria in exchange for peace treaties with these nations.

Israel's position regarding the territory won from Jordan was more complex. The cabinet quickly annexed to Israel those sections of Jerusalem that had been occupied by Jordan since the 1948 War. But when it came to the rest of the territory the Jordanians had controlled—what is now known as the West Bank—the government ministers were largely divided between two competing options. Unable to break their deadlock, they postponed a final decision.

One group of ministers wanted to return most of the West Bank to Jordan in exchange for a peace treaty. But another bloc feared that King Hussein would soon be overthrown and that Jordan's new masters would not honor any peace commitments he made. Instead of giving the West Bank to the Jordanians, these ministers proposed creating an autonomous Palestinian entity on the West Bank that could develop into a Palestinian state.

Israeli Prime Minister Levi Eshkol favored the Palestinian option. Eager to make this entity a reality, he sent a team into the West Bank that summer to see if the local leaders would accept self-rule. Israeli author (and later ambassador to the United States) Michael Oren summarized their findings: "Eighty Palestinian notables were interviewed that summer…and each of them came back, more or less, with the same answer. They said, 'Gee, you know, we'd really like to be autonomous. We'd love to be independent someday. But if we make a treaty with Israel at this time, Arab radicals will kill us. We'll get a bullet in the head.' So that initiative withered on the vine and never got anywhere."[3]

These local leaders were hardly exaggerating. King Hussein, who wanted the West Bank returned to Jordan, worked to undermine Eshkol's efforts at every turn. Egypt's Nasser rejected any option that did not include the return of East Jerusalem to the Arabs.[4] And the PLO and its leaders violently opposed any compromise whatsoever with Israel.

Before long, the Arabs dashed Israel's hopes that it could trade the land it had won in 1967 for peace. In late August, the Arab League met in Khartoum, Sudan, to formulate their post-war policy toward Israel. On September 1, they issued the infamous Khartoum Resolution. Article 3 of the resolution stated that there would be "no peace with Israel, no recognition of Israel, no negotiations with it." These "Three No's" could not have been any clearer. They closed the door to the negotiations the Israelis authorized on June 19th.

YASSER ARAFAT: NEW LEADER, SAME REJECTIONISM

Their crushing defeat in the 1967 War severely weakened most of the competitors for leadership of Palestine's Arabs. Following this debacle, Egypt's President Nasser experienced a steady political and physical decline. By 1970, he was dead. Syria and its Palestinian front groups suffered a similar post-war slump. And because he had lost the West Bank to Israel, Jordan's King Hussein could no longer exercise the direct control that had enabled him to compete for the hearts and minds of Palestine's Arabs.

Into this void stepped Yasser Arafat. Arafat had founded an organization called *Fatah* in 1959. Unlike the Palestine Liberation Organization
(PLO)—originally created and controlled by Nasser—Fatah was an
authentic Palestinian nationalist movement. Arafat and the other Fatah
founders argued that the Palestinians needed to stop waiting for Egypt,
Syria, or any other Arab power to liberate them; they needed to step up
and free themselves. With these rivals now sidelined, Arafat seized control of the PLO in 1968. For the first time since the heyday of the Mufti,
a Palestinian Arab was leading the Arabs of Palestine. Arafat would
continue to dominate the Palestinian national movement until his death
in 2004.

Now that the Palestinians had taken control of their fate, they could
have embarked on a practical path. They could have pursued a two-state
solution similar to those their leaders had rejected in 1937 and 1947.
There is every reason to believe that the Israelis would have welcomed
such an overture. After all, they had taken the lead in exploring this very
solution less than one year earlier.

Tragically, these new Palestinian leaders made a different choice. The
Mufti was now sidelined, and by 1974 he would be dead. But his spirit
was alive and well in his young successor. Arafat, like the Mufti, saw the
conflict over Palestine as a zero-sum game in which there could be only
one winner who would take all. Arafat, like the Mufti, was dedicated to
taking all by destroying Israel. And Arafat, like the Mufti, saw terrorism—the intentional murder of civilians—as a legitimate tool with which
to accomplish this goal.

The PLO Charter adopted following the Fatah takeover in 1968
could have been written by the Mufti himself. It refuses to recognize
Israel, stating, "The partition of Palestine in 1947 and the establishment
of the state of Israel are entirely illegal." The Charter also refuses to
recognize the existence of the Jewish people, claiming, "Judaism, being
a religion, is not a nationality." It even goes so far as to deny any "historical or religious ties" between the Jewish religion and Palestine.

Like the "Three No's" of Khartoum, the PLO Charter rejects not
only recognition of Israel, but also negotiations with Israel. "The Arab

Palestinian people," it states, "reject all solutions which are substitutes for the total liberation of Palestine." And if negotiations are out, then only one path remains. In the words of the Charter, "Armed struggle is the only way to liberate Palestine."[5]

Fatah's efforts at armed struggle had begun a few years earlier, in 1965, with a failed attempt to blow up Israel's National Water Carrier. Finding it difficult to strike hard targets in Israel, Fatah quickly shifted its focus to soft targets—that is civilians—both in Israel and abroad. Under Arafat's control, the PLO quickly became the chief pioneer and practitioner of international terrorism.

While the list of PLO atrocities is too long to catalogue here, it's worth reviewing some of the bloodier attacks that made the PLO the most notorious terrorist organization of the 1970s. In 1970, PLO terrorists fired a bazooka at an Israeli school bus, killing nine students and three teachers. In 1972, Fatah's "Black September" faction kidnapped and murdered eleven Israeli athletes at the Munich Olympics. In 1974, PLO terrorists attacked a school in the northern Israeli town of Ma'alot, killing twenty-one children and five adults. In 1978, PLO terrorists hijacked a bus on Israel's Coastal Highway and killed twenty-one Israelis.

Israel and the United States agreed that so long as the PLO's leaders were dedicated to Israel's destruction in both word and deed there was nothing to be gained from talking to them. It was clear to all that Israel—which had welcomed a two-state solution in 1937 and 1947 and seriously explored the prospect again in 1967—had no alternative but to wait for a Palestinian partner willing to compromise.

ARAFAT FLIRTS WITH COMPROMISE

In December 1987, the Palestinians of the West Bank and Gaza rose up in protest against Israel's continuing control of these territories. This uprising—which came to be known as the First Intifada—was a largely local initiative. It was thus seen as a sign that a new, homegrown Palestinian leadership might replace the aging PLO terrorists living abroad.

The PLO bosses realized that they needed to take radical action to remain relevant. The United States had long maintained that it would not recognize the PLO unless it first renounced terrorism and recognized Israel's right to exist. Thus in December 1988, Arafat held a press conference in Geneva in which he spoke a pre-negotiated set of words through which he appeared to do both.

The day after Arafat uttered these words, U.S. President Ronald Reagan announced the start of a "substantive dialogue" with the PLO. Israel was not as quick to take Arafat at his word. His conversion from arch terrorist to man of peace had been far too ambiguous. And the PLO Charter calling for an "armed struggle" to destroy Israel was still in full effect. Israel decided to wait and see if Arafat's reluctant words would be met with more persuasive action.

Israel's skepticism proved to be prescient. In 1990, the Palestine Liberation Front attempted to land a raft of armed terrorists on the Tel Aviv beach. Israel's navy thwarted the attack. The Palestine Liberation Front's leader Abu Abbas was a member of the PLO's executive committee. When Arafat refused to fire Abbas, the United States concluded that the PLO had failed to live up to its commitments. President George H. W. Bush suspended the dialogue between the U.S. and the PLO that had begun a mere two years earlier.

Despite the fiasco that was Arafat's renunciation of terrorism, the fact that he even made the effort fueled the hopes of many Israelis. In 1993, a group of Israeli negotiators met secretly with their PLO counterparts in Oslo, Norway. There these two teams made significant progress in delineating the broad outlines of a peace deal.

On September 9, 1993, Israeli Prime Minister Yitzhak Rabin and Arafat exchanged pre-arranged letters that removed the final barriers to direct negotiations between Israel and the PLO. Arafat wrote to Rabin that the PLO recognized "the right of the State of Israel to exist in peace and security" and renounced "the use of terrorism and other acts of violence." Rabin replied to Arafat that same day stating that, in light of these dual commitments, "the Government of Israel has decided to recognize the PLO as the representative of the Palestinian people and commence negotiations with the PLO within the Middle East peace process."

Arafat's letter to Rabin persuaded not only the Israelis to talk to the PLO; it also convinced the Americans. The next day, President Clinton resumed the U.S.-PLO dialogue that had been suspended in 1990.

In 1993, for the first time in their history, the Palestinians stopped insisting that their conflict with Israel was a zero-sum game. Instead of vowing to destroy and replace Israel, the PLO was now committing itself to share the land with Israel.

There was still plenty of cause for concern. While Arafat had made peaceful statements in English, he was quick to contradict them with troubling pronouncements in Arabic. And mere words had yet to be backed up with any kind of meaningful action. Yet, despite the warning signs, the Israelis were determined to pursue peace in both word and very risky deed.

THE OSLO PROCESS

On September 13, 1993, Israel and the PLO formalized their prior understandings by signing the Oslo Accords at a ceremony on the White House lawn. With some prodding from President Clinton, Rabin and Arafat shook hands for the first time. Expectations of peace and a new Middle East ran high.

The Oslo strategy was based on the premise that Palestinians and Israelis had been too hostile for too long to immediately settle their most contentious disagreements—namely Jerusalem, refugees, and settlements. The parties therefore decided to begin the peace process with an "interim period" of no more than five years during which they would undertake a series of confidence-building measures. As each side reaped the benefits of this process, it was hoped, public support for peace—and the painful concessions it required—would grow.

The core of the confidence-building measures was a phased exchange of land for peace. The Israelis agreed to cede increasing amounts of territory in Gaza and the West Bank to Palestinian control. In return, the Palestinians pledged to provide "peace" by preventing attacks against Israel from this territory.

Israel upheld its main Oslo commitments. Shortly after the 1993 signing ceremony, Israel withdrew from Gaza City and Jericho and ceded civilian authority over those areas to the PLO. Following the signing of the Oslo II Accords in September 1995, Israel surrendered control of the West Bank's major Palestinian cities—Bethlehem, Jenin, Nablus, Kalkilya, Ramallah, Tulkarem, and Hebron—as well as almost all of the West Bank's approximately 450 Palestinian towns and villages. By the end of the year, all of the West Bank's major Palestinian population centers were under Palestinian administration.[6]

From early in the process, however, the Palestinians proved unable to uphold their primary Oslo commitment to stop terror attacks from their territory. Following the signing of the Oslo Accords, terrorism against Israel did not stop or even decrease; *it dramatically increased.* In fact the horror of Palestinian suicide bombers blowing up Israeli buses, restaurants, and cafes was a purely post-Olso phenomenon. In their effort to derail the peace process, Palestinian terrorists made the suicide bomber their new weapon of choice.

At first, Prime Minister Rabin was determined not to let these attacks push Israel from the path of peace. After each bloody bombing, Rabin took to the airwaves to remind the Israeli public that the terrorists' goal was to undermine the peace process. Therefore, he argued, Israel must not reward the terrorists with the very prize they sought. As the death toll continued to mount, Rabin stoically persevered with the negotiations and the withdrawals.

Yet Arafat's behavior soon undermined Rabin's premise. It became increasingly apparent that Arafat was doing little to stop the terror. On occasion, usually in the aftermath of some of the bloodier attacks,

Arafat would arrest some of the perpetrators. But these killers would typically be released once the initial furor had passed. The serious security crackdown that could have ended the bloodshed simply never came.

We will never know how long Rabin's determination to press on despite the attacks would have lasted. On November 4, 1995, Rabin was assassinated by a Jewish fanatic opposed to Oslo's territorial concessions. In the elections that followed, Benjamin Netanyahu was chosen to replace him. In light of the suicide bombings and Arafat's refusal to battle those responsible, Netanyahu pledged to slow the pace at which Israel was handing territory over to Arafat's control.

EHUD BARAK TRIES AGAIN

Despite these setbacks, the Oslo process had unleashed messianic hopes for peace among Israelis, and these hopes did not easily die. Thus while they chose to slow the process, the Israelis never abandoned it. In fact, a few years after electing Netanyahu, the Israelis did something truly remarkable: they doubled down on peace.

When Israelis went to the polls in 1999, they ousted Netanyahu and gave a landslide victory to the Labor Party's Ehud Barak. Barak, the most decorated soldier in Israel's history, had a fabled background as an elite commando. Yet he had campaigned on a platform of reviving the stalled peace process and fulfilling the legacy of his slain mentor, Yitzhak Rabin. Barak soon proved to be as aggressive in pursuing peace as he had once been in hunting terrorists.

Barak's main critique of the peace process was that it was moving too slowly. Israel's gradual territorial concessions were failing to build Palestinian support for peace. Barak believed that the ultimate product of a peace deal—Palestinian independence—was the powerful prize that would finally empower Palestinian moderates to defeat their rejectionist rivals. Thus he proposed skipping the interim steps and jumping right to final status negotiations in order to bestow this prize upon the Palestinians as quickly as possible.

As the talks progressed, President Clinton offered to host both sides in the U.S. where he could help them bridge their remaining gaps. In July 2000, President Clinton, Prime Minister Barak, and Chairman Arafat arrived at the presidential retreat at Camp David for what would prove to be an intensive two weeks of negotiations.

Determined to seize what he saw as an historic opportunity, Barak made a series of increasingly generous offers to Arafat. At the start of the summit, Barak proposed giving the Palestinians all of the Gaza Strip and some 80 percent of the West Bank. By the summit's end, Barak had increased his offer to Gaza plus a full 91 percent of the West Bank, as well as territory from Israel proper equal to an additional one percent of the West Bank.[7] The land Barak offered to Arafat included most of Arab East Jerusalem, which could have served as the Palestinian capital.

Barak was risking his political future, and he knew it. His offer went far beyond what Rabin had ever proposed and what the Israeli public seemed willing to support. Indeed, Yitzhak Rabin's widow, Leah, criticized Barak's offer to relinquish East Jerusalem by noting, "Yitzhak never would have accepted this."[8] Chief U.S. negotiator Dennis Ross wrote that CIA director George Tenet was "astounded" by what Barak had offered and "asked incredulously, 'Why hasn't Arafat accepted this?'"[9]

Yet Arafat did not accept Barak's offer. Nor did he make a counteroffer. Instead, Arafat simply said "No" to each of the increasingly generous proposals that was made to him at Camp David. At the close of the summit, President Clinton "blew up" at Arafat, yelling that the Palestinian leader had "been here fourteen days and said no to everything."[10]

The real heartbreak was yet to come. Less than two months after Camp David, the Palestinians launched the Second Intifada. Unlike the First Intifada—in which the weapons had largely been limited to stones and petrol bombs—this uprising would be characterized by far more deadly methods. And before it was over, more than one thousand Israelis would be dead.

The Palestinians initially claimed that the Second Intifada was a spontaneous outburst of Palestinian rage. They suggested that Israeli opposition leader Ariel Sharon had provoked the uprising by visiting the

Temple Mount in Jerusalem, a sensitive site holy to both Jews and Muslims. But this claim ignored the fact that Sharon's visit had been pre-approved by the Palestinian security forces. It also overlooked the reality that other Israeli leaders had repeatedly visited the site without incident.

Before long, facts emerged that once again demonstrated Arafat's complicity in the very violence he condemned. For starters, Arafat never ordered his security forces to end the increasingly violent demonstrations that marked the start of the intifada. In fact, he never even ordered his security forces to stop *participating* in those demonstrations.[11] By failing to crack down on this unrest, Arafat gave those behind it a green light to keep going. As Dennis Ross has noted, "We now know that Arafat did not lift a finger to stop the demonstrations, which produced the second Intifada, the next day or in succeeding days."[12]

A number of sources close to Arafat—including Palestinian cabinet minister Imad Falouji[13] and Fatah commander Mamduh Nofal[14]—have claimed that Arafat not only permitted the intifada but was actually the one who ordered it. In 2010, Hamas leader Mahmoud Zahar told a gathering at Gaza's Islamic University, "President Arafat instructed Hamas to carry out a number of military operations in the heart of the Zionist entity after he felt that his negotiations with the Israeli government then had failed."[15]

In 2012, Arafat's widow Suha told a surprisingly similar story. In an interview with Dubai TV, she stated, "Immediately after the failure of Camp David, I met him [Arafat] in Paris upon his return.... Camp David had failed, and he said to me, 'You should remain in Paris.' I asked him why, and he said, 'Because I am going to start an intifada. They want me to betray the Palestinian cause. They want me to give up on our principles, and I will not do so.'"[16]

No matter what his role in starting the Second Intifada, there can be no denying that Arafat eventually became a full participant in it. The tragic fact is that these suicide attacks proved to be extremely popular on the Palestinian street. As Hamas and Palestinian Islamic Jihad bombed their way to prominence, Arafat and his colleagues decided to compete by launching attacks of their own. And Fatah proved to be a fierce competitor. Many of the bloodiest suicide bombings of the Second Intifada were carried out by two Fatah militias: the al-Aqsa Martyrs Brigade and the Tanzim.

Yet while these attacks boosted Fatah's popularity at home, they threatened its standing abroad as a serious partner for peace. Thus Arafat and his colleagues denied all responsibility for them. Try though they might, they claimed, they simply couldn't control the actions of their hotheaded young subordinates in these two Fatah militias. Those familiar with Arafat's iron grip over Fatah immediately dismissed such claims. And, before long, they had evidence to prove their point.

In March 2002, Israel raided Arafat's compound in Ramallah and removed reams of documents. Among these were records proving that one of Arafat's top deputies, Fouad al-Shoubaki, had regularly distributed funds to the al-Aqsa Martyrs Brigade.[17] The records further showed that Arafat himself had authorized a $20,000 payment to this militia.[18] In late 2003, a BBC investigation revealed that the Palestinian Authority was still sending "up to $50,000 a month" to the al-Aqsa Martyrs Brigade.[19]

THE CLINTON PARAMETERS

Arafat's complicity in the Second Intifada should have alerted both Israel and the United States that their "partner for peace" was not the man they hoped he was. Yet both Barak and Clinton were deeply invested in the peace process and determined to overcome what they believed to be the few remaining obstacles to an historic breakthrough. They pressed ahead despite the warning signs.

On December 23, 2000, President Clinton sent the Israelis and Palestinians a series of proposals for bridging the outstanding differences between them. These "Clinton Parameters" were for all intents and purposes the counteroffer that Arafat never made at Camp David. They called upon Israel to make even deeper concessions for peace, including transferring the following to the Palestinians:

- All of the Gaza Strip;

- Between 94 and 96 percent of the West Bank;
- Swaths of Israeli territory amounting to an additional 1 to 3 percent of the West Bank to offset the parts of the West Bank Israel would retain; and
- A safe passage corridor through Israeli territory that would connect the West Bank and Gaza.

In addition, the Clinton Parameters called for Jerusalem to be divided along ethnic lines. The Israelis would keep Jerusalem's Jewish neighborhoods and these would remain the capital of Israel. The Palestinians would be given Jerusalem's Arab neighborhoods and these would become the capital of Palestine.

Before presenting the Clinton Parameters to the parties, chief American negotiator Dennis Ross flew to London to share them with Saudi Arabia's ambassador to the U.S., Prince Bandar bin Sultan. Bandar was so impressed that he declared, "If Arafat does not accept what is available now, it won't be a tragedy, it will be a crime."[20] Egypt's President Mubarak described the parameters as "historic" and promised that he would "encourage Arafat to accept them."[21]

On the night of December 27, 2000, Prime Minister Barak and his security cabinet voted to accept the Clinton Parameters with certain reservations. According to Dennis Ross, "the reservations were within the parameters, not outside them."[22]

Arafat once again said "No." As always, he was indirect. At first he told President Clinton that he would accept the proposal, but that he had some reservations. According to Ross, however, these reservations were so far outside the parameters as to be "deal killers" and demonstrated that "Arafat was not going to say yes under any circumstances."[23] Ross concluded, "We now had to face a strategic reality: Arafat could not do a deal that ended the conflict. Partial deals were possible because they did not require him to adopt any irrevocable positions. But a comprehensive deal was not possible with Arafat. Too much redefinition was required. He was not up to it. He could live with a process, but not with a conclusion."[24]

Prince Bandar later told a reporter for the *New Yorker,* "It broke my heart that Arafat did not take that offer."[25] The violence of the Second Intifada continued unabated.

ARIEL SHARON AND DISENGAGEMENT

The Israeli consensus throughout most of the 1990s had been that seeking peace through a two-state solution was worth the risks and sacrifices. That consensus was shattered beyond repair when a series of painful concessions—and offers of still more—produced not peace but the unprecedented terror of the Second Intifada.

When the Israeli people next went to the polls in February 2001, they dumped Barak in a landslide. They replaced him with fabled Israeli hawk Ariel Sharon. With peace now beyond their grasp, the Israeli people chose security by an overwhelming margin.

Since Arafat refused to fight terror in the territory he controlled, Sharon concluded that the Israeli army would have to do it for him. On March 29, 2002, he launched Operation Defensive Shield. Over the course of the next month, Israeli troops returned to all of the major West Bank cities and towns from which they had so recently withdrawn. There they arrested wanted terrorists, battled those who refused to surrender, and destroyed the bomb factories that supplied them.

After the military operation was over, Sharon turned his attention to the problem of border security. Even during the height of the intifada, the border between the West Bank and Israel had remained surprisingly open. Suicide bombers could literally walk out their doors in the West Bank and stroll across open fields to reach their targets in Israel. At the end of 2002, Sharon's government approved construction of a security barrier between Israel and the West Bank to prevent such easy infiltration.[26]

These dual measures—the military operation and the security fence—eventually ended the Second Intifada. Terrorist incidents began a steady decline. Having delivered on his promise of security, Sharon was easily reelected in January 2003.

THE GAZA DISENGAGEMENT

For most of his career Sharon had argued that Israel—which is barely ten miles wide at its center—needed the strategic depth provided by the West Bank to survive an invasion. Sharon further believed that building Jewish settlements in the West Bank was the best way to maintain Israeli control over it. His relentless efforts to build these settlements earned him the nickname the "bulldozer."

But by his second term, Sharon had changed his mind. He now saw Palestinian terror at home and attacks on Israel's legitimacy abroad as the greatest threats to Israeli security. And he concluded that "disengaging" from the Palestinians—removing Israeli troops and civilians from Palestinian population centers—was the best way to defend against both dangers. The "bulldozer" now became as dogged in his pursuit of disengagement as he had once been in his promotion of settlements.

The peace process had offered the clearest path toward disengagement. Now that this effort had failed, however, Sharon decided to act unilaterally. In what he described as an effort to "break the stalemate," Sharon proposed, promoted, and passed a plan to withdraw all Israeli troops and civilians from the Gaza Strip and five West Bank settlements.

Sharon's disengagement plan was controversial. The Israeli Right, including a significant bloc from within his own Likud Party, angrily denounced it. Jewish residents of Gaza and their allies organized a series of massive demonstrations to protest it. Ultimately, Sharon had to send the Israeli army into Gaza to complete it. But by September 12, 2005, there were no Israelis left in Gaza. Sharon began to look toward the next phase of disengagement from the West Bank.

Given the lack of support for his policies from within his own party, Sharon made yet another dramatic move. He resigned as head of the Likud Party and launched a new party called *Kadima* ("Forward") as the vehicle through which he would pursue disengagement. New elections were scheduled for March 2006.

Just two months after founding Kadima, Sharon suffered a major stroke that left him in a vegetative state.[27] His deputy, former Jerusalem mayor Ehud Olmert, replaced him as party leader. Olmert's platform was simple: he would fulfill Sharon's legacy. He pledged to pursue negotiations toward a two-state solution so long as he had a Palestinian partner. But he also promised that, in the absence of such a partner, he would seek additional unilateral withdrawals from the West Bank.

Kadima won the March elections and formed the next government. Ehud Olmert came to office with a mandate to make serious concessions for peace. In Olmert's words, the "painful but necessary task" he was elected to carry out would require great sacrifice from Israelis: "We have to compromise in the name of peace, to give up parts of our promised land in which every hill and every valley is saturated with Jewish history and in which our heroes are buried. We have to relinquish our dream to leave room for the dream of others so that all of us can enjoy a better future."[28]

EHUD OLMERT TRIES AGAIN

By late 2006, disengagement seemed far less attractive a path than it once had. Israel's withdrawal from Gaza had not created the laboratory for Palestinian progress its proponents had promised. Palestinian mobs immediately demolished an extensive network of greenhouses the Israelis had left behind to jumpstart Gaza's economy. Even more ominously, the Israeli withdrawal was followed by a sharp *increase* in missile and mortar fire from Gaza into Israel. Once again, Israeli concessions had been met with an upsurge in terror.

Yet Prime Minister Olmert stubbornly followed the path of Rabin, Barak, and Sharon. Rather than abandon compromise in the face of increased terror, Olmert doubled down on it. He returned to peace negotiations and committed himself to making even more concessions more quickly in the hope that a final deal would change everything.

Over the almost two years from December 2006 to September 2008, Olmert met with Arafat's successor, Mahmoud Abbas, thirty-six times.[29] Their last meeting was on September 16, 2008, in Olmert's Jerusalem home. Here, Olmert went beyond the Clinton Parameters to make Abbas the most generous peace offer yet.[30] Among its highlights:

Territory. Olmert offered Abbas a Palestinian state on territory that would be equivalent in size to 100 percent of the West Bank and Gaza Strip. This would be accomplished through a land swap. Israel would give the Palestinians all of Gaza and 93.7 percent of the West Bank. In exchange for the 6.3 percent of the West Bank it retained, Israel would give the Palestinians land from Israel proper equal to 5.8 percent of the West Bank, along with a land link between the West Bank and Gaza equal to the remaining 0.5 percent.

Jerusalem. Olmert proposed sharing Jerusalem with the Palestinians. Jerusalem's Jewish neighborhoods would be the capital of Israel and its Arab neighborhoods would become the Palestinian capital.

The Holy Basin. Olmert was the first Israeli prime minister to offer to relinquish Israeli sovereignty over the "Holy Basin" (that part of Jerusalem containing the sites holiest to Jews and Muslims, including the Temple Mount and the Western Wall). He proposed ceding control of this area to a committee comprised of representatives from five countries: Saudi Arabia, Jordan, Palestine, the United States, and Israel.

Refugees. Olmert suggested that five thousand Palestinian refugees be allowed to return to Israel proper—one thousand a year for five years. He also proposed that the two sides work with international bodies and financial institutions to establish a fund to "generously compensate" refugees for their lost property.

Olmert's proposal was historic. And, coming from a lifelong leader of the Israeli Right, it was serious. But Abbas did not accept Olmert's offer. Nor did he make him a counteroffer. As Olmert later recounted, "Abu Mazen [Abbas's *nom de guerre*] said that he could not decide and needed time." Olmert pressed Abbas to accept his proposal, stressing that "you'll never get an offer that is fairer or more just."[31] But Abbas ended the conversation with an odd excuse: "Give me a few days. I don't know my way around maps. I propose that tomorrow we meet with two map experts, one from your side and one from our side. If they tell me everything is alright, we can sign."[32]

This meeting never took place. The next day, chief Palestinian negotiator Saeb Erekat called Olmert to cancel, claiming that they "had forgotten that Abbas had to go to Amman" that day. Erekat suggested that they meet the following week instead. But that call was the last time Olmert and his team ever heard from their Palestinian counterparts. As Olmert noted years later, "I've been waiting ever since."[33]

Olmert's account of these events has been confirmed by a number of reliable third parties. The *Washington Post*'s Jackson Diehl has reported that Abbas acknowledged receiving Olmert's offer and rejecting it because, in Abbas's words, "the gaps were wide."[34] According to Diehl, "Confronted with a draft deal that would have been cheered by most of the world, Abbas balked. He refused to sign on; he refused to present a counteroffer. Rice and Bush implored him to join Olmert at the White House for a summit. Olmert would present his plan to Bush, and Abbas would say that he found it worth discussing. The Palestinian president refused."[35]

In his autobiography *Decision Points*, President George W. Bush confirmed that Abbas refused to accept the deal.[36] In her autobiography *No Higher Honor*, former Secretary of State Condoleezza Rice wrote that "in the end, the Palestinians walked away from the negotiations."[37]

Why did Abbas turn down Olmert's offer? Some observers cite the fact that by this time Olmert faced a bleak political future. He was under investigation and facing possible indictment for a series of alleged financial improprieties. In fact, he had already announced that he would resign as prime minister as soon as his successor was elected.

Yet no matter how short Olmert's remaining tenure may have been, he was still the duly elected prime minister of Israel. There was still time for him and the Knesset majority he controlled to approve this deal. It was also quite reasonable to assume that Olmert's successor—who would come from Olmert's party—would support his policies. And since progress toward peace has historically boosted pro-peace candidates, a signed agreement would have gone a long way toward ensuring that any future government would have continued Olmert's work. Simply put, if Abbas liked Olmert's offer it would have made enormous sense for him to accept it.

The real reasons behind Abbas's refusal indicate a deeper problem. It seems that Abbas could not bring himself to go public with what he had contemplated in private. The concessions that Abbas would have had to make under this deal—especially disavowing the right of most Palestinian refugees to return to Israel—would have been highly controversial. They also would have been extremely dangerous. Palestinian leaders have been assassinated for far less.

As former deputy national security advisor Elliott Abrams concluded regarding Abbas, "He knew he would be accused of treason; he knew he would face physical risks; he knew he would be sowing the whirlwind if he signed. He was a nice and mild man and not a hero."[38]

Ehud Olmert echoed this view when he summed up Abbas's refusal to sign the deal: "They [the Palestinian leadership] were very worried. Abu Mazen is not a big hero. They were afraid."[39]

Thus, in the end, Abbas chose to follow the path of his predecessor and mentor Yasser Arafat. Abbas just said "No." He made no counteroffers. In so doing, he could never be accused of signing away any of his people's rights. And, in so doing, he ensured that his people would remain stateless.

Since 2008, there have been a number of efforts to resurrect these past offers and secure the elusive Israeli-Palestinian peace. But since Israel cannot offer more than it has already put on the table—territory equal to one hundred percent of the West Bank and Gaza Strip along with the Arab neighborhoods of East Jerusalem—it should come as little surprise that these efforts have thus far failed.

As recently as 2014, for example, the Obama administration engaged in an ill-fated round of shuttle diplomacy to establish a framework for renewed peace talks. Many observers, including the *New York Times'* Roger Cohen, have blamed Abbas for the failure of this Obama-Kerry initiative.[40] Others, blaming Israel, note that Abbas had reportedly agreed in private to accept certain key components of this framework.[41]

But the barrier to peace has never been Abbas's failure to contemplate compromise in private. The problem has always been his refusal—and the refusal of all Palestinian leaders before him—to commit to such compromises in public. Until this refusal to move beyond process to an actual agreement is overcome, there can and probably will be further peace talks. But there will never be a peace deal.

CHAPTER EIGHT

THE MOST MORAL
ARMY IN THE WORLD

*During Operation Cast Lead, the Israeli Defense Forces did
more to safeguard the rights of civilians in a combat zone than
any other army in the history of warfare.*

—Colonel Richard Kemp, 2009[1]

I n 1909, tensions were running high between two Galilee communities—the Jewish village of Sejera and the neighboring Arab village of Kafr Kanna. Repeated clashes culminated in Arabs from Kafr Kanna murdering two Jews from Sejera. But the residents of Sejera did not seek revenge. In the hope of preventing further bloodshed, they instead agreed to negotiate a *sulha*, or reconciliation, with their Arab neighbors.

While the talks were under way, a young Sejera resident named David Ben Gurion set off by foot to visit the nearby Jewish village of Yavniel. On the way, he was attacked by an Arab thief wielding a dagger. Despite his youth and fear, Ben Gurion responded admirably: "Because of their proximity to an Arab village, Ben Gurion did not shoot him with his pistol. But the robber attempted to wrest the gun away, and the two wrestled in the dirt. The Arab finally grabbed Ben Gurion's satchel and ran off, but not before wounding Ben Gurion with the dagger. Ben Gurion was proud that he had kept his wits about him and had not shot his assailant, thus reopening the circle of recrimination in the Galilee."[2]

Twenty-seven years later, in 1936, the Arabs of Palestine rebelled against British rule. But it was an odd sort of revolt. These rebels targeted not only their British rulers but also their Jewish neighbors. Life for Palestine's Jews grew increasingly dangerous.

By this time, Ben Gurion had risen from his humble roots to become the leader of Palestine's Jews. But his response to the violence of the Arab Revolt mirrored his response to the Arab robber so many years earlier. Ben Gurion imposed a policy of self-restraint—*havlaga* in Hebrew—upon his fellow Jews. He urged the Jews to defend themselves from attack. But he forbade them from taking any kind of offensive action against the Arabs.

The years that followed brought inevitable changes to Israeli military doctrine. Israel developed a far more aggressive strategy for confronting enemy armies in the field. And Israel learned to strike back at those who order or perpetrate terrorist attacks against it. But to a surprising extent, Israel's military is still governed by the ethos of the young David Ben Gurion. Israel exercises enormous self-restraint. It absorbs hundreds of blows without responding, in the hope of avoiding armed conflict. And when Israel finally does respond to attacks, it strives mightily to target the guilty and spare the innocent.

To proclaim the morality of Israel's army is not to insist upon its perfection. The Israel Defense Forces is an army of men, not angels. When they are under fire, even good men get frightened and make mistakes. And not every Israeli soldier is a good man.

Yet when judged by any realistic standard, Israel's army is among the world's most moral. The Israel Defense Forces has promulgated a strict code of ethics that places a high value on the lives of innocent civilians. And Israel's soldiers consistently implement this code with impressive success. When soldiers fail to uphold these rules, they are punished. When these rules are found wanting, they are improved.

But Israel is not always judged by realistic standards. Instead Israel is facing intensifying criticism from those who have never contemplated, let alone confronted, its challenges. As Israel's enemies grow increasingly skilled at using human shields to produce civilian casualties, Israel's efforts to defend itself grow ever more controversial. Images of dead Palestinian civilians do and should spark outrage. Unfortunately, this anger is automatically directed at Israel. Few care to follow the chain of causation back to the terrorist leaders hiding safely in their bunkers.

In recent years, Israel's critics have singled out two military operations for their harshest attacks and wildest claims. The first was Israel's 2002 effort to eliminate terror cells in the Jenin Refugee Camp. The second was Israel's winter 2008–09 campaign to stop missile fire from the Gaza Strip into her southern cities.

Yet when these operations are reviewed in detail—when fact is distilled from myth—both turn out to be examples not of excess but of exemplary restraint. These two campaigns thus serve as instructive case studies highlighting the great gap between rhetoric and reality when it comes to Israel's battlefield ethics.

THE JENIN "MASSACRE"

As we've seen, the 1990s were a decade of great hopes and risks for peace. Under the Oslo Accords, Israel withdrew its army from increasingly large portions of the West Bank and Gaza Strip and handed them over to Palestinian control. By December 1996, the IDF had pulled out of almost every major Palestinian population center.

At Camp David and again in response to the Clinton Parameters, Israeli Prime Minister Ehud Barak offered to withdraw from almost all of the remaining territory in the West Bank and Gaza, including the Arab neighborhoods of Jerusalem. Yasser Arafat rejected both offers and instead played a central role in the Second Intifada. Over the next two years, over a thousand Israelis were murdered as Palestinian suicide bombers blew themselves up in Israeli buses, cafes, and restaurants.

These attacks reached their bloody peak in March 2002. During that tragic month, Palestinian terrorists from the West Bank carried out fifteen attacks in Israel—an average of one every two days—killing over 130 Israelis.

This bloodiest of months ended with the deadliest of attacks. On the night of March 27, the dining room at the Park Hotel in Netanya was filled with people celebrating the first night of Passover. Then a suicide bomber carrying a suitcase packed with powerful explosives entered the dining room and detonated his device. He killed 30 and injured 140. Most of the dead were from eight families, including married couples and a father and his daughter.

The Passover massacre was the final straw. Most of the terrorists responsible for these attacks were operating from Palestinian-controlled territory. The Palestinians were either unable or unwilling to stop them. The Israelis concluded that they had no choice but to go in and do the job themselves. On March 29, 2002, Israel launched a military operation—Operation Defensive Shield—to end the carnage.

Among Israel's top priorities was to retake the West Bank city of Jenin. Of the approximately one hundred suicide bombers who had attacked Israel since the start of the Second Intifada, twenty-three were from Jenin. Another seven suicide bombers from Jenin had been intercepted before they could kill anyone.[3] The Palestinians themselves referred to Jenin as the "City of the Bombers" and "The Martyrs' Capital."[4]

Israeli troops entered Jenin on April 2. They finished their operation nine days later, on April 11. They lifted the military closure of the city on April 18.

Yet even before the closure was lifted and the facts ascertained, Palestinian sources were insisting that Israel had committed terrible atrocities in Jenin. As early as April 8, the Palestinian Authority news agency Wafa reported that Israel had committed the "massacre of the 21st century" in Jenin and that there were already "hundreds of martyrs" there.[5]

That same day, the Palestinian Authority's UN representative, Nasser al-Kidwa, described Israel's activities in Jenin as "a war crime, a clear war crime, witnessed by the whole world...I mean this is an all-out assault against the whole population."[6]

On April 10, chief Palestinian negotiator Saeb Erekat claimed on CNN that Israeli troops had killed "more than 500 people" in Jenin. On April 12, Erekat returned to CNN to add that "a real massacre was committed in the Jenin refugee camp" and that three hundred Palestinians had already been buried in mass graves.[7]

Not to be outdone, Ahmed Abdel Rahman—the secretary general of the Palestinian Authority Cabinet—took to the airwaves on April 13 to claim that "thousands" of Palestinians had been killed in Jenin. He added that the Israelis had taken "hundreds of bodies to northern Israel to hide their massacre they committed against our people."[8]

The international press was quick to echo these Palestinian claims. On April 16, the British newspaper the *Guardian* published an editorial comparing Israel's behavior in Jenin to that of al-Qaeda on September 11: "Jenin camp looks like the scene of a crime. Its concrete rubble and tortured metal evokes another horror half a world away in New York, smaller in scale but every bit as repellant in its particulars, no less distressing, and every bit as man-made.... Jenin already has that aura of infamy that attaches to a crime of especial notoriety."[9]

Writing in the *London Times* on April 16, war correspondent Janine di Giovanni exclaimed, "Rarely in more than a decade of war reporting from Bosnia, Chechnya, Sierra Leone, Kosovo, have I seen such deliberate destruction, such disrespect for human life."[10]

Philip Reeves began his April 16 article in the London *Independent* with the claim: "A monstrous war crime that Israel has tried to cover up for a fortnight has finally been exposed.... The sweet and ghastly reek of rotting human bodies is everywhere, evidence that this is a human tomb.... The people...say there are hundreds of corpses, entombed beneath the dust...."[11]

International officials soon joined in the frenzy. On April 18, UN envoy Terje Larsen described the scene in Jenin as "horrific beyond belief." He added, "We have expert people here who have been in war zones and earthquakes, and they say they have never seen anything like it."[12]

WHAT REALLY HAPPENED IN JENIN?

It's hardly uncommon for Palestinian officials to engage in hyperbole when describing Israeli behavior. And the press is likewise accustomed to exaggerating Israel's misdeeds. But the discussion of Israel's actions in Jenin was exceptional even for these actors. As journalist Joel Mowbray observed, "The only 'massacre' that took place at Jenin was that of the truth."[13]

At the outset, it's important to clarify the context. During Operation Defensive Shield, the Israeli army ultimately retook all of the West Bank's major Palestinian population centers. Most of these operations were completed without serious incident. In those cities and towns where the Israelis encountered no armed resistance, there was no fighting and the operation produced no casualties.[14] Those intent on perpetrating massacres, on the other hand, tend to do the opposite: they target precisely those places where there is no armed resistance—such as a Passover dinner.

Even in Jenin, the vast majority of the city was left unscathed. The city's extensive terrorist infrastructure was concentrated in the refugee camp on its outskirts. Thus all of the fighting took place there. In Jenin proper there were no battles, no deaths, and no destruction. As one observer commented after passing through Jenin, there was "not even a broken window anywhere in sight."[15]

Within the refugee camp, Israel made extensive efforts to protect innocent life and property. Before Israeli troops entered the camp, they used loudspeakers to repeatedly warn its residents to evacuate.[16] Over ninety percent of the camp's population followed these instructions and fled to safety. Only an estimated one thousand, three hundred civilians remained.[17]

Once inside the camp, Israeli troops gave a series of additional warnings before entering any particular residence. In one of many Palestinian confirmations of Israel's caution, an Arab grocer told *Time* that before entering his house, Israelis with megaphones called out in Arabic, "People in the house, get out. We don't want you to be hurt."[18]

These repeated house-by-house warnings gave the terrorists a chance to surrender. Those who did so were arrested, not killed. The only reason there were any deaths in the refugee camp is that an estimated two hundred militants from the most violent terrorist groups—al-Aqsa Martyrs Brigade, Tanzim, Palestinian Islamic Jihad, and Hamas—refused to surrender.[19] Instead, they decided to turn the camp into a killing field for the approaching Israelis.

Jenin's assembled terrorists were hardly shy about their intentions. On April 3, 2002, a Palestinian Islamic Jihad commander named Ali Safouri boasted, "We have prepared unexpected surprises for the enemy. We are determined to pay him back double, and teach him a lesson he will not forget.... We welcome them, and we have prepared a special graveyard in the Jenin camp for them."[20]

Safouri was not exaggerating. The terrorists had prepared an extensive array of mines and booby traps in the camp's cramped buildings and narrow alleys. A senior member of Palestinian Islamic Jihad, Tabaat Mardawi, later bragged to CNN that Palestinian fighters had placed between "1,000 to 2,000 bombs and booby traps" throughout the camp.[21]

A Palestinian Islamic Jihad bomb maker named Omar explained that most of these bombs were concentrated around a cluster of fifty houses. He noted that "We chose old and empty buildings and the houses of men who were wanted by Israel because we knew the soldiers would search for them.... We cut off lengths of water pipes and packed them with explosives and nails. Then we placed them about four meters apart throughout the houses—in cupboards, under sinks, in sofas."[22]

Prior to introducing ground troops into the camp, the Israelis sent a large bulldozer down a three-quarter-mile stretch of road to clear booby traps. An Israeli engineering corps officer logged 124 separate explosions set off by the vehicle.[23]

Thanks to these pronouncements and probes, the Israelis were well aware that the Jenin camp would be a death trap. Given that fact, they could have issued final warnings that specific structures were about to be destroyed. Then they could have called in air power or tank fire to strike these targets from a safe distance. This is what most modern armies facing comparable circumstances do.

But the Israelis decided that this approach carried too high a risk of civilian casualties. Instead of endangering innocent Palestinians, the Israelis decided to send their own soldiers into harm's way. Israel ordered ground troops into the Jenin camp's narrow alleys to go door by booby-trapped door to locate wanted terrorists.

Israel's decision to send its troops into the heart of the Jenin refugee camp elicited an interesting reaction from the terrorists holed up there. Many who had planned to flee decided to stay and take advantage of an unexpected opportunity to kill Israelis. Ata Abu Roumeileh, a Fatah leader in the camp, told a *Time* reporter that "it was only when his forces saw the Israelis advancing on foot that they decided to stay and fight."[24]

Palestinian Islamic Jihad leader Tabaat Mardawi shared a similar story with CNN. Mardawi said that he and his colleagues had expected Israel to attack with planes and tanks. When they instead saw Israeli troops entering the camp on foot, "It was like hunting…like being given a prize. I couldn't believe it when I saw the soldiers. The Israelis knew that any soldier who entered the camp like that was going to get killed. I've been waiting for a moment like that for years."[25]

On April 9, these terrorist dreams came true. On that day, a group of Israeli soldiers walked directly into a Palestinian ambush.

Shortly after escaping the Jenin camp, Omar—the Palestinian Islamic Jihad bomb maker—shared the details of the ambush with the Egyptian newspaper *Al-Ahram*. He bragged that he had used civilians to lure the Israeli soldiers into the trap. "We all stopped shooting, and the women went out to tell the soldiers that we had run out of bullets and were leaving."[26]

Thus encouraged, the Israelis continued their advance. At this point, the lead Israelis started triggering booby traps. A number of soldiers fell, dead or injured. According to Omar, "When the senior officers realized what had happened, they shouted through megaphones that they wanted an immediate cease-fire. We let them approach to retrieve the men and then opened fire. Some of the soldiers were so shocked and frightened that they mistakenly ran towards us."[27]

By the time the smoke had cleared, thirteen Israeli soldiers were dead. The Israeli army had suffered its deadliest single day since the 1982 Lebanon War.

After this ambush, the Israelis changed tactics. They still refused to risk civilian lives by calling in air power or tank fire. Instead, they sent Caterpillar D-9 armored bulldozers into the camp to clear paths, detonate booby traps, and provide safe entry into those buildings still occupied by militants.

To minimize casualties, the Israelis issued yet another set of warnings before permitting the bulldozers to demolish any structure. And, once started, it takes a D-9 at least a half-hour to bring down a building.[28] Thus even residents who had ignored the repeated warnings had plenty of time to flee once a bulldozer began its work.

To the extent civilians died in these bulldozed buildings, there may well have been another reason. A senior Palestinian military officer later confided to *Time* magazine that it was probably the gunmen's own booby traps—triggered by the bulldozers—that buried some of the civilians and fighters alive.[29]

With the D-9s in the lead, Israel quickly took control of the camp. Most of the remaining militants were arrested or killed.

THE REAL NUMBERS

A total of twenty-three Israeli soldiers were killed in the Jenin operation. Seventy-five were wounded.

As for the Palestinian casualties, the numbers were multiples below the initial inflated reports. Ultimately, the United Nations, Human Rights Watch, and Amnesty International concluded that no massacre had taken place in Jenin. *Time* magazine conducted an investigation and

likewise decided that "there was no wanton massacre in Jenin, no deliberate slaughter of Palestinians by Israeli soldiers."[30]

Israel reported that fifty-two Palestinians died in Jenin, and that the
majority of these were combatants. Every independent review has since
vindicated Israel's numbers. The United Nations concluded that fifty-two
Palestinians had been killed in Jenin.[31] Human Rights Watch likewise
counted fifty-two Palestinian fatalities.[32]

Even the Palestinians eventually revised their numbers dramatically
downward from their initial claims of five hundred or more dead. After
conducting his own investigation, the senior Palestinian Authority official in Jenin, Kadoura Mousa Kadoura, concluded that fifty-six Palestinians had been killed in Israel's Jenin operation.[33]

The only real disagreement was over the number of innocents among
the dead. The Israelis reported that fourteen civilians were killed and
that half of them were killed by Palestinian booby traps.[34] Human Rights
Watch, on the other hand, concluded that twenty-two civilians were
killed.[35]

Even if we use Human Rights Watch's number for the civilian casualties, and even if we assume that Israel was responsible for *all* of them,
the fact remains that the number of Israeli soldiers killed in Jenin surpassed the number of civilian deaths. This ratio of military to civilian
casualties is unprecedented in modern urban combat anywhere in the
world. By placing its own soldiers at risk, Israel succeeded in keeping
civilian deaths far below what other Western armies conducting similar
counterterror operations have been able to achieve.

In an interview after the fighting, Israeli commander Shlomo
Laniado recalled that one of his soldiers asked him, "Why aren't we using
more strength? Why do I have to go from house to house and maybe not
come back?"[36] Laniado answered this question when he told the reporter,
"We were injured and got killed since we have a heart. We paid this price
due to our morality that was seen all through the fighting."[37]

Israel's unprecedented measures to spare innocent Palestinian lives
were widely reported as a "massacre" of Palestinians. And while some
media outlets later issued corrections, they were made—as corrections

inevitably are—much more quietly than the initial sensational accusations. To this day, the "Jenin Massacre" remains a rallying cry for anti-Israel activists around the world.

POSTSCRIPT TO JENIN

Even though it kept civilian deaths to a record low in Jenin, the Israeli army did not behave perfectly. After the fighting, reports emerged that some Israeli soldiers had tried to protect themselves by using human shields. In particular, it was alleged that Israeli troops had compelled Palestinian civilians to knock on the doors of houses they intended to search and, in some instances, be the first to enter these homes.

On May 5, 2002, five Israeli, Palestinian, and international human rights organizations filed a petition with Israel's High Court of Justice objecting to this practice. In response, Israel's State Attorney's Office informed the Court, "In light of the various complaints received…and so as to avoid all doubt, the IDF has decided to immediately issue an unequivocal order…. that forces in the field are absolutely forbidden to use civilians of any kind as a means of 'living shield.'"[38]

GAZA—OPERATION CAST LEAD

Operation Defensive Shield was successful in breaking up the worst of the West Bank terror cells and reducing the number of suicide bombings in Israel. But it was hardly a long-term solution.

Since bilateral efforts to negotiate a two-state solution had failed to produce peace, Israeli Prime Minister Ariel Sharon embarked on a new course. He decided that he could best protect his citizens by unilaterally disengaging from the Palestinians. For Sharon "disengagement" meant removing Israeli troops and civilians from Palestinian population centers and then building a security barrier between the two communities.

Sharon launched his disengagement plan with a complete Israeli withdrawal from the Gaza Strip. This meant removing over eight thousand five hundred Israeli civilians from their homes in twenty-one Gaza communities. The scenes of Israeli soldiers pulling Israeli children from the only homes they had ever known sparked enormous controversy. But by September 2005, no Jews were left in Gaza.

Sharon had hoped that this withdrawal would be a down payment on peace. What followed was a heartbreaking disappointment. In 2007, Hamas seized the Gaza Strip from the Fatah-controlled Palestinian Authority in a bloody coup. Now free from any constraints, Hamas dramatically escalated its missile fire into southern Israel. By December 2008, Hamas and its allies had fired more than seven thousand rockets and mortar shells at Israeli towns and villages.[39] In short order, Israel's withdrawal from Gaza had produced not peace but a sharp spike in terror.

Not only was Hamas firing more missiles than ever, but it had also succeeded in increasing the range of these missiles so that they could reach Israel's largest southern cities, including Ashkelon, Ashdod, and Be'er Sheva. As a result, the number of Israelis living within range of Hamas missiles reached one million—almost fifteen percent of Israel's population.[40] Hamas missiles were also capable of hitting important infrastructure, including the power stations in Ashdod and Ashkelon that supplied southern Israel—and Gaza itself—with electricity.

On December 27, 2008, Israel launched Operation Cast Lead to stop the missile fire from Gaza. Days of air strikes were followed by a January 3 ground invasion. The fighting ended on January 17. By January 21, Israel had withdrawn all of its troops from Gaza.

The death toll in Gaza was much higher than in Jenin. The Israelis claimed that 1,166 people were killed in this operation, of whom 295 were civilians. The Palestinian Center for Human Rights counted 1,417 Palestinian dead, including 926 civilians. Most of the difference between these two figures results from the fact that Israel classified Hamas police officers as combatants, while the Palestinian Center for Human Rights counted them as civilians.

Given the scale of the suffering, it came as no surprise that this operation sparked immediate claims of Israeli atrocities and war crimes. News outlets condemned Israel's "naked brutality," its "deliberate targeting of civilian objects," and its "intentional killing of civilians."

South African Bishop Desmond Tutu later wrote that Israel's "bloody assault on the Gaza strip" was an episode "of such naked brutality that concerned observers must recoil in outrage and demand an end to the madness."[41]

In language reminiscent of the reporting from Jenin, Canadian author and social activist Naomi Klein wrote, "A sprawling crime scene. That is what Gaza felt like when I visited in the summer of 2009, six months after the Israeli attack. Evidence of criminality was everywhere— the homes, the schools that lay in rubble, the walls burned pitch black by white phosphorus, the children's bodies still unhealed for lack of medical care."[42]

Responding to the escalating outrage, the United Nations Human Rights Council sent a commission to investigate Israel's actions in Gaza. This team was led by former South African judge Richard Goldstone, who had served as the prosecutor for the international genocide tribunals in Yugoslavia and Rwanda. Both the commission and the report it later issued bore Judge Goldstone's name.

The Goldstone Report was released in September 2009. The document was a bombshell. Dismissing all other explanations for the presence of destroyed civilian structures in Gaza, the commission concluded that they were evidence of "a deliberately disproportionate attack designed to punish, humiliate and terrorize a civilian population."[43] More specifically, the Report accused Israel of the "direct targeting and arbitrary killing of Palestinian civilians."[44] In short, Israel was accused of the very terrorism that it claimed to be battling.

Unlike the UN Human Rights Council, Richard Goldstone enjoyed a sterling reputation as a human rights crusader. He was also Jewish and, therefore, supposedly without a bias against Israel. As a result, the Goldstone Report received enormous attention and enjoyed widespread credibility.

WHAT REALLY HAPPENED IN GAZA?

There is a branch of international law devoted to putting some humanitarian boundaries around the ugly enterprise of war. This "Law of Armed Conflict" does not outlaw war. Nor does it forbid the incidental killing of civilians in the course of battle. What the Law of Armed Conflict does prohibit is the *intentional* killing of civilians as an objective of war. This is the bright moral line that separates the legitimate use of force from terrorism.

There are two core legal principles that govern combatants in situations where they might harm civilians. The first is the principle of "distinction." This rule obligates the parties to a conflict to distinguish between civilians and combatants, as well as between civilian objects (houses and apartments, for example) and military objects (such as military bases and airfields). It is unlawful to *deliberately* target civilians or civilian objects. But it is not unlawful to accidentally harm civilians or civilian objects in the effort to strike a legitimate military target.[45] The critical component of any distinction analysis is therefore a combatant's *intent*.

The principle of distinction provides clear moral guidance in traditional battlefield situations, where civilians are typically miles from the front lines. But the rule is less helpful in urban warfare and counterterrror operations, when military and civilian targets are often closely intertwined. In these situations, efforts to strike legitimate military targets will often carry clear and foreseeable risks to nearby civilians. Under such circumstances, a second rule—the principle of "proportionality"—governs.

This rule does not prohibit harming civilians or civilian targets in the effort to strike legitimate military targets, so long as this harm is "incidental." What the principle of proportionality does prohibit is launching an attack "in the knowledge that" it will cause harm to civilians or civilian structures "which would be clearly excessive in relation to the concrete and direct overall military advantage anticipated."[46] As with the principle of distinction, a proportionality analysis rests on what an army "knew" and "anticipated" and therefore also focuses on the combatant's intent.

When the Goldstone commission came across a bombed house in Gaza, they made three indefensible logical leaps. First, they concluded that the house must have been a civilian object, even though Hamas used homes and other civilian structures throughout Gaza to store and launch missiles, thereby rendering them legitimate military targets. Second, they determined that Israel must have bombed the house intentionally, overlooking the possibility that Israeli soldiers may have made mistakes of intelligence or targeting. Finally, they decided that the destruction of the house was not "incidental" to any legitimate military objective even though this was often the case. Thus, in the absence of any facts, the Goldstone commission assumed sufficient Israeli intent to render the destruction of the house a violation of the Law of Armed Conflict.

These assumptions were unfounded. Hamas intentionally targeted civilians with each of the over seven thousand missiles and mortars they fired at Israel's population centers. Israel, in sharp contrast, went to exceptional lengths to distinguish between innocent civilians and the Hamas terrorists who tried so hard to blend in with them. Had the Israelis truly intended to harm civilians, they would never have taken so many steps to avoid doing exactly that.

The first thing that Israel did to avoid Palestinian civilian casualties was to wait. The Israelis understood that any military operation to stop the missile fire from Gaza would inevitably kill some of Hamas's human shields and other innocents. They therefore tried desperately to avoid having to conduct such a campaign in the first place. As missiles rained down on its southern cities, Israel mostly held its fire and absorbed the blows.

Such restraint is exceptional. Most countries simply don't permit their neighbors to fire missiles at them. To cite just one example, on October 3, 2012, a Syrian artillery shell landed in a Turkish border town killing five Turkish civilians. The Syrian army, which was battling Syrian rebels near the border at the time, had most likely overshot its intended target.[47] The Syrian government apologized for the incident and said it was investigating the source of the artillery fire.[48] But Turkey wasn't satisfied. It responded *that very day* by firing a barrage of mortars into Syria.

As Syria's battle with the rebels continued over the course of the next two weeks, additional Syrian shells landed in Turkey. In each case, Turkey immediately retaliated with artillery fire into Syria.[49] As Turkish Prime Minister Erdogan explained, "Soldiers loyal to Assad fired shells at us, we immediately reacted and responded with double force. We shall never stop responding."[50] By October 20, 2012, twelve Syrian soldiers had been killed by Turkish fire.[51]

The United Nations Security Council, NATO, and President Obama were all quick to condemn the violence. But it was the initial Syrian mortar fire—not Turkey's response—that they denounced.[52] NATO made it clear that it would defend Turkey, a member state, if Syria's strikes continued.[53]

Israel did not respond to Hamas rocket fire after one, one hundred, or even one thousand missiles had been fired at her southern cities from Gaza. Instead, Israel tried in vain to stop the aggression through diplomatic appeals and economic sanctions. In 2008 alone, Israel sent no less than twenty-nine letters to various UN officials and agencies complaining of the escalating attacks from Gaza.[54]

It was only after these peaceful measures failed—and over seven thousand missiles had been fired into its territory—that Israel decided to respond militarily. It is difficult to imagine any other country waiting so long to perform its fundamental duty to protect its citizens.

Even when Israel finally chose to strike Hamas, it took every step possible to protect Gaza's innocent civilians. The IDF began with general warnings. At the outset of the operation it flooded Gaza with media alerts and leaflet drops urging civilians to avoid any facilities being used by Hamas to fire or store weapons.

As the fighting progressed, the IDF issued a series of increasingly specific warnings. Hours before entering a particular neighborhood, Israel gave residents advance notice through radio broadcasts and leaflets. These warnings specified a timeframe during which residents could safely flee, as well as designated evacuation routes. The vast majority of people who received these alerts could and did move out of the danger zone.

Before striking a specific building within a targeted neighborhood, the IDF issued yet another set of warnings. The Israelis actually placed telephone calls or sent text messages—or both—to every resident of a targeted building, urging them to leave.

During Operation Cast Lead, the IDF dropped approximately 2.5 million leaflets in Gaza. They also made more than 165,000 phone calls warning civilians to evacuate buildings targeted for military strikes.[55]

Innocent civilians were not the only ones to receive these warnings. So did Hamas. In its concern for Palestinian civilians, Israel willingly and consistently gave up the element of surprise. As a result, wanted terrorists frequently escaped, along with their rockets, long before the IDF launched its operations against them. And these Hamas fighters often repaid the Israelis for their warnings by leaving behind booby-trapped homes and apartments to greet them.

Hamas eventually discovered an additional way to exploit Israel's concern for civilian safety. Once Israel had issued warnings that a particular building would be attacked, Hamas invited (or ordered) the building's residents to assemble on its roof. All involved were confident that Israel would be both responsible enough to watch for civilians and moral enough to abort the mission once they were spotted. They were right on both counts.

In response, the Israelis developed a new tactic called "knocking on the roof." The IDF designed an explosive device that would make a loud sound on impact but not otherwise damage buildings or endanger bystanders. They then dropped this device on an empty part of a roof on which civilians had gathered in order to frighten them into leaving.[56] These warnings were accompanied by real-time surveillance to ensure that everyone on the roof was seen leaving the building.[57] Only then did Israel proceed with the actual strike.

Finally, in cases where they couldn't sufficiently limit the risk to civilians, the Israelis typically aborted their attacks. At the outset of the fighting, for example, the IDF concluded that Hamas's military leaders had established their headquarters in the basement of Gaza's Shifa Hospital.[58] The Hamas brass bet their lives that Israel would never destroy Gaza's main hospital, when so many people needed medical care. This proved to be the safest of bets.

In addition to these safety precautions, the IDF also went to great lengths to ensure that humanitarian aid reached Gaza's population throughout the conflict. While the fighting was raging, Israel sent 1,511 trucks carrying 37,162 tons of food, medicine, and animal feed to Gaza. In addition, the IDF coordinated the entry of 706 trucks carrying donations from international relief organizations.[59] Finally, Israel transferred millions of liters of diesel fuel to Gaza for power generation, transportation, and heating.

Hamas took a less constructive approach to these aid convoys. It attacked them. Hamas launched a series of bombings at the very crossing points that Israel used to transfer food, fuel, and medicine to Gaza. This created the anomalous situation where Israeli truck drivers had to repeatedly risk being attacked by Palestinian terrorists in order to provide humanitarian aid to Palestinian civilians.

Once the aid did arrive, Hamas often stole it and sold it to the highest bidder. Such theft eventually drove the United Nations to suspend its aid shipments to Gaza.[60]

Finally, the IDF implemented daily three-hour humanitarian pauses in the fighting to allow the local population to safely shop and take care of their basic needs. Hamas refused to do likewise. It fired forty-four rockets and mortars at Israel during these pauses.[61]

Israel's commitment to protecting innocent Palestinian lives continued well after the Gaza operation was over. The Israelis made extensive efforts to investigate alleged violations of the rules of war by its soldiers. And they punished those found guilty of having violated them.

IDF policy requires that it investigate every allegation of wrongdoing by its soldiers *no matter what the source*. Such complaints are typically made by the commanders or comrades of the alleged offenders. But complaints also come through a variety of other channels, including Palestinian civilians, human rights organizations, the UN, and the media.

The Goldstone Report, for example, alleged thirty-four specific cases of wrongdoing by Israeli soldiers. Before the report was released, Israel had already initiated investigations of twenty-two of these cases. After the report was published, Israel immediately launched investigations of the remaining twelve incidents.[62]

Altogether, the IDF investigated over four hundred allegations of operational misconduct in Operation Cast Lead. Whenever any such investigation produced credible evidence of a violation, the IDF initiated criminal or disciplinary proceedings against the alleged offender. By July 2010, Israel had launched forty-seven criminal investigations into specific incidents in Gaza.[63] During the course of these investigations, evidence was taken from hundreds of Palestinian complainants and witnesses.[64] A number of these investigations resulted in criminal indictments, trials, and convictions of IDF soldiers.[65] Soldiers found guilty of lesser offenses were subject to military discipline.[66]

Anyone dissatisfied with the outcome of an investigation or prosecution can request that it be reviewed by Israel's civilian attorney general. And anyone disappointed with the attorney general's review can appeal it to Israel's Supreme Court. These rights of review and appeal are not

limited to Israeli citizens. Palestinian residents of the West Bank and
Gaza have frequently petitioned for—and received—such relief. And
Israel's Supreme Court has repeatedly ruled in favor of Palestinian civil-
ians over Israel's military.

POSTSCRIPT TO OPERATION CAST LEAD

The Goldstone Report was a sensational document that essentially
accused Israel of war crimes and crimes against humanity. These most
serious of allegations rested on the flimsiest of foundations, namely a
series of baseless assumptions about Israel's intent. As these assumptions
were steadily undermined by the facts, Judge Goldstone began to distance
himself from the report that bears his name.

In October 2009, Goldstone made a stunning statement to a reporter:
"Ours wasn't an investigation, it was a fact-finding mission.... We had
to do the best we could with the material we had. If this was a court of
law, there would have been nothing proven."[67]

Then, on April 1, 2011, Goldstone essentially repudiated his own
report. In an op-ed in the *Washington Post*, Goldstone admitted, "If I
had known then what I know now, the Goldstone Report would have
been a different document." He specifically retracted the Report's most
devastating allegation: that Israel had violated international law by
intentionally targeting civilians. Goldstone wrote that investigations
conducted and published by the Israeli military "indicate that civilians
were not intentionally targeted as a matter of policy."[68]

Goldstone also acknowledged that Israel had fulfilled its obligation
to seriously examine all allegations of misdeeds by its soldiers. By this
time a separate UN commission, chaired by former New York judge
Mary McGowan Davis, had reviewed these post-war investigations. As
Goldstone noted, the Davis Commission found that "Israel has dedicated
significant resources to investigate over 400 allegations of operational
misconduct in Gaza."[69]

Goldstone contrasted Israel's behavior with that of Hamas's leaders
who, according to the Davis Report, "have not conducted any investigations

into the launching of rocket and mortar attacks against Israel." This reality drove Goldstone to finally acknowledge the obvious. "In the end," he wrote, "asking Hamas to investigate may have been a mistaken enterprise."[70]

If a man as decent as Judge Goldstone saw Gaza's dead civilians and destroyed buildings and immediately blamed Israel, it's no wonder that most observers do the same. If it takes a man as intelligent as Judge Goldstone so long to understand the enormous challenges facing democracies seeking to defend themselves from terrorists wielding human shields, it should come as no surprise that most people never get that far. Hamas and its fellow terrorists have located the soft underbelly of Western democracies: compassion compounded by ignorance.

THE WEST CONFRONTS TERROR

Israel is not the only moral power forced to fight terrorists who operate in urban areas and use human shields. The United States, Great Britain, and other Western democracies have had to confront similar enemies in recent wars, including those in Somalia, Iraq, and Afghanistan. Yet the media coverage of these conflicts typically ignores civilian casualties. We rarely see photos of destroyed homes in Iraq or dead women and children in Afghanistan.

Especially in the United States, such reporting has unwittingly spread a fairytale version of modern warfare. Most Americans have come to believe that U.S. soldiers and drones target the bad guys with pinpoint precision while innocents are left unscathed. And if America can fight such pure wars, then certainly others can as well. Thus commentator after commentator insists that if Israel is killing civilians in its war on terror, it must not be trying hard enough to spare them.

But there are no pure wars. To its great credit, the U.S. strives mightily to spare innocent civilians as it combats insurgents and terrorists abroad. Yet American troops have nonetheless killed thousands of innocents in its recent conflicts, and the toll continues to mount. It turns out that, like Israel, the U.S. has yet to invent the perfect weapon by which it can both target terrorists and spare all of the surrounding civilians. Two examples illustrate the point.

BLACK HAWK DOWN

In December 1992, the United States sent troops to Somalia as part of an international coalition to facilitate the delivery of food and medicine to the people of that long-suffering county. When a Somali warlord named Mohammed Farrah Aidid began battling coalition forces, this humanitarian mission morphed into a military one.

In October 1993, an operation to capture Aidid went terribly wrong. A detachment of U.S. troops was attacked and pinned down on the streets of Mogadishu. The U.S. sent in reinforcements to rescue them. In the course of the fighting that followed, eighteen American soldiers were killed.

The number of Somali casualties was multiples larger. According to former U.S. Ambassador to Somalia Robert Oakley, by the time this battle was over between one thousand five hundred and two thousand Somalis had been killed or wounded.[71] Mark Bowden, author of the book *Black Hawk Down*, estimates that eighty percent of these Somali casualties were civilians.[72] Thus it's safe to assume that there were over a thousand Somali civilian casualties that day.[73]

These deaths were not intentional. As Ambassador Oakley makes clear, U.S. troops faced an extremely dangerous and chaotic situation on the streets of Mogadishu that day: "The Americans, and those who came to their rescue, were being shot at from all sides.... And women and children were being used as shields and in some cases women and children were actually firing weapons, and were coming from all sides. Sort of a rabbit warren of huts, houses, alleys, and twisting and turning streets, so those who were trying to defend themselves were shooting back in all directions."[74]

In other words, the Americans confronted a situation in Mogadishu strikingly similar to that encountered by the Israelis in Jenin. Israel's Jenin operation was universally condemned because Israeli troops may have killed as many as twenty-two Palestinian civilians. It is difficult to imagine the tidal wave of condemnation that would have engulfed the Jewish state had it killed or wounded over one thousand Palestinian civilians in Jenin.

THE BATTLE FOR FALLUJAH

In early 2004, Sunni insurgents drove U.S. forces from the Iraqi city of Fallujah. On March 31, these insurgents ambushed a convoy containing four American contractors working for the Blackwater Corporation. After the four men were killed, a mob set their bodies on fire and hung their burnt corpses from a bridge above the Euphrates River.

On April 1, 2004, U.S. Brigadier General Mark Kimmitt promised an "overwhelming" response to the Blackwater deaths. By the end of the month, American Marines had retaken Fallujah and handed control to allied Iraqi forces. When the Iraqis failed to hold the city, a force of U.S., British, and Iraqi troops took Fallujah for a third time in November.

Most of the city's civilians—between seventy and ninety percent—fled the city before the November offensive.[75] In the fierce house-to-house fighting that followed, coalition forces damaged half of Fallujah's thirty-nine thousand homes, rendering about ten thousand of them uninhabitable.[76] Among the buildings destroyed were over sixty mosques.[77] While the number of civilians killed was never verified, the best estimates surpass one thousand.[78]

During its 2008–09 Operation Cast Lead, the IDF destroyed a number of buildings in Gaza, including mosques. For this Israel was condemned, subject to repeated investigations, and accused of war crimes. It is difficult to fathom the outrage that would have engulfed Israel had it left *half* of Gaza's buildings damaged and a full *quarter* of them in ruins.

THE DESTRUCTION OF GROZNY

The fact that moral armies that strive to spare innocent civilians nevertheless harm so many is a tragedy. But the imperfection of these precautions does not disprove their value. These safeguards save lives by the thousands. One need only study the handiwork of an army that makes no such humanitarian efforts to understand how valuable they truly are.

In 1991, for example, the Chechen Republic declared its independence from the Russian Federation. In 1994, Russian President Boris Yeltsin sent his armed forces to crush this Muslim rebellion. The Russian offensive began with a massive aerial and artillery bombardment of the Chechen capital, Grozny. Thousands were killed, thousands more were forced to flee, and over half of the city was destroyed.[79]

When Chechen rebels resumed the fight in 1999, Russia's new president—Vladimir Putin—decided to crush them once and for all. Putin ordered a second and even more ferocious bombardment of Grozny that destroyed most of what had been left standing five years earlier. Russia dropped more bombs on the Chechen capital than had been unleashed on any European city since World War II.[80] In 2003, the United Nations called Grozny the most destroyed city on earth.[81] Not a single building remained undamaged.[82]

The extent of the bombing shows that Russia made little effort to distinguish between combatants and civilians. Chechen President Aslan Maskhadov claimed that two hundred fifty thousand Chechen civilians were killed in the course of these two wars.[83] The Russian-Chechen Friendship Society estimated that there were between one hundred and fifty and two hundred thousand civilian dead.[84] Memorial, a Russian human rights organization, placed the civilian death toll at seventy-five thousand.[85] By the time Putin had crushed the rebellion, roughly one out of every two Chechens had been killed or displaced.[86]

This approach—destroying the terrorists without regard to the civilian toll—is simply not an option for any moral nation. Israel and the United States cannot and will not do what Russia has done. But the contrast is instructive. The fact that most of those outraged by Israel's behavior in Gaza have never even heard of Grozny should prompt any thoughtful person to wonder why.

Ultimately, most analysts seem to have it exactly backward. Israel is not a criminal regime that targets civilians. Israel is actually a pioneer in developing the methods and technology with which the West can morally confront terrorists who employ human shields. When it comes to modern warfare, as in so many other spheres of life, Israel should be studied as a leader, not condemned as a villain.

THE FIVE NO'S

The Palestinian national movement has remained unchanged throughout the different periods of the struggle.... In the end, both sides of the Palestinian movement—the fundamentalists led by Hamas and the secular bloc led by Fatah—are interested in Muslim rule over all of Palestine, with no Jewish state and no partition.

—Benny Morris, 2012[1]

Conflicts between nations—or any other groups of fallible humans—are rarely black and white. The conflict between Israel and the Palestinians is no exception. Israeli society has produced some ugly extremists, while the Palestinians can count among their ranks many heroes of humanity. In this conflict, as in every other, no one can judge the individuals involved on the basis of their religious, national, or ethnic affiliation. There remains only one valid criterion for judging these or any other people: their actions.

Yet rejecting such simplistic absolutes does not require the complete suspension of judgment. Just because there are good people on both sides of a conflict doesn't mean that each side is equally to blame. There can be no peace without justice. And as any judge in any court of law would attest, there can be no justice without first placing blame.

As a general rule, most Israelis have viewed their conflict with the Palestinians as one between two peoples with valid claims to the same piece of land. They have thus repeatedly offered to end the conflict by sharing this land with the Palestinians. Yes, many Israelis reject such compromise. And yes, these hard-liners have occasionally won some battles. But Israel's moderates have won almost every war.

The Palestinians, on the other hand, have consistently insisted that there is only one valid claim to the land: their own. They have repeatedly refused Israeli offers to share the land. Yes, there are certainly Palestinian moderates. And yes, on occasion these moderates have proclaimed their willingness to pursue peace. But they have never risked the wrath of their extremists by actually signing on the dotted line. Thus far, Palestinian rejectionists have won every war.

This pattern of Jewish/Israeli peace offers met by Arab/Palestinian rejection began before there even was a State of Israel, and it has continued down to the present day. Palestinian rejectionism birthed this conflict. And Palestinian rejectionism has been the powerful engine driving this conflict forward ever since.

It's possible to pinpoint five critical junctures in the history of the conflict that illustrate this point. On these five occasions, the Jews/ Israelis officially offered to split the land with the Arabs/Palestinians. And on each of these five occasions the Arabs/Palestinians rejected the offer. More than any other factor, these "five no's" explain why this conflict—and Palestinian statelessness—persists to this very day.

Almost every time the Arabs rejected these compromises, innocent people—both Jews and Arabs—paid the price with their homes, their limbs, and their lives. We rarely see the Jewish victims of Palestinian rejectionism. The large majority of them were murdered before the birth of the State of Israel. The eight hundred thousand Jews forced from their homes in Arab countries between 1947 and 1967 have long ago been resettled. And Israel tends not to parade her mangled survivors of war and terror before television cameras.

In stark contrast, we are constantly bombarded with stories about the Palestinian victims of Palestinian rejectionism. Over time, such headlines trump history. Most casual observers see Israeli troops patrolling Palestinian towns and they chastise Israel for "occupying" them. They see Israel's security fence cutting through the countryside and they condemn Israel for building it. They see Palestinian civilians suffering from war and they blame Israel for harming them.

The reporting about Israel's conflict with the Palestinians is not only missing context; it's often missing one of its two protagonists. The Palestinians are increasingly portrayed as a uniquely passive people. Their history of aggression, terror, and rejectionism is downplayed or simply ignored. As a result, Israel's defensive measures—and Israel's very presence in the West Bank—appear in stark relief as inexplicable persecutions. With its opponent written out of the scene, all we see is an angry Israel shadowboxing with itself.

But the Palestinians are real people. They do act in the world. And their actions have sparked and perpetuated a conflict that need never have been. Once we return the Palestinians to history in all of their complexity, we realize that Israelis are not the villains their detractors would have us believe. Israel has behaved reasonably, even admirably, under the most difficult of circumstances.

Nobel Peace Prize winner and Holocaust survivor Elie Wiesel summed it up best. When asked about Palestinian suffering, he acknowledged it. He agreed that the Palestinians have every right to be angry. But, he added, they shouldn't be angry at Israel. The Palestinians should be angry at their grandparents, who turned down the offer of a Palestinian state back in 1947. And—to update Wiesel's formula—they should also be angry at their parents, who have continued to reject similar Israeli offers down to the present day.

THE FIRST "NO": THE 1937 PEEL PARTITION PLAN

In 1936, Palestine's Arabs rebelled against British rule. The British responded by sending a Royal Commission of Inquiry to Palestine to investigate the revolt's causes and propose policies to address them. This commission was chaired by Lord William Peel, and it quickly came to bear his name.

The Peel Commission concluded that the revolt had been caused by an irreconcilable conflict between Arab and Jewish national aspirations. It therefore proposed dividing Palestine into two states, one Arab and one Jewish, so that each side could achieve the sovereignty it sought. But the suggested split was far from equal. The Peel Commission recommended setting aside less than twenty percent of Palestine for the Jews and giving the Arabs almost all of the rest.

Palestine's Jewish leaders and the Zionist Organization accepted the Peel proposal while requesting a larger share of land. The Arab Higher Committee (representing Palestine's Arabs) and the neighboring Arab states rejected the proposal along with the very concept of partition. The Mufti of Jerusalem, Amin al-Husseini, and most of his associates were violently opposed to the creation of a Jewish state anywhere in Palestine, no matter what its size. They picked up their arms and resumed their revolt.

At this point, war with Nazi Germany loomed. With Arab leaders solidly opposed to partition, and Arab oil so crucial to modern warfare, Britain followed its already well-worn path of appeasement. On May 17, 1939, the British issued a "White Paper" in which they officially abandoned the goal of partition. Instead, they declared that an undivided Palestine would gain its independence within ten years.

Even more significantly, the 1939 White Paper placed tight limits on Jewish immigration to Palestine. It stipulated that over the course of the next five years, only seventy-five thousand Jews would be allowed to return. Any Jewish immigration beyond this token amount would be subject to Arab approval. This immigration cap guaranteed that the Palestine that would receive its independence in ten years would have an Arab majority and would therefore become yet another Arab state.

THE DAMAGE DONE

In 1939, Hitler had not yet decided to murder Europe's Jews; he merely wanted to expel them. Since coming to power in 1933, Hitler had pursued a set of discriminatory policies aimed at driving Germany's Jews to flee. Adolf Eichmann, the man who administered the Holocaust, first came to prominence as the head of a Nazi bureau called "the Central Agency for Jewish Emigration."

As increasing numbers of Jews sought to escape Europe, however, the number of countries willing to take them steadily shrank. The crisis of Europe's Jewish refugees grew so severe that in July 1938 an international conference was convened to address it. Delegates from thirty-two countries convened in the French resort of Evian and discussed the problem for eight days. Yet while delegate after delegate urged the other attendees to take in more refugees, each insisted that his own country was unable to do so. Of all of the nations represented—including the United States, Britain, and France—only the tiny Dominican Republic offered to take in more Jews.

For most of the 1930s, the Nazis had looked to Palestine as a possible dumping ground for Europe's Jews. In 1935, Adolf Eichmann actually traveled to Palestine to investigate this option for himself. As he noted, "We were most interested in the Palestine emigration and I wanted to find out at what point a Jewish state in Palestine might be set up."[2] But Husseini's Arab Revolt and the 1939 White Paper effectively shut the doors of the Jewish homeland to these Jewish refugees. The Mufti later conditioned his support for the Nazi war effort on this door staying shut.

Evian and the White Paper combined to render Hitler's expulsion plan impossible. It was only at this point that the Nazis began to contemplate a new solution—a "Final Solution"—to the Jewish question. This new policy was formally initiated on January 20, 1942, at a notorious meeting in the Berlin suburb of Wannsee. There, SS General Reinhard Heydrich announced that "emigration as a possible solution [to the Jewish question] has been superseded by a policy of evacuating Jews to the East." For those who didn't understand the euphemism, Heydrich added that once in the East the Jews would be worked to death and the survivors would be murdered outright. The Holocaust had begun.

This history clarifies a fact that is too often overlooked. When the Arabs of Palestine rejected the offer of their own state in 1937, they enabled a terrible tragedy. This tragedy did not befall the Arabs themselves; their suffering would come later. This first episode of Palestinian rejectionism brought disaster to the Jews of Europe.

If a Jewish state had been created in 1937, then Hitler's plan to expel the Jews would have worked; there would have been at least one place on earth willing to take them. And if Hitler's plan to expel the Jews had worked, he would not have needed to progress to his next and "Final Solution" to the Jewish problem. The Holocaust could have been avoided.

Instead, the Arabs rejected partition. They renewed their revolt. And they fought until the British appeased them with the 1939 White Paper. It was the White Paper that closed the doors of the Jewish homeland to the Jewish people. It was the White Paper that effectively trapped the Jews in Europe just when they most needed to escape.

Palestine's Arabs did not perpetrate the Holocaust. Neither did the British. But they both played an undeniable role in enabling it. As Israel's first Prime Minister David Ben Gurion observed twenty years later, "Had partition [under the Peel Commission plan] been carried out, the history of our people would have been different and six million Jews in Europe would not have been killed—most of them would be in Israel."[3]

When we look at the human tragedy that has flowed from the Palestinian refusal to share the land with the Jews, these six million Holocaust victims must not be forgotten. They too are part of this conflict's human toll.

THE SECOND "NO": THE 1947 UNITED NATIONS PARTITION PLAN

After World War II, hundreds of thousands of Holocaust survivors languished in displaced persons camps across Europe. As they clamored to go to their ancient homeland, world opinion turned against Britain and its White Paper policy. Weary of war and the burdens of empire, Britain searched for an exit from Palestine. In 1947, the United Nations agreed to decide Palestine's future.

The United Nations Special Committee on Palestine (UNSCOP) ultimately came to the same conclusion the Peel Commission had reached a decade earlier. It decided that both the Jews and the Arabs of Palestine had valid claims to the land of Palestine. It likewise recognized that the national aspirations of these two groups could never be reconciled. The committee therefore proposed that the land should be partitioned into two states, one Jewish and one Arab.

The United Nations proposal was more generous to the Jews than the Peel plan had been. The Jews were offered fifty-six percent of Palestine, although a majority of this was desert. The Arabs were offered forty-two percent, but with much less desert. The remaining portion of the land—a block surrounding Jerusalem and Bethlehem—was to be an international zone.

On November 29, 1947, the United Nations General Assembly voted to adopt the UNSCOP partition plan. The Jewish state thus approved was far from the Jewish dream. It was tiny, barely contiguous, and didn't include Jerusalem and its Jewish majority. Yet within the Jewish community there was no serious debate about whether to accept the offer. Jews around the world responded with spontaneous joy. The Jews of Palestine poured into the streets and danced until sunrise.

The Arabs said "No." The Mufti, the Palestinian Arab Higher Committee, and the Arab League all rejected the UN decision and the very concept of partition. The morning after the UN vote, Palestinian gunmen launched a civil war against their Jewish neighbors. When the British Mandate officially ended on May 15, 1948, the armies of four neighboring Arab countries joined the war to destroy the Jewish state.

THE DAMAGE DONE

Over five thousand seven hundred Israelis were killed in the 1948 War. One quarter of the fatalities were civilians. This death toll represented almost one percent of Palestine's Jewish population at the time. Few societies have ever had to pay such a high price for their independence.

This time, however, the Jews were not the only victims. The Arabs of Palestine also paid a heavy price for the intransigence of their leaders. They paid with the blood of their dead. And they paid with displacement. It was this war that the Palestinian Arabs started—and which their Arab neighbors later joined—that triggered the Palestinian refugee crisis.

Before the Arabs of Palestine attacked their Jewish neighbors in 1947, there were no Palestinian refugees. Not one. Then, in the almost half-year of civil war between the Arabs and Jews of Palestine, over three hundred thousand Palestinians became refugees. After the neighboring Arab states joined the fight, the number of refugees more than doubled, to approximately seven hundred thousand.

The large majority of these refugees voluntarily fled their homes to escape a war their leaders had launched and escalated. The wealthiest families—as well as most of the Palestinian Arab leadership—were the first to flee to safety. Then the middle-class merchants and artisans joined the exodus. The poor were the last to leave. Meanwhile, Palestine's Jews had nowhere else to go. Their backs to the sea, they stood their ground and fought.

But not all Palestinian refugees left voluntarily. Many were forced from their homes. In some cases, Arab leaders ordered Arab civilians to leave in order to clear the way for an attack or deny the Jews the recognition implied by surrender. In other cases, the Israelis expelled these Arabs in an effort to clear hostile villages from their rear as they prepared to confront an Arab onslaught on their borders.

The fact that Israel expelled tens of thousands of Palestinian Arabs cannot be denied. But these harsh actions can only be judged in their context. These expulsions were neither outbursts of racial animosity nor a calculated ethnic cleansing. They were simply part of the desperate strategy by which Israel's leaders hoped to survive an aggression they had not sought and were far from certain they would survive.

This doesn't mean that Israel's young army always acted admirably. Historians reviewing these events from the safe distance of the intervening years can and should continue debating the strategic necessity of some of these expulsions. But such errors in no way shift the ultimate responsibility for the conflict that necessitated such self-defense in the first place. As Israel's second Prime Minister Moshe Sharett noted, "There are those who say that we uprooted Arabs from their places. But even they will not deny that the source of the problem was the war; had there been no war, the Arabs would not have abandoned their villages, and we would not have expelled them."[4]

Sharett was right about everything except the ability of Israel's enemies to deny these facts.

THE THIRD "NO": THE 1967 SIX-DAY WAR

The effort to destroy the Jewish state did not stop with Israel's victory in 1948. On the contrary, Arab leaders responded to this humiliating defeat by pledging to launch a "second round" of war in which they would accomplish what they had failed to do the first time.

This threatened second round finally came in 1967. That spring, Egypt's President Nasser took a series of provocative steps that made war all but inevitable. On May 14, Nasser began massing his troops in Sinai next to the United Nations buffer zone between Egypt and Israel. Within a few days, he had over one hundred thousand soldiers in place. On May 16, Egypt ordered United Nations forces to evacuate the buffer zone, and the UN quickly complied. Now nothing stood between Israel and Nasser's massive army.

On May 21, Egyptian forces seized Sharm el-Sheikh, a strategic point overlooking the Red Sea's Straits of Tiran. From this position, Nasser announced that he was closing the Straits to Israeli shipping. This action—technically an act of war—effectively shuttered Israel's Red Sea port of Eilat, through which it received almost all of its oil. On May 26, Nasser put these aggressive steps into their obvious context by publicly stating, "Recently we felt we are strong enough that if we enter a battle with Israel, with God's help, we could triumph. On this basis, we decided to take actual steps.... The battle will be a general one and our basic objective will be to destroy Israel."[5]

Israel feared an imminent, devastating attack. Anticipating mass casualties, the government ordered fourteen thousand hospital beds prepared and dug mass graves in Tel Aviv's Yarkon Park.[6] Israeli commanders eventually decided that their best hope for survival lay in a surprise attack. On June 5, 1967, Israel launched a preemptive strike against Egypt's air force. Within hours, Israel had destroyed almost all of Egypt's fighter jets on the ground. Having achieved complete air supremacy, Israel proceeded to crush Egypt's army in the Sinai desert.

Desperate for help against Israel's lightning advance, Nasser sent false reports to both Syria and Jordan informing them that he had the Israelis on the run. He urged his neighbors to join the fight and share in the spoils. Both Syria and Jordan fell for Nasser's trick and attacked Israel from the north and the east. Iraq sent planes, tanks, and troops into battle.

The fighting was over by June 10. Within six days, Israel had won a stunning military victory on all three fronts. Israel had conquered the Sinai Peninsula from Egypt, the Golan Heights from Syria, and the West Bank from Jordan. Jerusalem—half of which was occupied by the Jordanians in 1948—was reunited under Israeli rule. The Jewish state now controlled territory three times larger than it had before the war.

The Israelis were ecstatic. Within the space of one week, they had gone from the dread of imminent destruction to the exhilaration of miraculous salvation. Many Israelis dared to dream that after such a decisive defeat their neighbors might finally despair of destroying them. And where the hope of annihilation ends, the possibility of peace begins.

Less than ten days after the war's end, on June 19, 1967, Israel's cabinet met to decide what to do with these newly conquered territories. Given the existential peril they had just survived, these leaders made a surprising decision. They voted to authorize the government to return Sinai to Egypt and the Golan to Syria in exchange for peace treaties with these countries.

When it came to the West Bank, the cabinet was largely divided between those who wanted to return it to Jordan and those who preferred to empower its residents to govern themselves. Unable to reach a consensus, the cabinet postponed its ultimate decision. In the meantime, however, Prime Minister Eshkol sent a high-level team into the West Bank to determine whether the Palestinian Arabs living there were interested in autonomy and ultimate independence from Jordan.

These dreams of peace were quickly dashed. In late August 1967, the Arab League met in Khartoum, Sudan, and adopted a hard anti-Israel line. Among the resolutions these Arab states approved was one specifying that there would be "no peace with Israel, no recognition of Israel, no negotiations with it." The West Bank Arabs who had been negotiating with Israel decided to fall in line and end their talks.

THE DAMAGE DONE

This third Arab rejection of an Israeli peace offer hurt all sides. Most immediately, it set the stage for further rounds in the war to destroy Israel. In an effort to regain by force the very territories that they refused to accept through peace, Egypt and Syria went to war with Israel again in 1973. This time they launched a surprise attack on Yom Kippur, the holiest day of the Jewish year, while most Israeli soldiers were home with their families. The Israelis were eventually able to mobilize their troops, seize the strategic initiative, and reverse the Arabs' initial advances. But the price they paid in blood was high. Israel lost over 2,500 dead and 7,250 wounded.

This third "No" also hurt the Palestinians. Before the 1967 War, Jordan and Egypt occupied the West Bank and Gaza, respectively. Neither Arab state permitted any Jews to live in these territories. Thus two of the three central Palestinian grievances—the Israeli occupation and Israeli settlements—simply did not exist prior to 1967. Neither of these alleged transgressions would have occurred had Egypt and Jordan not gone to war with Israel in 1967. And neither would have continued had the Arabs not unanimously refused to negotiate with Israel in September 1967.

THE FOURTH "NO": EHUD BARAK, CAMP DAVID, AND THE CLINTON PARAMETERS

In 1999, the Israelis responded to the stalled Oslo peace process by electing Ehud Barak prime minister. As a candidate, Barak had promised to revive the peace process with the Palestinians. Upon taking office, Barak worked hard to fulfill his pledge.

In July 2000, President Clinton hosted Barak and PLO Chairman Yasser Arafat at Camp David to help them bridge their remaining gaps. During the course of this summit, Barak placed a number of increasingly large concessions on the table. Eventually, Barak offered Arafat one hundred percent of the Gaza Strip, ninety-one percent of the West Bank, and sovereignty over Jerusalem's Arab neighborhoods.

Arafat didn't accept Barak's offer. Nor did he make a counteroffer. He simply let the clock run out. At the close of the summit, President Clinton "blew up" at Arafat, shouting at the Palestinian leader that he had "been here fourteen days and said no to everything."[7]

Shortly after Camp David, the Palestinians launched their bloody Second Intifada. Historians still debate whether Arafat started this uprising or merely permitted it. But there is no denying that once it began, Arafat decided to become a full participant. Before long, the PLO and its al-Aqsa Martyrs Brigade were competing with Hamas to see who could blow up more Israelis.

Yet neither Barak nor Clinton responded to this violence by abandoning negotiations. On the contrary, in their effort to salvage the peace process they actually offered Arafat deeper concessions than ever before. On December 23, 2000, Clinton sent the parties a bridging proposal in a last ditch effort to reach a final deal. These "Clinton Parameters" called for Israel to give the Palestinians the following:

- All of the Gaza Strip;
- Between ninety-four and ninety-six percent of the West Bank;
- Israeli territory amounting to an additional one to three percent of the West Bank;
- A safe passage corridor between the West Bank and Gaza through Israeli territory; and
- The Arab neighborhoods of Jerusalem.

Barak accepted the Clinton Parameters. Arafat rejected them.

Once again, a Palestinian leader had rejected an offer of a Palestinian state. As U.S. negotiator Dennis Ross later commented, "Those who argue that we just ran out of time ignore the many opportunities Arafat had refused. They ignore that with the Clinton ideas practically on the table at the end of September, Arafat either let the intifada begin or, as some argue, actually gave orders for it. They ignore his actual rejection of the specifics of the Clinton ideas. They ignore his extraordinary rebuff of the President's extraordinary offer to come to the area in his final days as President."[8]

THE DAMAGE DONE

Arafat's rejection of this fourth offer to create a Palestinian state brought immediate tragedy to Israel. This "No" came in the form of a bloody wave of Palestinian suicide bombings that killed over one thousand Israelis.

But the Palestinians suffered as well. This fourth Palestinian rejection of a Palestinian state led to the perpetuation of the very occupation and settlements that they claim are driving the conflict. Had the Palestinians accepted Barak's offer, Israeli administration would have been replaced by full Palestinian independence. And if Palestinians, not Israelis, controlled the West Bank, they would have the power to prohibit Jews from building houses in their territory.

Finally, this Palestinian rejection produced a new Palestinian complaint: Israel's West Bank security barrier. Had the Palestinians accepted independence instead of launching an intifada, the border between Israel and the Palestinians would likely have remained as open as that between the United States and Canada. Instead, the bloody suicide bombings of the Second Intifada forced Israel to build a barrier—mostly wire fence but with some sections made of concrete slabs—between its civilians and the Palestinian population centers from which the suicide bombers came.

THE FIFTH "NO": EHUD OLMERT'S 2008 OFFER

Shortly after the start of the Second Intifada, Ehud Barak was voted out of office by an electorate that had received terror as the only return on their risks for peace. They replaced him with Ariel Sharon, a storied general who promised to restore security to a traumatized nation.

Once Sharon's policies began to work and a semblance of safety had been restored, the Israeli people did something incredible. They decided to once again give peace a chance. In 2006, Israelis elected Sharon's handpicked successor, Ehud Olmert, as prime minister.

As a candidate, Olmert had stressed the need to disengage from the Palestinians through a peace deal or by unilateral actions. He thus came to office with a mandate to pursue peace talks, and he wasted little time in doing so.

From December 2006 to September 2008, Olmert met with Palestinian President Mahmoud Abbas thirty-six times. At a final meeting in September 2008, Olmert made an historic offer to Abbas. Among its highlights:[9]

- Territory. Olmert offered Abbas all of the Gaza Strip (already under Palestinian control) as well as the territorial equivalent of 100 percent of the West Bank. In particular, Israel would retain the 6.3 percent of the West Bank that included the major Jewish settlement blocks and related roads. In exchange, however, it would give the Palestinians land from Israel proper equal to 5.8 percent of the West Bank, along with a land link between the West Bank and Gaza essentially equal to the remaining 0.5 percent of the West Bank.
- Jerusalem. Olmert proposed sharing Jerusalem with the Palestinians. Jerusalem's Jewish neighborhoods would be the capital of Israel and its Arab neighborhoods would become the Palestinian capital.
- The Holy Basin. Olmert was the first Israeli leader to offer to relinquish Israeli sovereignty over the "Holy Basin"— that part of Jerusalem that contains the sites holiest to Jews and Muslims, including the Temple Mount and the Western Wall. He proposed that this area be governed by

a committee comprised of representatives from five countries: Saudi Arabia, Jordan, Palestine, the United States, and Israel.

- Refugees. Olmert suggested that five thousand Palestinian refugees be allowed to return to Israel; one thousand a year for five years. He also proposed that the two sides work with international bodies and financial institutions to establish a fund to "generously compensate" all Palestinian refugees for their lost property.

Olmert's offer was the most generous any Israeli leader had ever made to the Palestinians, exceeding even the Clinton Parameters in its concessions. Yet Abbas refused to accept it. And Abbas never made a counteroffer. He later noted that "the gaps were wide."[10]

As recently as March, 2014, Abbas stated that even if the Palestinians were given a state he would not agree to declare an end to the conflict with Israel or abandon the Palestinian right of return to Israel.[11] In other words, Israel can give land, but the Palestinians will not give peace. The best one can say for Abbas is that he delivers his "No's" with words instead of bombs.

THE DAMAGE DONE

So far, this fifth Palestinian rejection of a Palestinian state has not produced the death toll of its predecessors. Abbas has not used terror as a negotiating tactic. He is simply unwilling—or unable—to stop others from engaging in terror. Instead of battling Hamas or arresting its operatives, he continues to partner with Hamas and largely ignores its violence. Instead of preparing the Palestinian people for compromise, he continues to legitimize rejectionism and terror through his government's public pronouncements, textbooks, television broadcasts, and cash payments to terrorists and their families.

The main losers in Abbas's refusal of Olmert's offer are the Palestinians themselves. By once again refusing to accept an independent state, the Palestinians have chosen to perpetuate the very things about which they complain most bitterly: Israeli rule, Israeli houses, and Israel's security fence.

THE THREE WITHDRAWALS

In recent years, the Israelis have done much more than *offer* to withdraw from disputed territories in exchange for peace. They have repeatedly withdrawn from such territories. Since the start of the Oslo peace process in 1993, Israel has pulled out of contested areas on three separate occasions. Each of these withdrawals was intended to satisfy an Arab claim, reduce tensions with an Arab adversary, and spark a virtuous cycle toward peace. Instead, each exit had the opposite effect of emboldening Israel's enemies and increasing attacks against Israel.

In the mid-1990s, under Oslo II, Israel withdrew its troops from every major Palestinian population center in the West Bank and Gaza. But these withdrawals did not produce peace. Quite to the contrary, Israel soon suffered the bloodiest wave of Palestinian terror in its history. Almost all of the Second Intifada's suicide bombers came from the very cities and towns Israel had so recently vacated. Eventually, Israel had to send its troops back into these areas to dismantle the terror cells that had flourished in their absence.

In 2000, Israel completely withdrew from the security zone it had maintained in southern Lebanon. But this withdrawal did not deliver quiet. Instead, the Iranian-backed terrorist group Hezbollah took over this territory and turned it into a forward base from which to strike Israel. In 2006, during the Second Lebanon War, Hezbollah fired approximately four thousand Katyusha rockets from southern Lebanon into northern Israel. By 2016, Hezbollah was estimated to have an arsenal of well over one hundred thousand missiles capable of striking every city in Israel.

In 2005, Israel withdrew all of its soldiers and civilians from the Gaza Strip and handed control of this territory to the Palestinian Authority. But this withdrawal neither strengthened Palestinian moderates nor reduced the number of terrorist attacks. Instead, Hamas seized power in a 2007 coup and turned Gaza into a virtual terrorist base. Between 2005 and 2016, Hamas and its allies fired more than eleven thousand rockets into Israel from Gaza. Israel has had to fight three wars in six years—2008–09, 2012, and 2014—to stop this missile fire. And while each war produced temporary quiet, none has restored the relative security that existed before Israel's withdrawal.

WHY THE WEST BANK IS DIFFERENT

Gaza is of relatively little strategic significance. This small strip of flat land is located on Israel's southwestern border, relatively far from Israel's major population centers. Yet within a year of taking over Gaza, Hamas had obtained a stockpile of missiles that could reach all of Israel's major southern cities and send over one million Israelis rushing to the bomb shelters. By 2014, Hamas had obtained missiles that could reach Tel Aviv and Jerusalem and terrorize the large majority of Israelis.

The West Bank, by contrast, is of overwhelming strategic significance. The West Bank is the elevated hill country that dominates Israel's coastal plain directly below it. And this coastal plain is the narrow strip of land—a mere nine miles wide at points—that contains over seventy percent of Israel's population and economic infrastructure. Even with the crudest of homemade missiles, anyone who controls the West Bank can easily shell any point in the coastal plain, from the cafes of Tel Aviv to the runways of Ben Gurion Airport. The West Bank also surrounds Israel's capital, Jerusalem, on three sides.

In short, whoever rules the West Bank effectively controls life in Israel. Thus the risks involved in withdrawing from the West Bank cannot be overstated. This is why an increasing number of Israelis—including many who passionately support a two-state solution in principle—are hesitant to roll the land-for-peace dice yet again. First they want some assurance that this time their sacrifices won't simply strengthen the extremists and multiply the number of missiles and bombs raining down on them. They want to know that the West Bank won't become another Gaza.

Yet there is no evidence that anything has changed for the better since Israel withdrew from Gaza in 2005. President Abbas is no more popular, no stronger, and no more determined to fight terror today than he was a decade ago. The Israeli military must constantly intervene to thwart the terror plots that Abbas's forces are unable or unwilling to stop. Far from cracking down on Hamas, Abbas joined with them to form a unity government in June 2014.

Abbas is so weak that Hamas would probably have taken over the West Bank by now had it not been for Israel's ongoing military presence there. In August 2014, for example, Israel's Shin Bet security service revealed that it had discovered and disrupted a Hamas plot to topple Abbas. During the course of a three-month operation, the Shin Bet arrested ninety-three Hamas operatives in the West Bank and seized stockpiles of weapons, ammunition, and cash intended for the coup.[12] Abbas confirmed these reports later that month, when he told Hamas leader Khaled Mashal, "You are smuggling money and ammunition into the West Bank, not for a confrontation with Israel but to carry out a coup against me."[13]

Israelis have a well-founded fear that a West Bank withdrawal would be a Gaza rerun. They also know that Hamas is no longer the most vicious of the barbarians at their gates. ISIS has taken over large swaths of Syria and Iraq and threatens Jordan. At the same time, al-Qaeda affiliates have taken up positions on Israel's borders with Syria and Egypt. Israelis now have every reason to believe that their departure from the West Bank would bring the most bloodthirsty of murderers to the hills overlooking their homes.

THE FUTURE

This long history of rejectionism has taught Israelis that their concessions don't bring peace, only more violence. Most Israelis, no matter how idealistic, now understand that it isn't enough to dream of peace, visualize peace, or make painful concessions for peace. The only way Israel will know peace is if it has a partner that is both willing and able to deliver it. And no such Palestinian partner currently exists.

This difficult lesson has been taught with particular cruelty and clarity to Israel's millennials, the cohort that came of age during the Second Intifada. This is a generation that spent their teen years effectively grounded, as their parents refused to let them out to shopping malls or restaurants when so many of them were so often blown up. This is a generation that still holds its breath when a bus passes, hoping it won't explode. These are people who still avoid sitting near windows in restaurants since shattered glass flying at high velocity often kills more people than the bomb blast itself.

As they've grown up, these millennials have graduated from confinement in their homes to confinement in the safe rooms of their homes. Every Israeli home must be built with a reinforced safe room designed to withstand nearby missile and rocket explosions. In recent conflicts with Hamas and Hezbollah, almost every citizen of every city in Israel has experienced the terror of repeated air raid sirens giving them between fifteen and thirty seconds to seek shelter in their safe rooms.

These Israelis did not suffer these attacks because of their parents' intransigence. Quite to the contrary, they were subject to these attacks because of their parents' compromises. They can trace each wave of suicide bombings or barrage of missiles to concessions that Israeli leaders made in the hopes of peace.

It should surprise no one that a generation thus schooled has developed doubts about the land-for-peace formula. This Israeli skepticism toward peace may be the most bitter fruit of Palestinian rejectionism. Like the occupation, the settlements, and the security fence, Israel's young hawks are very much a problem of the Palestinians' own making.

Yet the same polls that show these young Israelis questioning the wisdom of land for peace also indicate that their concerns are largely pragmatic. Their life experience has made these young Israelis "cynical" and "skeptical" that concessions will bring peace, and rightly so. But they remain surprisingly open to compromise *if such compromise would actually deliver peace.*[14] History teaches that a sincere gesture of Arab goodwill can overcome years of bloodshed and persuade Israelis that, finally, their sacrifices may actually improve their lives.

Israel's first Likud prime minister, Menachem Begin, was no dove. Begin's life experience—from losing his family in the Holocaust to losing his friends in Israel's struggle for independence—planted deep within him a suspicion of the world beyond Israel's borders. Yet even Begin's profound doubts melted when confronted with an Arab leader genuinely committed to compromise. When Egyptian President Anwar Sadat flew to Jerusalem and spoke from his heart about forging an historic peace, Begin embraced him and agreed to return the entire Sinai Peninsula to Egypt.

Few leaders are as courageous as Sadat. But it doesn't take a Sadat to convince most Israelis to give peace yet another chance. Yasser Arafat was a lifelong terrorist. As it turned out, he was a completely unrepentant terrorist. Yet for a brief period he removed his holster from his hip and spoke of peace. Prime Minister Yitzhak Rabin agreed to enter into historic negotiations with him. Public support for territorial concessions to Arafat, previously nonexistent, became widespread.

Yes, young Israelis have been schooled in skepticism. But if past is prologue, any doubts they have developed from bitter experience will fade in the face of a sincere Palestinian offer of peace. The only problem—what has always been the problem—is that such an offer is not likely to be forthcoming any time soon.

NOTES

PREFACE

1.   Thomas L. Friedman, "Campus Hypocrisy," *New York Times*, October 16, 2002.

2.   Anna Hiatt, "Abbas in NY: We Have All Made mistakes," *Jerusalem Post*, September 24, 2014.

3.   James Minihan, *Encyclopedia of the Stateless Nations* (Westport, CT: Greenwood Press, 2002).

4.   Ibid., xx.

5.   Mikael Bodlore-Penlaez, *Atlas of Stateless Nations in Europe* (Ceredigion Wales: Y Lolfa, 2012).

6.   Palash R. Ghosh, "Ahwazis: Iran Persecution of Its Arab Minority," *International Business Times*, July 24, 2012; Khalef Ahmad Al Habtoor, "Al Ahwaz Will Always Be Arab," *Egyptian Gazette*, April 11, 2011.

7.   "Arabistanis" in Minihan, *Encyclopedia of the Stateless Nations*, 161.

8.   "Arrest of 244 Ahwazi Arabs in Recent Weeks Says NGO," *Ahwaz News Agency*, April 2, 2013; "Khatemi Denies the Existence of Ahwazi Arabs," *Ahwaz News Agency*, January 23, 2013.

9.   "Amnesty Urgent Action: Iranian Ahwazi Arabs on Hunger Strike over Death Sentences," Amnesty International, March 27, 2013.

10. Ghosh, "Ahwazis"; Al Habtoor, "Al Ahwaz Will Always Be Arab."

11. "Iran: New Government Fails to Address Dire Human Rights Situation," Amnesty International, February 16, 2006, MDE 13/010/2006.
12. Ibid.
13. Ghosh, "Ahwazis"; Al Habtoor, "Al Ahwaz Will Always Be Arab."
14. Jerry Z. Muller, "Us and Them: The Enduring Power of Ethnic Nationalism," *Foreign Affairs*, March/April 2008.
15. Cited in Alfred M. de Zayas, *Nemesis at Potsdam: The Expulsion of the Germans from the East* (Lincoln, NE: University of Nebraska Press, 1988), 11.
16. Cited in Alfred Maurice de Zayas, *A Terrible Revenge: The Ethnic Cleansing of the East European Germans* (New York, NY: Palgrave Macmillan, 2006), 83.
17. Cited in Zayas, *Nemesis at Potsdam*, 11.
18. Cited in ibid., 87.
19. Ibid., xix.
20. Cited in ibid., 135.
21. Ibid., 141.
22. Ibid., 134.
23. "Introduction" in Steffan Prauser and Arfon Rees, eds., *The Expulsion of the 'German' Communities from Eastern Europe at the End of the Second World War* (San Domenico, Italy: European University Institute, 2004), 2.
24. Michael Levitin, "Germany Provokes Anger over Museum to Refugees Who Fled Poland During WWII," *Telegraph*, February 26, 2009.
25. "Who Are Palestine Refugees?," UNWRA, http://www.unrwa.org/palestine-refugees.
26. Ari Ben Goldberg, "US Senate Dramatically Scales Down Definition of Palestinian 'refugees,'" Times of Israel, May 25, 2012,
27. While Hitler saw Jews as racial inferiors like Africans, Arabs, and Slavs, his genocidal rage was fueled by his belief that Jews had taken actions to corrupt, betray, and control Germany.
28. Khaled Abu Toameh, Speech at the Eyal Hotel, Jerusalem, September 6, 2014.

INTRODUCTION: PEACE THROUGH TRUTH

1. Albert Memmi, *Jews and Arabs* (Chicago, IL: J Philip O'Hara, Inc., 1975), 14–15.
2. Albert Memmi, *The Colonizer and the Colonized* (Boston, MA: Beacon Press, 1991), 127–28. The book was originally published in 1957 as *Portrait du Colonisé, Précédé par Portrait du Colonisateur* and first translated into English two years later.
3. Memmi, *Jews and Arabs*, 20.
4. Ibid., 20–22.

5. Ibid., 21.
6. Ibid., 22
7. Ibid., 12.
8. Ibid., 14–15.
9. These smaller, nation-state nationalisms were born before 1967. Most trace their roots back to the years following the fall of the Ottoman Empire at the end of World War I. But it was only after the 1967 War that these new identities finally came to dominate the prior, pan-Arab view.
10. Memmi, *Jews and Arabs*, 35.
11. Ibid., 111.
12. See David Samuels, "In a Ruined Country," *Atlantic*, September 2005.
13. Mahmoud Abbas, "The Long Overdue Palestinian State," *New York Times*, May 16, 2011.
14. Cited in Sarah Honig, "Another Tack: Self-Exiled by Guilt," *Jerusalem Post*, July 17, 2009. Video of this interview is available at www.memritv. org/clip/en/2212.htm.
15. David Hacohen, *A Time to Tell: An Israeli life 1898–1984* (New York, NY: Herzl Press, 1985), 38.
16. Benny Morris, *Righteous Victims: A History of the Zionist-Arab Conflict, 1881–2001*, 115.
17. Hacohen, *A Time to Tell*, 40.
18. *Report of the Palestine Royal Commission*, 50.
19. Ibid.
20. Benny Morris, *1948* (New Haven, CT: Yale University Press, 2008), 90–91.

CHAPTER 1: THE JEWISH CLAIM

1. Cited in Dan Bahat, ed., *Twenty Centuries of Jewish Life in the Holy Land* (Jerusalem, Israel: The Israel Economist, 1976), 49.
2. Tudor Parfitt estimates the Jewish population in 1882 at thirty-two thousand. See Tudor Parfitt, *The Jews in Palestine 1800–1882* (Exeter, England: The Royal Historical Society, 1987), 126. Ben Gurion places the Jewish population at twenty-four thousand. See David Ben Gurion, "From the Founding of Petach Tikva to the Present Day," in David Ben Gurion, ed., *The Jews in Their Land* (Garden City, NY: Doubleday, 1966), 272. James Parkes places the Jewish population at forty-five thousand in 1888. James Parkes, *Whose Land?* (New York: Taplinger, 1970), 47. Jacob De Haas gives forty thousand Jews out of a total population of two hundred thousand. See Jacob De Haas, *History of Palestine—the Last Two Thousand Years* (New York: Macmillan Company, 1934), 442.
3. Cited in De Haas, *History of Palestine*, 55.
4. Cited in Bahat, ed., *Twenty Centuries of Jewish Life*, 16.

5.   Peter Schafer, *The History of the Jews in Antiquity* (Luxembourg: Harwood Academic, 1995), 181.
6.   Parkes, *Whose Land?*, 47.
7.   Cited in Jewish National Council, "Second Memorandum: Historical Survey of the Jewish Population in Palestine from the Fall of the Jewish State to the Beginning of Zionist Pioneering (Presented to the United Nations in 1947)."
8.   S. Klein, *Safer ha-Yishuv*, cited in Jewish National Council, "Second Memorandum."
9.   Schafer, *The History of the Jews in Antiquity*, 187–90.
10. Cited in Bahat, ed., *Twenty Centuries of Jewish Life*, 23.
11. De Haas, *History of Palestine*, 115.
12. H. H. Ben-Sasson, ed., *A History of the Jewish People* (Cambridge, MA: Harvard University, 1976), 362.
13. Ben-Sasson, ed., *A History of the Jewish People*, 362–63.
14. Sefer ha-Yishuv, cited in Norman Stillman, *The Jews of Arab Lands* (Philadelphia, PA: The Jewish Publication Society of America, 1979), 152; Moshe Gil, *A History of Palestine 634–1099* (Cambridge, UK: Cambridge University, 2010), 57.
15. Ha-Yishuv, cited in Stillman, *The Jews of Arab Lands*, 152; and Gil, *A History of Palestine*, 58.
16. De Haas, *History of Palestine*, 137; Martin Gilbert, *In Ishmael's House* (New Haven, CT: Yale University, 2010), 39: Gil, *A History of Palestine*, 59.
17. Stillman, *The Jews of Arab Lands*, 154–55; Benzion Dinur, "From Bar Kochba's Revolt to the Turkish Conquest," in Ben Gurion, ed., *The Jews in Their Land*, 202; Bahat, ed., *Twenty Centuries of Jewish Life*, 24.
18. Parkes, *Whose Land?*, 112–13.
19. Dinur, "From Bar Kochba's Revolt," 205.
20. Parkes, *Whose Land?*, 96.
21. Dinur, "From Bar Kochba's Revolt," 205.
22. Cited in ibid., 214.
23. Gil, *A History of Palestine*, 829.
24. Cited in Bahat, ed., *Twenty Centuries of Jewish Life*, 37; Dinur, "From Bar Kochba's Revolt," 215.
25. Ibid., 214; Parkes, *Whose Land?*, 97; and Jewish National Council, "Second Memorandum."
26. Dinur, "From Bar Kochba's Revolt," 215.
27. Ibid., 217; Gilbert, *In Ishmael's House*, 60
28. Dinur, "From Bar Kochba's Revolt," 217–18; and Gilbert, *In Ishmael's House*, 60.

29. Ibid., 60; and Bahat, ed., *Twenty Centuries of Jewish Life*, 41; Dinur, "From Bar Kochba's Revolt," 217.
30. Gilbert, *In Ishmael's House*, 60.
31. Bahat, ed., *Twenty Centuries of Jewish Life*, 41–42; and Dinur, "From Bar Kochba's Revolt," 221–22.
32. Jewish National Council, "Second Memorandum."
33. Cited in Stillman, *The Jews of Arab Lands*, 278.
34. Parkes, *Whose Land?*, 113.
35. Dinur, "From Bar Kochba's Revolt," 218.
36. Arie Morgenstern, "Dispersion and the Longing for Zion 1240–1840," in David Hazony, Yoram Hazony, and Michael Oren, eds., *New Essays in Zionism* (Jerusalem, Israel: Shalem, 2006), 318.
37. Dinur, "From Bar Kochba's Revolt," 223; Morgenstern, "Dispersion and the Longing for Zion," 318.
38. Parkes, *Whose Land?*, 129. See also Jewish National Council, "Second Memorandum."
39. Ibid.
40. Cited in Stillman, *The Jews of Arab Lands*, 290.
41. Cited in Cecil Roth, *The Duke of Naxos* (Philadelphia, PA: The Jewish Publication Society of America, 1948), 104.
42. Abraham David, *To Come to the Land* (Tuscaloosa, AL: The University of Alabama, 1999), 32.
43. Cited in Bahat, ed., *Twenty Centuries of Jewish Life*, 52.
44. Cited in Roth, *The Duke of Naxos*, 126–29.
45. Cited in David, *To Come to the Land*, 19.
46. De Haas, *History of Palestine*, 345; Izhak Ben-Zvi, "Under Ottoman Rule," in David Ben Gurion, ed., *The Jews in Their Land*, 237–38.
47. Stillman, *The Jews of Arab Lands*, 91.
48. Jacob Barnai, *The Jews in Palestine in the Eighteenth Century* (Tuscaloosa, AL: The University of Alabama Press, 1992), 172.
49. De Haas, *History of Palestine*, 363.
50. Ibid.
51. Barnai, *The Jews in Palestine*, 148–53.
52. Ibid., 18–19.
53. Jewish National Council, "Third Memorandum: Historical Survey of the Waves of Jewish Immigration into Palestine from the Arab Conquest to the First Zionist Pioneers (640–1882)" (Presented to the United Nations in 1947).
54. Cited in Ben-Zvi, "Under Ottoman Rule," 257.
55. Yehoshua Ben-Arieh, *Jerusalem in the Nineteenth Century* (Tel Aviv, Israel: MOD Books, 1989), 12.
56. Ibid., 13.

57. Mark Twain, *The Innocents Abroad, or the New Pilgrim's Progress* (Wordsworth Classics, 2010), 313, 335, 360. Originally published in 1869, the book gives an account of Twain's 1867 tour of Palestine.

58. Tudor Parfitt cites sources that place the number of Jewish dead at two thousand. See Parfitt, *The Jews in Palestine*, 64–66.

59. Ibid., 69–70.

60. Andrew Alexander Bonar and Robert Murray M'Cheyne cited in ibid., 68.

61. Cited in Bat Ye'or, *The Dhimmi* (Cranburry, NJ: Associated University Press, 1985), 225–26.

62. J. S. Buckingham, cited in Ye'or, *The Dhimmi*, 220.

63. Stillman, *The Jews of Arab Lands*, 329.

64. Cited in Ye'or, *The Dhimmi*, 220.

65. Cited in Gilbert, *In Ishmael's House*, 106.

66. Ben-Arieh, *Jerusalem in the Nineteenth Century*, 27. Tudor Parfitt places the date on which the Jews outnumbered the Muslims in Jerusalem one year earlier, in 1839. See Parfitt, *The Jews in Palestine*, 22.

67. Ibid., 50.

68. Ben-Arieh, *Jerusalem in the Nineteenth Century*, 32; and Parkes, *Whose Land?*, 230. Tudor Parfitt places the date at which the Jews constituted an outright majority in Jerusalem earlier, in 1850. See Parfitt, *The Jews in Palestine*, 29.

69. Report of James Finn cited in Stillman, *The Jews of Arab Lands*, 356. Tudor Parfitt places the date of Jewish majority in Safed later, in 1882. See Parfitt, *The Jews in Palestine*, 74.

70. De Haas, *History of Palestine*, 438.

CHAPTER 2: THE PALESTINIAN CLAIM

1. George Antonius, *The Arab Awakening* (reprinted in Safety Harbor, FL by Simon Publications, 2001), 390.

2. Woodrow Wilson, "Address to Congress, Analyzing German and Austrian Peace Utterances," February 11, 1918, downloaded from the World War I Document Archive, http://wwi.lib.byu.edu/index.php/President_Wilson%27s_Address_to_Congress,_Analyzing_German_and_Austrian_Peace_Utterances.

3. Robert Lansing, *The Peace Negotiations—A Personal Narrative* (Lexington, KY: Filiquarian, 2012), www.Qontro.com, 52.

4. Ibid., 53.

5. Cited in Alfred Cobban, *National Self-Determination* (Chicago: The University of Chicago Press, 1944), 21.

6. Cited in Lloyd E. Ambrosius, *Wilsonianism* (New York, NY: Palgrave MacMillan, 2002), 127.

7.   See Muhammad Muslih, *The Origins of Palestinian Nationalism* (New York: Columbia University Press, 1988), 1, 15.

8.   Antonius, *The Arab Awakening*, 99.

9.   Ibid., 99.

10. Cited in Martin Kramer, *Arab Awakening and Islamic Revival* (New Brunswick, NJ: Transaction Publishers, 1996), 24.

11. Muslih, *The Origins of Palestinian Nationalism*, 96.

12. C. Ernest Dawn, "The Origins of Arab Nationalism," in Rashid Khalidi, Lisa Anderson, Muhammad Muslih, and Reeva S. Simon, eds., *The Origins of Arab Nationalism* (New York: Columbia University Press, 1991), 13.

13. Muslih, *The Origins of Palestinian Nationalism*, 97.

14. Ibid.

15. Cited in Isaiah Friedman, *British Pan-Arab Policy 1915–1922* (New Brunswick, NJ: Transaction Publishers, 2010), 69.

16. Ibid., 70.

17. Muslih, *The Origins of Palestinian Nationalism*, 103.

18. Kramer, *Arab Awakening and Islamic Revival*, 26.

19. Antonius, *The Arab Awakening*, 304; Muslih, *The Origins of Palestinian Nationalism*, 128.

20. Ibid., 181.

21. Ibid., 181–82.

22. Rashid Khalidi, *Palestinian Identity* (New York: Columbia University Press, 1997), 162–66.

23. Daniel Pipes, "The Year the Arabs Discovered Palestine," *Middle East Review*, Summer 1989, as downloaded from danielpipes.org on February 23, 2013.

24. Muslih, *The Origins of Palestinian Nationalism*, 126.

25. Ibid., 187.

26. Muhammad Muslih, "The Rise of Local Nationalism in the Arab East," in Khalidi, Anderson, Muslih, and Simon, eds. *The Origins of Arab Nationalism*, 178.

27. Pipes, "The Year the Arabs Discovered Palestine."

28. Friedman, *British Pan-Arab Policy*, 293.

29. Muslih, *The Origins of Palestinian Nationalism*, 207.

30. Hillel Cohen, *Army of Shadows* (Los Angeles, CA: University of California Press, 2008), 3; and Issa Khalaf, *Politics in Palestine: Arab Factionalism and Social Disintegration, 1939–1948* (Albany, NY: State University of New York Press, 1991), 208.

31. Cohen, *Army of Shadows*, 263–64.

32. Benny Morris, *1948* (New Haven, CT: Yale University Press, 2008), 91.

33. Ibid., 210.

34. Khalidi, *Palestinian Identity*, 194.

35. Ibid., 178.

36. Zvi Elpeleg, *The Grand Mufti* (London, England: Routledge, 1993), 123.

37. Ibid.

38. On September 28, 1961, a group of Syrian officers staged a coup and declared Syria's independence from the UAR.

39. Khalidi, *Palestinian Identity*, 182.

40. Rashid Khalidi, "The 1967 War and the Demise of Arab Nationalism," in Wm. Roger Louis and Avi Shlaim, eds., *The 1967 Arab-Israeli War: Origins and Consequences* (New York: Cambridge University Press, 2012), 281.

41. Fouad Ajami as cited in Kramer, *Arab Awakening*, 35.

42. Khalidi, *Palestinian Identity*, 27.

43. Ibid., 149.

44. Elpeleg, *The Grand Mufti*, 3.

45. Ibid., 4

46. Ibid.

47. Cited in ibid., 202–5.

48. Ibid., 65; Barry Rubin and Wolfgang Schwanitz, *Nazis, Islamists and the Making of the Modern Middle East* (New Haven, CT: Yale University Press, 2014), 125, 177.

49. Rubin and Schwanitz, *Nazis, Islamists*, 177.

50. Edwin Black, *The Farhud* (Washington, DC: Dialog Press, 2010), 272–73; Rubin and Schwanitz, *Nazis, Islamists*, 125, 177.

51. Cited in Elpeleg, *The Grand Mufti*, 202–5.

52. Zvi Elpeleg, *Through the Eyes of the Mufti* (London, England: Valentine Mitchell, 2009), 151.

53. Elpeleg, *The Grand Mufti*, 170.

54. Cited in ibid., 158.

55. The more specific term for Leonardo's error is "prochronism."

CHAPTER 3: THE JEWS COME HOME

1. Cited in David Ben-Gurion, *My Talks with Arab Leaders* (New York: The Third Press, 1973), 7.

2. Rashid Khalidi, *Palestinian Identity* (New York: Columbia University Press, 1997), 101.

3. See Diana Muir, "A Land without a People for a People without a Land," *Middle East Quarterly* (Spring 2008).

4. Theodor Herzl, *The Jewish State* (reprinted by Filiquarian Publishing, 2006), 8.

5. Ibid., 8.

6. Ibid., 27.

7. Theodor Herzl, *Altneuland* (reprinted in Lexington, KY by WLC, 2011), 97.
8. Ibid., 97–99.
9. Ibid., 99.
10. Cited in Barnet Litvinoff, ed., *The Essential Chaim Weizmann* (New York, NY: Holmes and Meier Publishers, 1982), 17.
11. Chaim Weizmann, *Trial and Error* (London, England: Hamish Hamilton, 1950), 566.
12. Cited in Efraim Karsh, *Palestine Betrayed* (New Haven, CT: Yale University Press, 2010), 26.
13. Ben-Gurion, *My Talks*, 44.
14. Cited in Shabtai Teveth, *Ben-Gurion and the Palestinian Arabs* (New York: Oxford University Press, 1985), 38.
15. Cited in Ben-Gurion, *My Talks*, 7.
16. Cited in Shimon Peres, *Ben-Gurion: A Political Life* (New York, Nextbook, 2011), 62.
17. Cited in Teveth, *Ben-Gurion*, 189.
18. Ibid., 27, 43.
19. Ibid., 43
20. David Ben-Gurion, *Memoirs* (Cleveland, Ohio: The World Publishing Company, 1970), 50.
21. Teveth, *Ben-Gurion*, 9.
22. Ben-Gurion, *Memoirs*, 51.
23. Ibid., 51.
24. Walter Clay Lowdermilk, *Palestine: Land of Promise* (New York: Harper & Brothers Publishers, 1944), 137.
25. Ben-Gurion, *Memoirs*, 25–26.
26. Ibid., 136.
27. Ibid., 147.
28. Cited in Karsh, *Palestine Betrayed*, 24.
29. Cited in ibid., 24.
30. Cited in Arthur Hertzberg, ed., *The Zionist Idea* (New York: Atheneum, 1984), 562.
31. Vladimir Jabotinsky, *The War and the Jew* (New York: The Dial Press, 1942), 211.
32. Cited in ibid., 215.
33. Cited in ibid.
34. Report of the Palestine Royal Commission (henceforth "Peel Commission Report") (London, England: His Majesty's Stationery Office, 1937; reprinted in 1947), 90.
35. Arieh L. Avneri, *The Claim of Dispossession* (New Brunswick, NJ: Transaction Books, 1984), 254.

36. Ibid., 255.
37. Ibid.
38. Ibid., 258.
39. Peel Commission Report, 93.
40. Avneri, *The Claim of Dispossession*, 282.
41. Peel Commission Report, 90.
42. Peel Commission Report, 92–93; Avneri, *The Claim of Dispossession*, 259–63; and Efraim Karsh, "1948, Israel and the Palestinians: The True Story," *Commentary* (May 1, 2008).
43. Peel Commission Report, 94.
44. Peel Commission Report, 91–93.
45. Kenneth W. Stein, "Legal Protection and Circumvention of Rights for Cultivators in Mandatory Palestine," downloaded from Emory University at http://www.ismi.emory.edu.
46. Kenneth W. Stein, *The Land Question in Palestine, 1917–1939* (Chapel Hill, NC: University of North Carolina, 1984), 51. At first this legislation also applied to owner-occupiers, but it was quickly amended to restrict its protection to tenant farmers.
47. Stein, "Legal Protection," 11.
48. Stein, *The Land Question*, 52.
49. Stein, "Legal Protection," 14.
50. Ibid.
51. Stein, *The Land Question*, 143.
52. Ibid., 59.
53. Ibid., 142.
54. Ibid., 158–59.
55. Peel Commission Report, 271.
56. Ibid., 95.

CHAPTER 4: ZIONISM ENCOUNTERS ARAB NATIONALISM

1. David Ben-Gurion, *My Talks with Arab Leaders* (New York, NY: The Third Press, 1973), 222.
2. Amy Dockser Marcus, *Jerusalem 1913* (New York, NY: Penguin, 2007), 129.
3. Cited in Aharon Cohen, *Israel and the Arab World* (New York, NY: Funk & Wagnalls, 1970), 97.
4. Cited in ibid.
5. Vladimir Jabotinsky, "Evidence Submitted to the Palestine Royal Commission (1937)," in Arthur Hertzberg, ed., *The Zionist Idea* (New York, NY: Atheneum, 1984), 562.
6. Shabtai Teveth, *Ben Gurion and the Palestinian Arabs*, 93–94.

7. Ben-Gurion, *My Talks*, 21.
8. Teveth, *Ben Gurion*, 94.
9. Ben-Gurion, *My Talks*, 21.
10. Teveth, *Ben Gurion*, 94.
11. Ben-Gurion, *My Talks*, 210; and Isaiah Friedman, *British Pan-Arab Policy 1915–1922*, 193.
12. Chaim Weizmann, *Trial and Error* (London, England: Hamish Hamilton, 1950), 293.
13. Weizmann, *Trial and Error*, 293.
14. "Emir Feisal and Chaim Weizmann: Agreement (January 3, 1919)," in Walter Laqueur and Barry Rubin, eds., *The Israel-Arab Reader* (New York, NY: Penguin Books, 2008), 17.
15. Ibid., 17–18.
16. Ibid., 18.
17. Ibid., 19–20.
18. Cited in Friedman, *British Pan-Arab Policy*, 177.
19. Cited in ibid., 178.
20. Ronald Florence, *Lawrence and Aaronsohn: T. E. Lawrence, Aaron Aaronsohn, and the Seeds of the Arab-Israeli Conflict*, 61.
21. Cited in Friedman, *British Pan-Arab Policy*, 177.
22. Cited in ibid., 176–77.
23. Cited in ibid., 178.
24. Ben-Gurion, *My Talks*, 16, 260.
25. Ibid., 20.
26. Teveth, *Ben Gurion*, 130.
27. Ben-Gurion, *My Talks*, 15.
28. Ibid., 15.
29. Ibid., 32.
30. Teveth, *Ben Gurion*, 136.
31. Cited in Dore Gold, *The Fight for Jerusalem* (Washington, DC: Regnery Publishing, 2007), 130.
32. Ben-Gurion, *My Talks*, 32.
33. Teveth, *Ben Gurion*, 138.
34. Ibid., 138.
35. Ibid., 145.
36. Ibid., 146–48.
37. Ben-Gurion, *My Talks*, 51.
38. Teveth, *Ben Gurion*, 161.
39. Ben-Gurion, *My Talks*, 194.
40. Cited in Walter Laqueur and Barry Rubin, eds., *The Israel-Arab Reader: A Documentary History of the Middle East Conflict* (New York, NY: Penguin Books, 2008), 17.

CHAPTER 5: PALESTINE'S ARABS RESPOND

1. Cited in Efraim Karsh, *Palestine Betrayed* (New Haven, CT: Yale University Press, 2010), 1.
2. Cited in Shabtai Teveth, *Ben Gurion and the Palestinian Arabs* (New York, NY: Oxford University, 1985), 159.
3. Cited in Karsh, *Palestine Betrayed*, 18.
4. See Edwin Black, *The Farhud* (Washington, DC: Dialog Press, 2010), 348–50; Zvi Elpeleg, *The Grand Mufti: Haj Amin Al-Hussaini Founder of the Palestinian National Movement* (London: Routledge, 1993), 69–70; Barry Rubin and Wolfgang G. Schwanitz, *Nazis, Islamists and the Making of the Modern Middle East* (New Haven, CT: Yale University, 2014), 165–66.
5. Cited in Elpeleg, *The Grand Mufti*, 72.
6. Ibid.
7. Cited in ibid., 73.
8. Cited in Ronald Florence, *Lawrence and Aaronsohn: T. E. Lawrence, Aaron Aaronsohn, and the Seeds of the Arab-Israeli Conflict* (New York, NY: Penguin Books, 2007), 32.
9. Ibid., 33.
10. Ibid.
11. Ibid.
12. David Ben-Gurion, *My Talks with Arab Leaders* (New York, NY: The Third Press, 1973), 243.
13. Florence, *Lawrence and Aaronsohn*, 66.
14. Report of the Palestine Royal Commission (henceforth "Peel Commission Report") (London, England: His Majesty's Stationery Office, 1937; reprinted in 1947), 10.
15. Muhammad Muslih, *The Origins of Palestinian Nationalism* (New York, NY: Columbia University Press, 1988), 72; Neville Mandel, *The Arabs and Zionism before World War I* (Berkeley, CA: The University of California Press, 1976), 39–40.
16. Muslih, *The Origins of Palestinian Nationalism*, 73; Mandel, *The Arabs and Zionism*, 21.
17. Ibid., 72.
18. Ibid., 103–4.
19. Ibid., 112; Rashid Khalidi, *Palestinian Identity* (New York, NY: Columbia University Press, 1997), 31, 80–81.
20. Arieh L. Avneri, *The Claim of Dispossession* (New Brunswick, NJ: Transaction Books, 1984), 95.
21. Black, *The Farhud*, 193.
22. Benny Morris, *Righteous Victims* (New York, NY: Vantage Books, 2001), 95.

23. Florence, *Lawrence and Aaronsohn,* 442; and Black, *The Farhud,* 193; and Morris, *Righteous Victims,* 95.
24. Tom Segev, *One Palestine Complete* (New York, NY: Henry Holt and Co., 1999), 127–38; Morris, *Righteous Victims,* 95–96.
25. Peel Commission Report, 37.
26. Segev, *One Palestine,* 136; Morris, *Righteous Victims,* 96.
27. Black, *The Farhud,* 217.
28. Segev, *One Palestine,* 177.
29. Morris, *Righteous Victims,* 101–2.
30. Ibid., 102.
31. Peel Commission Report, 37.
32. Segev, *One Palestine,* 180; Morris, *Righteous Victims,* 102.
33. Ibid., 102–3.
34. British White Paper of 1922 as reprinted in Walter Laqueur and Barry Rubin, eds., *The Israeli-Arab Reader* (New York, NY: Penguin Books, 2008), 28.
35. Peel Commission Report, 48; Benny Morris, *Righteous Victims,* 112; Segev, *One Palestine,* 295–97.
36. Ibid., 112; Segev, *One Palestine,* 303–4.
37. Elpeleg, *The Grand Mufti,* 20.
38. Morris, *Righteous Victims,* 114; and Segev, *One Palestine,* 314.
39. Cited in Morris, *Righteous Victims,* 114.
40. Segev, *One Palestine Complete,* 322–23.
41. Ibid., 324.
42. Ibid.
43. Morris, *Righteous Victims,* 115.
44. Ibid.
45. Peel Commission Report, 50.
46. Ibid.
47. Ibid., 70.
48. Morris, *Righteous Victims,* 130.
49. Segev, *One Palestine,* 365.
50. Morris, *Righteous Victims,* 158.
51. Peel Commission Report, 76–77.
52. Cited in Morris, *Righteous Victims,* 138.
53. Cited in Benny Morris, *One State, Two States* (New Haven, CT: Yale University Press, 2009), 99.
54. Cited in Peel Commission Report, 102 and Karsh, *Palestine Betrayed,* 32–33.
55. Segev, *One Palestine Complete,* p. 414.
56. Morris, *Righteous Victims,* 145.
57. Segev, *One Palestine Complete,* 415, 432.

58. Morris, *Righteous Victims*, 159.
59. Ibid., 158.
60. Cited in Black, *The Farhud*, 228.
61. Elpeleg, *The Grand Mufti*, 57.
62. Black, *The Farhud*, 305.
63. Ibid., 304–5.
64. Elpeleg, *The Grand Mufti*, 62.
65. Black, *The Farhud*, 322.
66. Ibid.,325; Rubin and Schwanitz, *Nazis, Islamists*, 140.
67. Black, *The Farhud*, 333; Rubin and Schwanitz, *Nazis, Islamists*, 150–52.
68. Ibid., 8–9, 163.
69. Black, *The Farhud*, 345–46; Rubin and Schwanitz, *Nazis, Islamists*, 8–9, 163.
70. Ibid., 138–39.
71. Ibid., 9; Tony Paterson, "'Chivalrous' Rommel Wanted to Bring Holocaust to Middle East," *Independent*, May 25, 2007.
72. Rubin and Schwanitz, *Nazis, Islamists*, 9.
73. Ibid., 164, 225.
74. Cited in ibid., 185.
75. Ibid., 161.
76. Ibid.
77. Ibid., 9, 162.
78. Ibid., 163.
79. Hillel Cohen, *Army of Shadows* (Los Angeles, CA: University of California Press, 2008), 3.
80. Segev, *One Palestine*, 325–26.
81. Ibid., 325.
82. The Muslim National Associations accepted contributions from Zionist sources. But their acceptance of this support hardly discredits these leaders or the sincerity of the beliefs for which they repeatedly risked their lives.
83. Cited in Cohen, *Army of Shadows*, 15.
84. Ibid., 58–59.
85. Ibid.,117.
86. Ibid., 122.
87. Ibid.,
88. Ibid., 124.
89. Ibid., 202.
90. Ibid., 203.
91. Morris, *Righteous Victims*, 260; and "Assassination of King Abdullah," *Guardian*, July 21, 1951.
92. Cohen, *Army of Shadows*, 106.
93. Ibid., 100–2.

94. Ibid., 171.
95. Ibid., 144.

CHAPTER 6: 1948: PALESTINE'S ARABS ATTACK

1. Benny Morris, *The Birth of the Palestinian Refugee Problem Revisited* (Cambridge, England: Cambridge University Press, 2004), 588.
2. Mahmoud Abbas, "The Long Overdue Palestinian State," *New York Times*, May 16, 2011.
3. Cited in Benny Morris, *1948* (New Haven, CT: Yale University Press, 2008), 76.
4. Martin Gilbert, *Israel: A History* (New York: Harper Perennial, 2008), 155; Efraim Karsh, *Palestine Betrayed* (New Haven, CT: Yale University Press, 2010), 100; and Morris, *1948*, 76.
5. Ibid.
6. Gilbert, *Israel*, 154 and Karsh, *Palestine Betrayed*, 101.
7. Ibid.
8. Morris, *The Birth of the Palestinian Refugee Problem*, 596.
9. Most of these volunteers served in the "Arab Liberation Army" which operated in Galilee.
10. Morris, *1948*, 90–91.
11. Gilbert, *Israel*, 162; Morris, *The Birth of the Palestinian Refugee Problem*, 76–85, 343.
12. Ibid., 76–85.
13. Cited in Karsh, *Palestine Betrayed*, 114.
14. Cited at ibid.
15. Cited in ibid., 177.
16. Morris, *1948*, 117–18, and Morris, *The Birth of the Palestinian Refugee Problem*, 76–77.
17. Cited in Karsh, *Palestine Betrayed*, 115.
18. Ibid., 118.
19. Cited in ibid., 119.
20. Morris, *1948*, 90–91.
21. Ibid., 125.
22. Cited in ibid., 162.
23. Karsh, *Palestine Betrayed*, 128.
24. Cited in ibid., 138.
25. Cited in ibid., 139.
26. Cited in Morris, *1948*, 145.
27. Cited in ibid., 145.
28. Cited in ibid., 146. See also Karsh, *Palestine Betrayed*, 136–37.
29. Morris, *1948*, 146; Karsh, *Palestine Betrayed*, 140–41; Morris, *The Birth of the Palestinian Refugee Problem*, 198–99.

30. Cited in Karsh, *Palestine Betrayed*, 137.
31. Ibid., 155.
32. Morris, *1948*, 154; Karsh, *Palestine Betrayed*, 155.
33. Cited in ibid., 159.
34. Cited in Morris, *The Birth of the Palestinian Refugee Problem*, 219.
35. Benny Morris, *Righteous Victims* (New York, NY: Vintage Books, 2001), 209; Benny Morris, "The Historiography of Deir Yassin," *Journal of Israeli History*, 24:1 (March 2005), 79, 87.
36. Morris, "The Historiography of Deir Yassin," 85; and Morris, *1948*, 126.
37. Morris, *Righteous Victims*, 207; Benny Morris, *The Birth of the Palestinian Refugee Problem*, 126; Morris, "The Historiography of Deir Yassin," 85.
38. Morris, *Righteous Victims*, 208; Morris, *1948*, 126; and Morris, "The Historiography of Deir Yassin," 86.
39. Morris, "The Historiography of Deir Yassin," 104, note 63.
40. Benny Morris, *Righteous Victims*, 207–8.
41. Morris, *1948*, 126.
42. Morris, *Righteous Victims*, 207; Morris, "The Historiography of Deir Yassin," 86.
43. Morris, *The Birth of the Palestinian Refugee Problem*, 237; Morris, *1948*, 126; Morris, "The Historiography of Deir Yassin," 86.
44. Morris, *The Birth of the Palestinian Refugee Problem*, 238.
45. Morris, "The Historiography of Deir Yassin," 93.
46. Morris, *Righteous Victims*, 208; Morris, "The Historiography of Deir Yassin," 87.
47. Ibid., 95, 100–1.
48. Morris, *1948*, 127; Morris, "The Historiography of Deir Yassin," 92.
49. Gilbert, *Israel*, 170.
50. Cited in Karsh, *Palestine Betrayed*, 209.
51. Cited in Gilbert, *Israel*, 181
52. Cited in Morris, *1948*, 175.
53. Ibid., 170.
54. Ibid., 409.
55. Ari Shavit, *My Promised Land* (New York, NY: Spiegel and Grau, 2013), 107, 116–17.
56. Morris, *The Birth of the Palestinian Refugee Problem*, 426.
57. Morris, *1948*, 289.
58. Morris, *The Birth of the Palestinian Refugee Problem*, 427..
59. Dan Kurzman, *Genesis 1948* (New York, NY: Da Capo Press, 1992), 514.
60. Karsh, *Palestine Betrayed*, 216–17.

61. Morris, *Righteous Victims*, 240; Morris, *The Birth of the Palestinian Refugee Problem*, 427; and Morris, *1948*. 289. Karsh, *Palestine Betrayed*, 217.

62. Shavit, *My Promised Land*, 121.

63. Ibid., 124.

64. Hundreds of residents of these two towns remained in their homes. Hundreds more returned in the weeks and months following the expulsion. Today, each city has an Arab population roughly equal to that which existed prior to the 1948 War.

65. Shavit, *My Promised Land*, 125.

66. Morris, *The Birth of the Palestinian Refugee Problem*, 433.

67. Morris, *1948*, 290.

68. Cited in Martin Gilbert, *Israel*, 486.

69. Morris, *The Birth of the Palestinian Refugee Problem*, 426, 489.

70. Ibid., 489.

71. Cited in Karsh, *Palestine Betrayed*, 223.

72. Ibid., 237; Morris, *The Birth of the Palestinian Refugee Problem*, 67.

73. Morris, *1948*, 96.

74. Ibid., 97.

75. Benny Morris, "The Origins of the Palestinian Refugee Problem," in Laurence Silberstein, ed., *New Perspectives on Israeli History* (New York: New York University Press, 1991), 43–44.

76. Benny Morris, *The Birth of the Palestinian Refugee Problem*, 165.

77. Morris, *1948*, 344–46.

CHAPTER 7: ISRAEL ENCOUNTERS PALESTINIAN NATIONALISM

1. Ehud Olmert, Speech to the United States Congress, May 24, 2006.

2. Golda Meir interview with Frank Giles, *Sunday Times*, June 15, 1969, as reprinted in "Golda Meir Scorns Soviets," *Washington Post*, June 16, 1969.

3. Michael Oren interview with Terry Gross, "Michael Oren Discusses His New Book 'Six Days of War' and the Events Leading Up to Today's Israeli-Palestinian Conflict," *Fresh Air*, June 11 2002.

4. Michael Oren, *Six Days of War* (New York, NY: Presidio Press, 2003), 316.

5. The PLO Charter may or may have not been amended by the Palestine National Council in 1993 to cancel those articles "contrary to" certain commitments made by Yasser Arafat to Israeli Prime Minister Rabin. Unfortunately, like so many of Arafat's peace efforts, this amendment process was reluctant, vague, and never fully implemented.

6. The redeployment from Hebron was delayed until the parties worked out the final details in January 1997.

7. Dennis Ross, *The Missing Peace* (New York: Farrar, Straus and Giroux, 2004), 717.

8. Cited in ibid., 715.

9. Cited in ibid., 699.

10. Cited in ibid., 705.

11. Ibid., 732.

12. Ibid., 730.

13. See Charles Krauthammer, "Why Arafat Will Not Stop His War," *Washington Post*, May 18, 2001.

14. See David Samuels, "In a Ruined Country," *Atlantic*, September 2005.

15. Cited in Khaled Abu Toameh, "Arafat Ordered Hamas Attacks against Israel in 2000," *Jerusalem Post*, September 28, 2010.

16. Cited in "Suha Arafat Admits Husband Premeditated Intifada," *Jerusalem Post*, December 29, 2012.

17. "Israel: Documents Link Al-Aqsa to Palestinian Finance Official," CNN. com, April 3, 2002.

18. Todd S. Purdum and Patrick E. Tyler, "Mideast Turmoil: Diplomacy; Aides to Bush say Arafat Financed a Terrorist Group," *New York Times*, June 26, 2002; David E. Sanger, "Bush Says Palestinians Will Lose Aid if They Keep Arafat," *New York Times*, June 27, 2002; Robert Siegel, "Interview: Todd Purdum Discusses an Intelligence Report Indicating that Yasser Arafat Paid the Al-Aqsa Martyr's Brigade $20,000," *All Things Considered*, NPR, June 26, 2002; Elliott Abrams, *Tested by Zion* (New York: Cambridge University Press, 2013), 41.

19. "Palestinian Authority Funds Go to Militants," BBC News, November 7, 2003.

20. Ross, *The Missing Peace*, 748.

21. Ibid., 754.

22. Ibid., 755.

23. Ibid., 13, 756.

24. Ibid, 13.

25. Elsa Walsh, "The Prince," *New Yorker*, March 24, 2003.

26. Over 95 percent of this barrier is a wire fence. The use of concrete slabs is limited to urban areas where there is not enough land for the trenches and guard paths that wire fences require.

27. Sharon died in January 2014 without ever having regained consciousness.

28. Olmert, Speech to the United States Congress.

29. Bernard Avishai, "A Plan for Peace That Still Could Be," *New York Times*, February 7, 2011.

30. This summary is based upon information contained in the following sources: Avi Issacharoff, "Exclusive: Olmert: I Am Still Waiting for Abbas to Call," The Tower.org, May 24, 2013; Ehud Olmert, "Peace Now, or

Never," *New York Times*, September 21, 2011; Ethan Bronner, "Olmert Memoir Cites Near Deal for Mideast Peace," *New York Times*, January 27, 2011; Ben Birnbaum, "The End of the Two-State Solution," *New Republic*, March 11, 2013; Bernard Avishai, "A Plan for Peace That Still Could Be," *New York Times*, February 7, 2011; Abrams, *Tested by Zion*, 287–88.

31. Bronner, "Olmert Memoir Cites Near Deal for Mideast Peace."
32. Ibid.
33. Issacharoff, "I Am Still Waiting."
34. Jackson Diehl, "Abbas's Waiting Game," *Washington Post*, May 29, 2009. In a July 2012 interview with Israel's Channel 2 news, Abbas denied saying these words. But Diehl insists that the quote is accurate. See Raphael Ahern, "Rebutting Abbas: Condoleezza Rice Confirms Her Account of Their 2008 refugee conversation, Times of Israel, July 11, 2012.
35. Jackson Diehl, "A Familiar Obstacle to Mideast Peace: Mahmoud Abbas," *Washington Post*, March 22, 2010.
36. Hilary Leila Krieger, "Abbas Was Ready to Back Olmert Deal, Bush Memoir Says," *Jerusalem Post*, October 13, 2011.
37. Condoleezza Rice, *No Higher Honor* (New York: Crown Publishers, 2011), 724.
38. Abrams, *Tested by Zion*, 292.
39. Issacharoff, "I Am Still Waiting."
40. Roger Cohen, "Why Israeli-Palestinian Peace Failed," *New York Times*, December 23, 2014.
41. Avi Issacharoff, "When Netanyahu Closed the Door on Peace Talks," Times of Israel, February 13, 2015.

CHAPTER 8: THE MOST MORAL ARMY IN THE WORLD

1. Colonel Richard Kemp, Testimony before the United Nations Human Rights Commission, Geneva, Switzerland, October 16, 2009, www. unwatch.org.
2. Shabtai Teveth, *Ben-Gurion and the Palestinian Arabs* (New York, NY: Oxford University Press, 1985), 15.
3. Israel Ministry of Foreign Affairs, "Suicide Bombers from Jenin," April 24, 2002, http://mfa.gov.il/MFA/MFA-Archive/2002/Pages/Suicide%20 Bombers%20from%20Jenin.aspx.
4. Jerusalem Center for Public Affairs, "What Really Happened in Jenin?," Jerusalem Issue Brief, 1: 22 (May 2, 2002); Jonathan Cook, "The 'Engineer,'" *Al-Ahram Weekly Online*, April 18–24, 2002; Yigal Henkin, "Urban Warfare and the Lessons of Jenin, *Azure*, Summer 2003, 53.

5. Cited in Richard Starr, "The Big Jenin Lie," *Weekly Standard*, May 8, 2002.

6. Cited in ibid.

7. Jerusalem Center for Public Affairs, "What Really Happened?"

8. United Press International, "Palestinians: Hundreds in Mass Graves," *NewsMax*, April 13, 2002.

9. "The Battle for the Truth: What Really Happened in Jenin Camp?" *Guardian*, April 16, 2002.

10. Cited in Sharon Sadeh, "How Jenin Battle Became a 'Massacre,'" *Guardian*, May 5, 2002; Martin Sieff, "Part One: Documenting the Myth," *United Press International*, May 20, 2002; Ros Taylor, "The Wrap: 'Monstrous War Crime' Alleged in Jenin," *Guardian*, April 16, 2002; Tom Gross, "Jeningrad," National Review Online, May 13, 2002.

11. Phil Reeves, "Amid the Ruins of Jenin, the Grisly Evidence of a War Crime," *Independent*, April 16, 2002.

12. "Jenin Camp 'Horrific beyond Belief,'" BBC News, April 18, 2002.

13. Joel Mowbray, "Muslim Mythology," *Front Page Magazine*, April 20, 2005.

14. "Anatomy of Anti-Israel Incitement: Jenin, World Opinion and the Massacre That Wasn't," Anti-Defamation League, June 2002, 19.

15. Daniel Gordon, How the Times Distorted Jenin," *Jewish Journal*, May 2, 2002.

16. United Nations General Assembly, "Report of the Secretary-General Prepared Pursuant to General Assembly Resolution ES-10/10," July 30, 2002, 11; John Lancaster, "Ill-Prepared for a Battle Unexpected," *Washington Post*, April 26, 2002.

17. Matt Rees, Bobby Ghosh, Jamil Hamad and Aharon Klein, "Untangling Jenin's Tale," *Time*, May 13, 2002.

18. Ibid.

19. General Assembly, "Report of the Secretary-General," 11.

20. Anti-Defamation League, "Anatomy of Anti-Israel Incitement," 22.

21. "Palestinian Fighter Describes 'Hard Fight' in Jenin," CNN, April 23, 2002.

22. Cook, "The 'Engineer.'"

23. Rees, Ghosh, Hamad and Klein, "Untangling Jenin's Tale."

24. Ibid.

25. "Palestinian Fighter Describes 'Hard Fight.'"

26. Cook, "The 'Engineer,'"

27. Ibid.

28. Rees, Ghosh, Hamad and Klein, "Untangling Jenin's Tale."

29. Ibid.

30. Ibid.

31. General Assembly, "Report of the Secretary-General, 12.

32. Paul Wood, "'No Jenin Massacre' Says Rights Group," BBC News, May 3, 2002.

33. "Jenin 'Massacre' Reduced to Death Toll of 56," *Washington Times*, May 1, 2002.

34. Jerusalem Center for Public Affairs, "What Really Happened in Jenin?"; General Assembly "Report of the Secretary-General, 12.

35. Wood, "'No Jenin Massacre.'"

36. John Lancaster, "Ill-Prepared for a Battle Unexpected," *Washington Post*, April 26, 2002.

37. "Anatomy of Anti-Israel Incitement," Anti-Defamation League, 20.

38. General Assembly, "Report of the Secretary-General," 8.

39. Michael Oren, "UN Report a Victory for Terror, *Boston Globe*, September 24, 2009.

40. The State of Israel, "The Operation in Gaza, Factual and Legal Aspects," July 2009, 1, 18.

41. Desmond Tutu, "A Call to the Community of Conscience," in Adam Horowitz, Lizzy Ratner and Philip Weiss, eds., *The Goldstone Report: The Legacy of the Landmark Investigation of the Gaza Conflict* (New York: NY: Nation Books, 2011), vii.

42. Naomi Klein, "The End of Israeli Exceptionalism," in Horowitz, Ratner and Weiss, eds., *The Goldstone Report: The Legacy*, xi.

43. UN Human Rights Council, "Report of the United Nations Fact-Finding Mission on the Gaza Conflict," UN Doc. A/HRC/12/48 (September 25, 2009) [hereinafter the Goldstone Report], paragraphs 1884 and 1893.

44. The Goldstone Report, paragraphs 810 and 816.

45. See the Additional Protocol to the Geneva Conventions (June 8, 1977), Article 48.

46. The Rome Statute of the International Criminal Court, Article 8(2)(b)(iv). See also the Additional Protocol to the Geneva Conventions, Article 51(5) (b).

47. Jeffrey White, Soner Cagaptay, and Andrew Tabler, "Military Implications of the Syria-Turkey Border Incident," The Washington Institute for Near East Policy, October 5, 2012.

48. Ivan Watson, "Turkey Strikes Targets in Syria in Retaliation for Shelling Deaths," CNN.com, October 4, 2012; "Turkey on Edge as Syria Widens Offensive," Associated Press, October 6, 2012.

49. "Turkish Artillery Strikes Back After Syrian Mortar Bomb Hit," *Daily Star*, October 17, 2012.

50. "NATO Says Plans in Place to Defend Turkey from Syrian Attacks," Associated Press, October 9, 2012.

51. "Turkish Retaliatory Fire Has Killed 12 Syrian Soldiers," *Daily Star*, October 20, 2012.
52. "Turkey Strikes Targets inside Syria after Mortar Attack," Ynetnews.com, October 4, 2012; "Turkey Shells Syria for Sixth Day," *Telegraph*, October 8, 2012.
53. "NATO Says Plans in Place"; "Syria Clashes Intensify Near Turkey Border," Reuters, October 9, 2012.
54. The State of Israel, "The Operation in Gaza," 19–21.
55. Ibid., 99.
56. Steven Erlanger, "A Gaza War Full of Traps and Trickery," *New York Times*, January 11, 2009; Moshe Halbertal, "The Goldstone Illusion," *New Republic*, November 6, 2009; "IDF Phones Gaza Residents to Warn Them of Imminent Strikes," *Haaretz*, January 2, 2009.
57. The State of Israel, "The Operation in Gaza," 100.
58. Erlanger, "A Gaza War Full of Traps."
59. The State of Israel, "The Operation in Gaza," 102–3.
60. Ibid., 75–76.
61. Ibid., 72.
62. The State of Israel, "Gaza Operation Investigations: An Update," January 2010, 36.
63. The State of Israel, "Gaza Operation Investigations: Second Update," July 2010, 3.
64. The State of Israel, "Gaza Operation Investigations: An Update," 35.
65. The State of Israel, "Gaza Operation Investigations: An Update," 36, note 112; The State of Israel, "Gaza Operation Investigations: Second Update," 3.
66. Ibid., 3.
67. Gal Beckerman, "Goldstone: 'If This Was a Court Of Law, There Would Have Been Nothing Proven,'" *Forward*, October 7, 2009.
68. Richard Goldstone, "Reconsidering the Goldstone Report on Israel and War Crimes," *Washington Post*, April 1, 2011.
69. Ibid.
70. Ibid.
71. Interview with Ambassador Robert Oakley, "Ambush in Mogadishu," *Frontline*, http://www.pbs.org/wgbh/pages/frontline/shows/ambush/interviews/oakley.html.
72. Jeffrey Goldberg, "Does 'Black Hawk Down' Portray an American War Crime?," *Atlantic*, January 13, 2009.
73. Ibid.
74. Interview with Ambassador Oakley, "Ambush in Mogadishu."
75. Dexter Filkins and James Glanz, "With Airpower and Armor, Troops Enter Rebel-Held City," *New York Times*, November 8, 2004.

76. Ann Scott Tyson, "Increased Security in Fallujah Slows Effort to Rebuild," *Washington Post*, April 19, 2005.

77. Asa Kasher, "A Moral Evaluation of the Gaza War," Jerusalem Center for Public Affair, February 4, 2010; Mike Marqusee, "A Name that Lives in Infamy," *Guardian*, November 9, 2005.

78. See Alan Dershowitz, "Wikileaks and the Goldstone Report," Huffington Post, April 19, 2011; "No Longer Unknowable: Fallujah's April Civilian Toll is 600," *Iraq Body Count*, October 26, 2004; "Red Cross Estimates 800 Iraqi Civilians Killed in Fallujah," *Democracy Now*, November 17, 2004.

79. Brian Glyn Williams, "The Russo-Chechen War: A Threat to Stability in the Middle East and Eurasia?," *Middle East Policy* 8:1 (March 2001), 130.

80. Susan B. Glasser and Peter Baker, "Chechnya War a Deepening Trap for Putin," *Washington Post*, September 13, 2004.

81. IrakliI Kakabadze, "The Roots of Caucasian Terrorism," *Unrest Magazine*, October 30, 2013.

82. "Scars Remain Amid Chechen Revival," BBC News, March 3, 2007.

83. Liz Fuller, "Analysis: Look Back in Anger—Ten Years of War in Chechnya," Radio Free Europe, December 11, 2004.

84. Kakabadze, "The Roots of Caucasian Terrorism."

85. Cited in Olga I. Vendina, Vitaliy S. Belozerov, and Andrew Gustafson "The Wars in Chechnya and Their Effects on Neighboring Regions," *Eurasian Geography and Economics*, 48: 2 (2007), 178.

86. Matthew N. Janeczko, "The Russian Counterinsurgency Operation in Chechnya," *Small Wars Journal*, October 30, 2012.

CONCLUSION

1. Cited in Coby Ben-Simhon, "Benny Morris on Why He's Written His Last Word on the Israel-Arab Conflict," Haaretz.com, September 20, 2012.

2. Adolf Eichmann, "I Transported Them to the Butcher," *Life* 49:22 (November 28, 1960), 21–22.

3. Cited in Tom Segev, *One Palestine Complete* (New York, NY: Henry Holt and Company, 2000), 414.

4. Cited in Benny Morris, *1948* (New Haven, CT: Yale University Press, 2008), 410.

5. Cited in Walter Laqueur and Barry Rubin, *The Israel-Arab Reader* (New York, NY: Penguin Books, 2008), 99.

6. Michael Oren, "Did Israel Win the Six-Day War?," *Azure*, Volume 7, Spring 1999.

7. Cited in Dennis Ross, *The Missing Peace* (New York: Farrar, Straus and Giroux, 2004), 705.

8. Cited in ibid.

9.   This summary is based upon information contained in the following: Avi Issacharoff, "Exclusive: Olmert: I Am Still Waiting for Abbas to Call," The Tower.org, May 24, 2013; Ehud Olmert, "Peace Now, or Never," *New York Times*, September 21, 2011; Ethan Bronner, "Olmert Memoir Cites Near Deal for Mideast Peace," *New York Times*, January 27, 2011; Ben Birnbaum "The End of the Two-State Solution," *New Republic*, March 11, 2013; Bernard Avishai, "A Plan for Peace That Still Could Be," *New York Times*, February 7, 2011; and Elliott Abrams, *Tested by Zion* (New York: Cambridge University Press, 2013), 287–88.

10.   Jackson Diehl, "Abbas's Waiting Game," *Washington Post*, May 29, 2009. In a July, 2012 interview with Israel's Channel 2 news, Abbas denied saying these words. But Diehl insists that the quote is accurate. See Raphael Ahern, "Rebutting Abbas: Condoleezza Rice Confirms Her Account of Their 2008 Refugee Conversation, Times of Israel, July 11, 2012.

11.   "TV report: Abbas Said 'No' to Obama on 3 Core Peace issues,"Times of Israel, March 22, 2014.

12.   Mitch Ginsburg and AP, "Israel Says it Foiled Hamas Plan for Massive Attacks on Israel, Coup Against PA," Times of Israel, August 18, 2014; Yaakov Lappin, "Hamas in West Bank 'Planned to Topple Palestinian Authority,'" *Jerusalem Post*, August 18, 2014; Gili Cohen, "Israel Arrested 93 Hamas Men in West Bank over Terror Network Targeting PA, Israel," *Haaretz*, August 18, 2014.

13.   Quoted in Terrence McCoy, "After Israel-Hamas War in Gaza, Palestinian Unity Government on Rocks," *Washington Post*, September 10, 2014.

14.   See Edmund Sanders, "Obama Message May Not Resonate with Israeli Youth," *Los Angeles Times*, March 20, 2013; Uri Friedman, "The Problem with Obama's Appeal to Israeli Youth," *Foreign Policy*, March 22, 2013; Jeff Moskowitz, "The Next Generation of Israeli-Palestinian Conflict," *Atlantic*, July 9, 2014.

INDEX